Girl Gro
Girl Culture

Girl Groups, Girl Culture

Popular Music and Identity in the 1960s

Jacqueline Warwick

Dalhousie University, Canada

New York London

Routledge
Taylor & Francis Group
270 Madison Avenue
New York, NY 10016

Routledge
Taylor & Francis Group
2 Park Square
Milton Park, Abingdon
Oxon OX14 4RN

Printed in the United States of America on acid-free paper
10 9 8 7 6 5 4 3 2 1

International Standard Book Number-10: 0-415-97113-6 (Softcover) 0-415-97112-8 (Hardcover)
International Standard Book Number-13: 978-0-415-97113-3 (Softcover) 978-0-415-97112-6 (Hardcover)

Library of Congress Cataloging-in-Publication Data

Warwick, Jacqueline C., 1969-
Girl groups, girl culture : popular music and identity in the 1960s / Jacqueline Warwick.
p. cm.
Includes bibliographical references (p.) and index.
ISBN 0-415-97112-8 -- ISBN 0-415-97113-6
1. Rock music--1961-1970--History and criticism. 2. Girl groups (Musical groups)--History and criticism. I. Title.

ML3534.W35 2007
781.64082'0973--dc22 2006031350

Visit the Taylor & Francis Web site at
http://www.taylorandfrancis.com

and the Routledge Web site at
http://www.routledge-ny.com

For my sisters

Contents

Preface and Acknowledgments

In the chapters that follow, I explore interconnected themes of adolescent female identity and vocality as they exist in the 1960s' girl group repertoire. Girl group music as I define it comprises several distinct elements: an emphasis on the concerns and interests of teenage girls in its lyrics (i.e., boys, the strictness of parents, etc.); material prepared for the most part by professional songwriters; origins in the recording studio and dependent upon professional session musicians; an instrumental sound often dominated by orchestral instruments rather than the minimal rock'n'roll band lineup of guitar, bass guitar, and drum kit; and above all, the audibly adolescent voices of girls interacting in dialogues between lead and backing vocalists. Some nominally solo artists are associated with the girl groups, while some all-girl groups make music that does not adhere to the hallmarks of the genre. Thus, Little Eva and Lesley Gore are part of the girl group sound, while all-female 60s bands such as the Liverbirds and Goldie and the Gingerbreads are not, because they were self-contained units of instrumentalists/songwriters/singers and also because they did not present identities understood strictly as adolescent.

While the music identified with the girl group category encompasses a wide variety of sounds and styles, a unifying feature is the presence of female adolescent voices. Accordingly, Part 1 of this book,

"Girl Talk," examines vocal types and vocal relationships in some of the earliest girl groups, exploring the dynamics of lead and backup singers. The call-and-response form of girl group songs is often understood as a musical representation of "girl talk," a conversational method considered central to girl culture. I explore the relationships between these concepts and consider also the different musical styles that influenced the developing girl group sound, concentrating particularly on how the nonsense syllables of doo wop were subtly exploited to create a kind of girlspeak and considering the possibilities for understanding girl group music as a proto-feminist forum. The chapters in this section include readings of songs such as the Chantels' "Maybe" (1958), the Bobbettes' "Mr. Lee" (1958), the Shirelles' "I Met Him on a Sunday" (1958), the Marvelettes' "Please Mr. Postman" (1961), the Crystals' "Da Doo Ron Ron" (1963), Betty Everett's "Shoop Shoop Song" (1964), and the Dixie Cups' "Iko Iko" (1965).

In Part 2, "A Brand New Dance Now," I explore the vocabulary of girl movements and gestures developed and codified by Cholly Atkins, the choreographer who trained many of the important girl groups of the early 1960s, at Motown Records and elsewhere, and I analyze the ways in which these gestures came to signify physical markers of femininity. My work here is informed by feminist scholarship into body politics, for control over the body emerges clearly as a central issue in girl culture. Coaching girl singers into specific ways of being in the body can be understood as a form of repression and violence, and in these chapters I also analyze songs that have explicit themes of violence, such as the Crystals' "He Hit Me (and It Felt Like a Kiss)" (1962), the Cookies' "Chains" (1962), and Martha and the Vandellas' "Nowhere to Run" (1965). I also address Little Eva's "The Locomotion" (1962) and the Supremes' "Stop! In the Name of Love" (1965).

In the third section, "He Makes Me Say Things I Don't Want to Say," I tackle the politics of music production in the girl group genre. When the creation of the songs involves so many people, to what extent is it possible and appropriate to consider the lead singers as the speaker? At the same time, when the songs exist in most listeners' ears only because of highly individual vocal performances, should we attach too much importance to the roles of producers, songwriters, and recording engineers? Finally, why do these questions arise so immediately in relation to girl group music but so seldom in connection to bands such as the Beatles, whose producers also made many important artistic decisions? I explore the careers of several young women working behind the scenes in the girl group genre, complicating the widespread assumption that the only females involved in creating girl group records were the singers themselves. My discussion pays close attention to songs such as the Shirelles' "Will You Love Me Tomorrow?" (1960), the Crystals' "Uptown" (1962), and the Ronettes' "Be My Baby" (1963).

The chapters of Part 4, "Look Here, Girls, and Take This Advice," address some of the complexities of race and class in girl groups and girl culture. I have already noted that many of the best-known girl groups of the 1960s consisted of African American girls from urban, working-class backgrounds who came to exemplify glamour, sophistication, and ladylike respectability for a generation of youth from diverse class backgrounds and ethnic identities. During the most active years of the Southern Civil Rights movement, young female singers such as Diana Ross of the Supremes were among the most visible African Americans in the United States, and they represented notions of black identity as well as girl identity to fans and detractors alike. In marked contrast to the male rockers who would dominate popular music culture later in the decade, girl group singers worked hard to appear demure and respectable, adhering closely to societal expectations of "proper," well-brought-up young ladies (even "bad girl" groups like the Shangri-Las and the Ronettes were generally compliant and polite in their interviews and public appearances). At the same time that so much girl group material seems to reinforce the most repressive notions of femininity under patriarchal control, these songs also function as enactments of sisterhood embraced by many for their feminist potential. I consider the tradition of "advice songs," where girl singers shared their wisdom and experience with listeners in songs such as the Exciters' "Tell Him" (1962), the Shirelles' "What Does a Girl Do?" (1963), the Ronettes' "I Saw Mommy Kissing Santa Claus" (1963), the Marvelettes' "Little Girl Blue" (1963) and "Too Many Fish in the Sea" (1964), and the Velvelettes' "Needle in a Haystack" (1964).

In the final section, "Out in the Streets," I consider the issues surrounding girls and public space. If middle-class respectability insists that girls and women belong in the domestic sphere, how do we respond to the phenomenon of girls who venture outside of safe containment? I examine girl groups that projected a rebellious "bad girl" image, exploring the different kinds of rebellion possible to girls in 1960s youth culture, and I also discuss the experiences of girl groups who traveled with rock'n'roll tours, often making themselves vulnerable to sexual aggression and racist hostility. Although recent analysis has tended to consider girls' friendships detrimental to individual self-esteem, I suggest that group membership can actually be a valuable, empowering part of girls' self-fashioning strategies. In the concluding pages, I also investigate the legacy of the girl groups for later generations of females in popular music and for broader social understandings of female adolescent identity. Songs studied in these chapters include the Crystals' "He's a Rebel" (1962), the Chiffons' "He's So Fine" (1962), the Angels' "My Boyfriend's Back" (1963), the Shangri-Las' "Leader of the Pack" and "Give Him a Great Big Kiss" (both 1964), and the Girls' "Chico's Girl" (1966).

Throughout the book, I am concerned with challenging some of the methods and priorities of music scholarship that posit instrumentalists and composers as the most important players in music-making, while the work of singers and listeners is dismissed. I take as a given that auditors of music are integral participants in any musical experience, as Lisa Lewis and others have indicated in publications such as *The Adoring Audience*.[1] My emphasis on vocalists as the central musicians is distinct from the approaches of most genre studies in popular music, and it will, I hope, participate in a growing interest in the work of singers evident in writings such as Gage Averill's history of barbershop singing.[2] Finally, and most importantly, I hope that my focus on girls' voices and their experiences and strategies will dignify girls and girl culture.

Much of the information in this book came from singers and other experts on 60s' girl group music, and I gratefully acknowledge Ron Barrett, John Grecco, Fanita James, Billy Wilson, and Mary Weiss for their contributions—any errors are mine alone. May I also thank my research assistant Sarah Feltham, who searched tirelessly for pictures and information.

My work on girl groups began as a doctoral project in musicology at the University of California, Los Angeles, where it was guided by a peerless dissertation committee: co-advisors Susan McClary and Robert Walser, Mitchell Morris and Sandra Harding. I consider myself blessed indeed that these distinguished scholars took an interest in me and my half-baked ideas! Through seminars, teaching or research assistantships, and impromptu debates in the hallways of Schoenberg Music Building, I benefited also from rubbing shoulders with Philip Brett, Robert Fink, Raymond Knapp, Elisabeth LeGuin, and Tamara Levitz. I gratefully acknowledge the fellowships generously funded by Jean Stone, Mary Bianco, and the Pauley Foundation that made my studies at UCLA possible. My life as a doctoral student in Los Angeles would have been unimaginably impoverished without the constant stimulation and support of my friends and fellow grad students, in particular: Kate Bartel, Andy Berish, Durrell Bowman, Dale Chapman, Maria Cizmic, Charles Hiroshi Garrett, Daniel Goldmark, Jonathan Greenberg, Gordon Haramaki, Erik Leidal, Olivia Mather, Louis Niebur, Caroline O'Meara, Glenn Pillsbury, Cecilia Sun, and Stephanie Vanderwel.

In its journey from dissertation to book, this project grew and flourished with the encouragement of many friends and colleagues, as well as a generous grant from the Dalhousie University Research Development Fund. My colleagues at Dalhousie graciously commented on chapter drafts and opened my eyes and ears to new areas of inquiry: Jennifer Bain, Roberta Barker, Sue Campbell, Dennis Farrell, Liesl Gambold Miller, Ann Martin, David Schroeder, Sue Sherwin, and Shirley Tillotson have all helped me to refine my thinking. I am also grateful for the energy and fresh ideas of my students at Dalhousie, especially Paul Aitken, Jennifer Bentley, Angelica Blenich, Gina Burgess, Andrea Curry, Jacob Danson-Faraday, Bob Garrish, Brenna Holeman, Devin Krauskopf, and Rose Lipton. A group of "girl music" scholars has been invaluable as a source of information, ideas, and emotional support, and I thank Norma Coates, Susan Fast, Martha Mockus, Annie Janeiro Randall, Robynn Stilwell, Patricia Juliana Smith, and Laurie Stras for their wisdom and their friendship. My own adolescent years were brightened by a group of girls who are still my dear friends: Deborah Koenig, Heather Macfarlane, Samantha Scroggie, Debra Stein, Megan Wells, and Marina Santin, still in my heart every day despite her death in 1993.

Through all the years of my thinking about girls and music, Steven Baur has been a partner in every sense of the word, making great sacrifices to stick by me, insightfully helping me work through my ideas, and bearing repeated listenings of girl group songs with fortitude and even enthusiasm. I cannot imagine a life without him in it. My parents and sisters have unfailingly supported my creative endeavors in writing and in music, and I rely on their love and encouragement. And how could I proceed without acknowledging the girl and boy most precious to me—my children Sophie and Adam, whose births punctuated my work on this project. Their own years of adolescence are still a long way off, but every day they teach me about girlhood and boyhood. Through watching them grow and develop their own special ways of interacting with music, I too am learning new ways to listen to and learn about the world.

Introduction

> One is not born a woman, but becomes one.
>
> *Simone de Beauvoir,* The Second Sex

When I was nine, I had an experience that I have come to consider a feminist awakening. It happened on a Sunday morning; the Brownie troupe of which I was a member was preparing to take part in a special annual church service, awaiting the signal to march up the aisle and gather in front of the altar, singing "All Things Bright and Beautiful." A puny and dreamy child, I had not been entrusted with an important job such as carrying a cross or flag at the head of the procession, so instead I sulked resentfully in the narthex with the other undifferentiated Brownies, hideous in our mud-brown and orange uniforms. I noticed the flag of the church's Cubs troupe displayed prominently on the sanctuary wall (Cubs, if you don't know, are a boys' organization junior to Boy Scouts, in the same way that Brownies are to Girl Guides or Girl Scouts).[1] I was immediately offended that there was no equivalent emblem of Browniedom anywhere in sight, but closer inspection revealed a far greater injustice: the Cub motto, "Do Your Best," emblazoned magnificently in dark green silk. The Brownie motto, I knew only too well, was "Lend a Hand."

As an adult, I have often told the story of the Brownie Incident in order to account for my evolution as a feminist as well as to demonstrate that children are indoctrinated from very early on into rigid gender positions. As I perceived in a flash of clarity that morning, boys in Western society are urged to strive for excellence and independence, whereas girls are more likely to be directed toward helpful, supporting roles. Brownie dogma, I have warned, prepares us to conform to patriarchal institutions like traditional marriage, wherein wives are expected to be nurturing helpmeets to their ambitious and hardworking husbands. Thus, organizations like Brownies and Girl Guides are not merely anodyne after-school clubs for girls, but rather they are training grounds for repressive womanhood.

In making this dramatic claim, I have sought to emphasize the importance of girls, a social group that is generally dismissed and overlooked in cultural analyses, whether of women or of youth. Girls have little social power, and their interests and concerns are often regarded with derision (if they are noticed at all). Sherrie Inness observes wryly that even in the realm of toys for boys and girls, "G.I. Joe is concerned with life and death and war, while Barbie's main interest is what color bikini to wear to the beach."[2] Indeed, an enthusiasm for Barbie is regarded by some as the very nadir of girliness, to the extent that many girls routinely deny having any interest in the doll, and some even profess intense loathing for her that leads to "Barbie torture," as a study from the University of Bath reports.[3]

Rejecting the trappings of girl culture seems, then, to be the best route to earning respect and power. By problematizing the notion of "girl," tomboys cast doubt on the value of womanhood, and they suggest that the price of success in a man's world is suppressing stereotypically feminine character traits such as helpfulness and supportiveness. Tomboys can thus earn grudging admiration for their jettisoning of girly tropes, particularly from quarters where the superiority of masculinity is assumed. Adolescent and preadolescent females who adhere to conventional, clichéd understandings of what girls ought to be, on the other hand, appear to present no challenge to societal norms, so they can be considered reactionary. These kinds of girls are adorable, innocent, and fetching, and their culture seems frivolous and ultimately inconsequential. At the same time, however, the emblem of the conventional girl has been and is a powerful emblem in cultural discourse. She has served and continues to serve as a token of nostalgia for some idealized past; an icon for a bright future; an embodiment of innocence to be protected at all costs; a symbol of hope and inspiration; a helpless and tragic manifestation of pathos; an unspoiled object of lust; and a model of pouting selfishness and egocentrism.

Clearly, the emblem of the girl is highly complex and contradictory. The growing scholarly field of girl studies works to reclaim "girl" from being a term of condescension and belittlement. Girl theorists consider the phenomenon of female childhood and adolescence as it intersects with issues of race and class, and girl studies identify the subject position of "girl" as distinct from both "woman" and "youth," an ostensibly gender-neutral term that often signifies only male adolescents.[4] In this book I explore the phenomenon of pre-adolescent and adolescent girl identity as it was constructed and negotiated in the popular music of the 1960s, specifically in girl group music, a genre that played a crucial role in youth culture in the early part of the decade. The tremendous popularity of girl groups such as the Shirelles, the Ronettes, the Crystals, and the Shangri-Las marked the first instance in U.S. history of a music centered around adolescent girls and their experiences coming of age, in a society where teenagers were emerging as a newly significant group.

Throughout this project my thinking is governed by an understanding of "girlhood" and "girlness"—as well as their attending adjectives "girlish" and "girly"—as related but distinct concepts. Girlhood and girlish, in my usage, refer to a phase of the female life cycle, the period between childhood and womanhood, during which most females undergo the hormonal changes of puberty and prepare to be sexual adults. Girlness, on the other hand, is not a liminal phase but a set of behaviors and attributes available to females at any time during their lives. Children as well as adult women (and men, for that matter) can adopt a girly manner for strategic purposes, and they can play with the characteristics of girlness for their own enjoyment. In the following chapters I will make use of these terms freely.

Music and Youth in the 1960s

The 1960s are generally recognized as a turning point in youth culture, and the popular music of the decade has been considered particularly worthy. Members of the baby boom generation who came of age during the 60s celebrate the power and beauty of music, and they readily acknowledge the important role that music played in the cultural events of their adolescent years. Yet it is difficult not to notice that most of the celebrations of 1960s music in histories of the period are lopsided, focusing disproportionately on the music that was important to white, middle-class males who participated in (or at least sympathized with) left-wing political movements.

Indeed, so total is the fascination with the Beatles, the Rolling Stones, Bob Dylan, Jimi Hendrix, and the Grateful Dead that—in my experience, at least—the term "sixties' music" in general conversation often refers exclusively to their works, ignoring altogether music that emerged from the worlds of jazz, the avant-garde, and mainstream radio. Even within the realm of histories explicitly addressing popular music, most begin their narratives of the 1960s with the so-called British Invasion of the North American music charts by artists such as the Beatles and Rolling Stones and conclude with the counterculture festivals at Monterey (1967) and Woodstock and Altamont (both 1969).

Two well-regarded histories of the decade exemplify this approach.  Durwood Ball's article "Popular Music" in *The Columbia Guide to America in the 1960s* extols the importance of the Beatles, Bob Dylan, and artists associated with psychedelic culture and briefly mentions only three artists representing other styles of popular music (the Shirelles, Fabian, and Connie Francis) in order to dismiss them as trivial and politically irrelevant.[5] Similarly, Todd Gitlin's best-selling reflections on the 60s include a discussion of popular music, heavily weighted toward the Beatles, Bob Dylan, the Rolling Stones, and the participants in counterculture festivals such as Monterey Pop and Woodstock.[6] When these kinds of accounts are accepted as representative and complete, they distort our understanding of the early 60s. Because this period is generally considered such a pivotal moment in the evolution of the teenager, this distortion has significant consequences for the ways in which we understand popular music and youth culture in the present day.

Commenting on this kind of male bias in accounts of 1960s youth culture, Susan Douglas observes trenchantly that

> According to the prevailing cultural history of our times, the impact of the boys was serious, lasting, and authentic. They were the thoughtful, dedicated rebels, the counterculture leaders, the ones who made history. The impact of the girls was fleeting, superficial, trivial. The supposedly serious cultural documents of teenage rebellion…emphasized male alienation and malaise…while [girls] appear as nothing more than mindless, hysterical, out-of-control bimbos who shrieked and fainted while watching the Beatles or jiggled our bare breasts at Woodstock.[7]

Both examples that Douglas provides of pejorative attitudes to girls relate to the consumption of popular music, and they refer to the often unquestioned view of girls as mere fans and recipients of the creative and important music of boys. This kind of treatment typically posits girls as reactionary, passive devotees, in marked contrast to the innovative and rebellious boys whose music they are privileged to enjoy. Similarly, music associated primarily with audiences of girls tends to be considered girly by association, regardless of the actual sex of the performers. Thus, their numerous girl fans guaranteed that the Monkees were excoriated as peddlers of inane "bubblegum" music, and the group struggled to restore masculine credibility by touring with Jimi Hendrix as their opening act in 1967 and by collaborating with Jack Nicholson on their 1968 feature film *Head*.

Girls find themselves caught in a double bind: choosing to participate in the musical discourses of important male culture limits them to the subject position of groupie or perhaps honorary male, but subscribing to an identifiably girl-centered music earns them contempt for embracing mainstream fluff.[8] No surprise, then, that Mary Weiss, the former lead singer of the wildly popular and influential Shangri-Las, prefers to distance her group from the girl group category altogether. She states firmly that "We never thought of ourselves as a 'girl group.' We were rock and rollers, same as the guys. True rock and roll has no sex—it's rock and roll."[9]

Nevertheless, I would argue that rock'n'roll is much concerned with sex and sex identity, as indeed are other genres and styles of music. As Susan McClary argued in her path-breaking *Feminine Endings*, even the most casual listener can quickly distinguish stereotypically masculine music (aggressive, rhythmically energetic, created with instruments such as brass, percussion, low strings, distorted electric guitar) from stereotypically feminine music (soft, melodic, made by instruments such as flute, harp, acoustic guitar).[10] These musical codes are instantly recognized and accepted as part of most people's everyday soundscapes, whether heard in a nineteenth-century European symphony, a classic hard rock song, or a television commercial for Barbies. For the most part, the gender associations reinforced are absorbed without question, and the characteristics of masculine music are generally ceded greater cultural authority.

The vocabulary of musical gestures and sounds used in popular music during the 1960s communicated a great deal to its listeners about gender, race, and class, and these lessons were arguably the more effective for being invisible and intangible. If our histories of the period valorize the activities of boys and men, they also valorize the aesthetic priorities of popular music associated with maleness: extended forms, long solos that showcase virtuosity and technical skill, the use of distortion, harmonic complexity, and powerful rhythms. By contrast, music that adheres to conventional harmonic language, accessible hooks and lyrics, sweet-sounding voices and instruments, and an emphasis on the ensemble rather than the soloist is treated summarily (sometimes even vindictively) as trifling and immaterial. It is surely not coincidence that this kind of mainstream, radio-friendly music is associated largely with female or feminized listeners and that it commands large audiences, if little prestige. In *Air Guitar*, art critic Dave Hickey notes that "ninety percent of the pop songs ever written [are] love songs, while ninety percent of rock criticism [is] about the other ten percent."[11] Those pop songs that make use of conventional harmonic language, clichéd grooves, and standard instrumentation have generally been ignored or despised by both popular music scholars and rock critics, like an elephant in the room that everyone pretends not to see.

The fetishization of popular music that styles itself as complex, challenging, and oppositional is parallel to the desirability of the "terminal prestige" that Susan McClary has observed in the sphere of academic composers, the importance of whose music is measured according to how few people understand it.[12] Countercultural musics earn valorization and admiration because they rail against the codes of mainstream pop; however, this resistance would hardly be worth celebrating were it not for the enormous cultural clout of commercially successful, middle-of-the-road (MOR) pop music—indeed, opposition is scarcely comprehensible unless we understand what is being opposed. In an influential essay, Andreas Huyssen has noted that the idea of important, "authentic" culture existing somehow apart from mainstream commercial society is invariably gendered in any epoch.[13] Certainly, we can discern a sexist bias in the extolling of countercultural music and the zealous dismissal of a mass culture largely associated with girls.

Girl Groups and Girl Culture

The well-known girl groups of the 1960s are clearly archetypes of girlness set to music, so much so that their musical vocabulary, choreographed moves, and matching outfits, as well as many of their actual songs, have transcended their initial social and historical context and continue to be significant forty years after their original moment. Quite apart from girl groups popular at the turn of the twenty-first century (such as Destiny's Child, the Spice Girls, and All Saints, all defunct at the time of writing), echoes of 60s girl groups abound in popular culture. As I write this, I am energized by listening to my brand-new, four-CD box set *One Kiss Can Lead to Another: Girl Group Sounds, Lost and Found*, a 2005 release that has garnered much positive attention in the international press.[14] Doubts about the relevance of my work can be assuaged by visiting the Spectropop website dedicated to circulating information about girl groups and solo girl singers from the 1960s. I am further heartened by the continued appearance of the girl group in various cultural forums, from the girl-group-as-Greek-chorus in the 1982 Broadway musical *Little Shop of Horrors* (given a film treatment in 1986 and continuing to attract audiences in touring theatrical productions in 2006) to the girl-group-as-source-of-inner-strength that bolstered Ally McBeal's self-esteem in the popular television series *Ally McBeal* (1997–2002), to say nothing of the girl-group-as-children's-cartoon in many "Elmo's World" segments of *Sesame Street* (1998–present). The presumed recognizability of girl groups in these various contexts attests to the enduring relevance of the sound and image of the 1960s girl group.[15]

My study focuses on the output of groups such as the Shangri-Las, the Shirelles, the Crystals, and the Marvelettes, groups that emerged from inner-city and suburban backgrounds, were black and white, came together through audition processes, or formed based on family relationships and friendships. What these groups have in common is that all of them comprise three to five adolescent female singers who seem to articulate highly personal sentiments and concerns, but each has also been regarded as a group of puppets masterminded by some behind-the-scenes Svengali.

This formation becomes more complicated when we acknowledge that members of many of the prominent 1960s girl groups were African American girls from working-class backgrounds—in many cases managed and controlled by white men—who became emblems of girlhood for white, middle-class suburbia during the years of the Southern Civil Rights movement. What are we to make of this multifaceted configuration? Many of the most popular groups came into being through careful planning, management, and coaching, but at the same time, we measure the success of a girl group song (and any other pop song for that matter) by the extent to which it rings true with its intended audience. Carefully staged though they may have been, songs like "Will You Love Me Tomorrow?," "Give Him a Great Big Kiss," and "Sweet Talkin' Guy" resonated with legions of girls from diverse class and race backgrounds who recognized themselves in the texts.

One of the problems girl group music poses to historians and critics of popular music, therefore, is its unique ability to combine shameless artifice with truthfulness and honest attention to real experience. A preoccupation with veracity and authenticity will naturally enough lead to this music begin denigrated, so I challenge the reader to listen differently. My analysis of representative songs aims to demonstrate how songs work as multilayered cultural documents articulating complex notions of the self through words, music, and movement, and I strive also to problematize the murky relationships between authenticity and mediation. Girl group songs are always both examples of unsophisticated girl singers performing material written and produced by others, usually under the direction of adult men, and compelling emblems of sisterhood, female collectivity, and—in the post–Spice Girls era—"girl power."

If we accept the idea that girlness exists as a social construct and concur with Mary Russo that "to put on femininity with a vengeance suggests the power of taking it off," then it becomes possible to understand girl group songs as potent rather than simply passive and reactionary.[16] I approach girl group music with this understanding of girl identity in mind, treating songs as cultural texts and making use of them to explore various issues pertaining to female adolescence. My close attention to musical detail allows me to address aspects of this repertoire that have not been examined by other writers.[17] Given that so many girl group songs from the 1960s still constitute part of our contemporary soundscape, I also address the ways in which some musical devices and strategies continue to resound with the conventional understandings of girl identity.

The girl group genre has been at the forefront of popular music at two different historical periods: the rock'n'roll era of the late 1950s and early 1960s and the late 1990s, when the children of the baby boom generation were themselves coming of age. In between these historical periods, other manifestations of femininity in popular music have been prominent, but the poetic, acoustic instrument–based songs of confessional singer/songwriters such as Joni Mitchell; the sassy, sexy reportage of streetwise rappers like Missy Elliott; and the raw, punk-influenced anger of Riot Grrrls like Kathleen Hanna have little in common with the girl group style. In spite of its popularity and importance, however, girl group music has been one of the most underresearched repertories in popular music history. I focus on the complex nature of a music culture that is too often dismissed as vapid and reactionary, and I consider ways in which girls can and do negotiate their gender and generational identities through music.

PART I
Girl Talk

A founding member of the Supremes, the most successful and well-known female vocal ensemble of all time, Mary Wilson has published a best-selling memoir recounting the trajectory of a career that emerged against the backdrop of the girl group phenomenon of the early 1960s.[1] At one point, she recalls indignantly that at the height of the Supremes' commercial success, some considered the three singers to have lost their inherent black "soulfulness," to the point that a British journalist even urged them to "Get back to church, baby!" In fact, none of the Supremes had ever sung in church, and Wilson complains about "the misguided notion that a black who was singing and didn't sound like Aretha Franklin or Otis Redding must have been corrupted in some way."[2] As I will show in this section, the girl group sound developed by drawing on many musical styles, of which gospel singing was by no means the only one, or even the most important. I want above all to refute still-widespread assumptions that black singers of soul, R&B, and rock'n'roll all draw on some instinctive, intuitive vocal ability that is simply a by-product of their genetic makeup, rather than a learned artistry requiring considerable skill and effort. My discussion considers the still-developing adolescent voices in girl groups, the relationships they enacted in their records, and the possibilities they present for an understanding of the Voice of the Girl.

1

The Emerging Girl Group Sound

With their glamorous gowns, elegant choreography, theatrical vocal style, and songs dealing with adult themes such as marital infidelity ("Stop! In the Name of Love," 1965), illegitimate children ("Love Child," 1968), and filial guilt ("Livin' in Shame," 1969), the Supremes were in many ways never really a *girl* group, although they are often named first in a list of girl groups from the 60s. Even their earliest hits, "Where Did Our Love Go?," "Baby Love," and "Come See about Me" all appeared in 1964, a year in which the girl group "moment" was, for all intents and purposes, over. The girl group sound and style occupied a prominent position in mainstream popular culture at the very beginning of the 1960s, emerging in 1957 and dominating the pop charts from 1960 to 1963. The style was predicated on the sounds of adolescent female voices audibly going through hormonal development—most girl group singers really were *girls*, with ages ranging from eleven to eighteen in the most representative groups. Girl group records had lyrics addressing themes of special importance to teenage girls, such as boys, the strictness of parents, and the complexities of imminent womanhood. The genre generally involved young vocalists backed by studio musicians, performing material written by professional songwriters (though this book will present several examples of groups that operated differently). Girl group music was at the forefront of popular music during the early 1960s, an unprecedented instance of teenage girls occupying center stage of mainstream commercial culture. This phenomenon was not repeated until the late 1990s and early twenty-first century, when latter-day girl groups and solo singers including the Spice Girls, Britney Spears, and Avril Lavigne, among others, were immensely successful in bringing girl's voices and concerns back to prominence in mainstream music.

One of the first ensembles to achieve critical and commercial success as a girl group was the Chantels, who really had sung in church: members of the quintet were Catholic convent school girls from the Bronx who were trained in chant and choral singing. Lead singer Arlene Smith would go on to pursue formal music studies at the Juilliard School, and as teenagers, all group members took lessons in piano, were musically literate, and were adept at close harmony singing, thanks to a steady diet of motets and hymns. The Chantels were the first group of black girl singers to attract a significant following, beginning in 1957, only a year after the eruption of rock'n'roll into mainstream culture. When their career took off, members of the Chantels ranged in age from fourteen to seventeen, and they had been singing together at school for more than seven years.[1]

The Chantels

There are conflicting accounts of how the Chantels came to prominence. Charlotte Grieg and Alan Betrock, both of whom draw on interviews with Arlene Smith, assert that the group lay in wait backstage at Loew's Theatre one night for well-established producer/manager Richard Barrett to emerge after an episode of *The Alan Freed Show*, and then caught his attention by singing either a unison hymn or their own composition "The Plea."[2] Michael Redmond, Steven West, and Jay Warner, on the other hand, state that the group happened to recognize Barrett and his group, the Valentines, walking on Broadway one afternoon and approached them for autographs. Hearing these young girls boast that they were singers, too, Barrett challenged them to sing something then and there; under the awning of the Broadway Theatre, they performed a hymn in Latin and impressed him with their angelic sound.[3] In both versions of the story, Barrett was intrigued by the possibilities of blending these choirgirl voices with R&B grooves and doo wop harmonies, and he eventually took the group in hand, cowriting their material with lead singer Arlene

Smith, producing their records with George Goldner, and guiding the group to considerable chart success over the next four years.

The voices of the Chantels were an exciting sound in 1958, the year their song "Maybe" rose to #15 on the pop charts and #2 on the R&B charts. Their choirgirl diction and the focused, ringing timbres of their upper vocal registers were novel, resembling in some ways the sweet-voiced sounds of urban black teenage boys singing doo wop, and in other ways the barbershop aesthetics of white, mid-Western women like the Chordettes, and even the polished recordings of white, adult starlet/pop singers such as Debbie Reynolds or Patti Page. Their African American identity also invited superficial comparison with blues shouters such as Ruth Brown, LaVern Baker, and Etta James, although the Chantels never emulated a bluesy, gritty vocal style. Ultimately, the Chantels' music could not be categorized with any other style of the day, and their success spawned many imitators and precipitated a new genre in popular music. However, the girl group sound of the early 60s would develop a markedly different aesthetic from the Chantels' sound of the late 50s, as even a cursory listening of records by the Shirelles, the Crystals, the Cookies, or the Marvelettes reveals.

The Chantels' success with "Maybe" paved the way for other girls to enter the world of the music industry, hitherto populated largely by adults and a few teenage boys. "Maybe" set the benchmark for the Chantels and many other female harmony groups. The song is credited variously to Richard Barrett and to Arlene Smith and George Goldner, although Jay Warner asserts that this and many other Chantels songs were composed by Arlene Smith alone and then credited to Barrett and George Goldner—this is, of course, a common claim about many popular songs, particularly in the girl group repertoire.[4]  Stylistically, "Maybe" closely resembles songs credited solely to Smith such as "He's Gone" and "The Plea" (both 1957). These songs make use of close harmony singing, featuring Smith's full and impassioned sound supported by the comforting tones of her sister Chantels. In "The Plea" the protagonist begs forlornly for her lover to remain at her side, while in "Maybe" she yearns for his return—in both songs, she prays ardently for the return of her affections, a religious allusion also present in "Every Night (I Pray)" and "Prayee" (both 1958).

Based on song titles and lyrics alone, these songs reinforce the seldom-examined assumptions that all young African American singers at mid-century were heavily steeped in gospel music traditions and that vocal ensembles like the Chantels came together through singing in black Pentecostal churches. The dialogic style typical of what would be called the girl group sound is assumed to derive from the singers' musical education of rote learning with call and response, building songs through collective improvisation from a shared vocabulary of memorized riffs, with careful reaction to a leader's spontaneous singing, which is in turn dictated by congregational behavior. This mistaken belief often led white music critics in the late 1960s to condemn girl groups and other African American acts erroneously for abandoning their gospel roots and "selling out," as Mary Wilson recalls on page 11. Further confounding this simplistic assessment, the Blossoms, a Los Angeles trio who became emblematic of girl groups because of their position as regular backing singers on the popular television variety show *Shindig!*, comprised members raised in very different liturgical traditions. Darlene Love was a preacher's daughter brought up in the Pentecostal Church of God in Jesus, whose father was so displeased by her singing secular music that she was forced to leave home at an early age; Jean King grew up singing chant in the Roman Catholic tradition; and Fanita James was raised in the Methodist church by a father who was a jubilee singer.[5]

The Chantels met at choir practice in the Bronx, but rehearsals were led by a nun at their Roman Catholic convent school, St. Anthony of Padua.[6] Indeed, the choral influence was so strong that, according to composer Arlene Smith, "The Plea" was based on Gregorian chant.[7] Some features of the melody do suggest the influence of chant; for example, the melody is centered around a repeated pitch that is a fifth higher than the final resting place of the tune. This is similar to the function of a reciting tone in chant repertoire, in which most of the text is sung on a single repeated pitch a fourth or fifth above the final.[8] Furthermore, the melodies of "Maybe" and "The Plea" are grounded in a high tessitura that is unusual for pop songs, and they feature tutored choirgirl diction—Smith's "ee" vowels in particular are more in line with choral pronunciation than with American conversational English. Her controlled vibrato with lowered larynx is not typical of the straight, vibrato-less sound favored by most choral directors, but it is strikingly different from gospel and blues singing styles and suggests that her vocal training was at least in part focused on singing solo with classical technique. Smith recalls the musical education of the Chantels:

> When I was about seven I became a member of the St. Anthony of Padua Cherub Choir. We were all trained in music from a very early age; we all took piano and voice lessons from the same nun. By about '53 or '54, just as we were coming up to our teens, we started to be interested in pop—and boys, of course. At that time I played basketball because I was tall. I was second string so I had a chance to sit on the bench and fool around with my friends. We grouped together and sang; and a sound kept evolving.[9]

A picture of nicely brought up convent schoolgirls singing together while under supervision at school activities suggests that the soundscape of the Chantels' world did not include the aggressive, raw sounds of jump blues or R&B and that the pop music Smith was interested in probably comprised mainstream Tin Pan Alley standards. Similarly, Mary Wilson insists that

> [the Supremes'] roots were in American music—everything from rock to show tunes—and always had been. We weren't recording [Tin Pan Alley] standards because they were foisted on us by Motown; we loved doing them and had since we were fourteen years old.[10]

The close harmony style of Chantels recordings also evokes barbershop quartet singing, and "The Plea" in particular features many hallmarks of the barbershop sound: liberally used seventh chords; echo effects at the end of verses, resembling the classic "Sweet Adeline"; and a vocal arrangement that places the lead singer second from the top, with a higher voice contributing to the backing vocals, in a style standardized by the Andrews Sisters and other vocal harmony groups in the 1940s.

Close Harmony Singing: Barbershop

With regard to female singing groups in the 50s, this distribution of vocal parts typifies the work of the Chordettes, a quartet of young white women from Wisconsin whose hits include 1954's "Mr. Sandman," "Eddie my Love" in 1956, and 1958's "Lollipop" (by teenage songwriter Beverly Ross, a Jewish New Yorker who would go on to cowrite Lesley Gore's "Judy's Turn to Cry" and several other 1960s hits). The Chordettes were explicitly linked to the barbershop genre; their founder Jinny Lockard was the daughter of a president of the Society for the Preservation and Encouragement of Barber Shop Quartet Singing in America (SPEBSQSA). Following barbershop nomenclature, they described their voices as tenor, baritone, and bass rather than using more customary terms such as soprano or alto for females in choral music. The Chordettes' nimble voices and ringing harmonies were enormously popular to adult and adolescent listeners alike in the post-war era, but their appeal became more limited after the rise of teen genres in the late 1950s; although they embraced rock'n'roll more enthusiastically than many of their peers, their sound and image connected them strongly to ideas of young suburban wives in Middle America.

The possibility that African American girls in the Bronx might have been influenced by barbershop singing might seem farfetched; this genre is commonly understood as the province of fresh-faced, white, male singers from Smalltown USA, thanks largely to cultural texts such as Norman Rockwell's illustrations of barbershop quartets in the 1920s and 30s, and Meredith Willson's 1957 Broadway musical *The Music Man*, made into a popular Hollywood film in 1962. The sounds that we now think of as barbershop were, however, a significant feature of black quartet singing in the late nineteenth century, well documented in newspaper accounts and reviews from the period.[11] Gage Averill argues that in American vernacular culture, "close harmony [singing is] a music of racial encounter, of a profound cultural intimacy, a short circuit in the hardwiring of racial separation and segregation, and the product of cultural transgressions, borrowings, mimicry, miscegenation, and cross-cultural homage."[12] Averill's notion of close harmony singing as an overlooked ancestor of rock'n'roll history is crucial to an examination of the girl group genre. I want also to follow his example in my consideration of the racial encounters involved in girl group music, arguing that notions of Girl Identity derive from multiple race and class origins, just as songs like "The Plea" and "Maybe" are shaped by numerous musical traditions.

Close Harmony Singing: Doo Wop

Jeffrey Melnick makes a similar case for doo wop, arguing for a nuanced understanding of racial encounter in this vocal genre: "How do we come to terms with the 'black' music made by Lee Andrews and The Hearts if we admit that its guiding imagery comes from the Shakespeare they learned in school? What if some African American teenagers turn out to have been a lot like some white ones, especially in their expressive practices?"[13]

The Chantels' "Maybe" makes skillful use of the vocabulary of doo wop songs: a 12/8 meter; a looping, descending harmonic pattern of I–vi–IV–V, the "doo wop progression" that characterizes such songs as Gene Chandler/the Dukays' 1962 "Duke of Earl" and "Heart and Soul" (a favorite with amateur pianists since the 1930s); and fervent singing about love lost. After an introduction of Fats Domino–styled triplets in the piano and voices on "ah" vowels establishing B-flat major, Arlene Smith sings a melody built on a stepwise descent, pondering that "maybe if I pray every night/you'll come back to me." At the end of this phrase, the harmonic framework has cycled through the doo wop progression to F major, the dominant, denying Smith the closure she seeks through her lyrics. She must repeat her melodic phrase insistently, enacting the wishful thinking that is her song's theme as she strives for the comfort of the tonic. At the end of each verse, as she contemplates the possible reciprocity of her love, the other Chantels mirror her sentiments with a barbershop-style echo: maybe, maybe, maybe.

Smith's high soprano (the entire range of "Maybe" sits on the top half of the staff, an unusual sound in pop singing) is in many ways like the falsetto virtuosity of groups such as the Platters ("Only You"), the Crests ("Sixteen Candles"), and, above all, Frankie Lymon and the

Teenagers ("Why Do Fools Fall in Love?"), whose influence on the girl groups was significant. In her autobiography, no less a girl group icon than Ronnie Spector identifies Lymon as the single most important inspiration for her career, declaring that "if [Lymon] hadn't made a record called 'Why Do Fools Fall in Love,' I wouldn't be sitting here writing this today."[14] Similarly, Arlene Smith recalls the first time she heard the song:

> It was a lovely high voice and a nice song. Then [DJ Alan] Freed announces that Frankie is just thirteen! Well! I had to sit down. It was a big mystery, how to get into this radio stuff. I thought if he could do it....It seemed so far removed, but I made a conscious decision to do the same.[15]

The imitation of Lymon's group could only go so far: male doo wop ensembles invariably comprised baritone and deep bass voices surrounding the falsettist, and this bottom range is naturally absent from records by the Chantels and other female harmony groups (the Chordettes' Janet Ertel, soloist on "Eddie My Love," referred to herself as the group's bass, but this term had more to do with her voice's harmonic function than with its husky alto range and timbre). By comparison with the broad range of male voice types, female vocal groups sing in a narrower tessitura with more overlap in the pitches that each voice can extend to—this is a partial explanation of why female groups often have only three singers. Within the realm of barbershop music, for example, female entrants in early singing competitions were "Gibson Girl Trios" who performed three-part arrangements of the same material as male foursomes.[16] Arranging parts for three voices is a significantly simpler task than writing for four, because there are no difficulties with voices doubling each other and very little need to involve sevenths. Three-part singing is also easier to stage and easier to rehearse, so that on the whole it is more accessible to girls, who typically have less leisure time and access to musical training than their brothers. However, this kind of ensemble singing does require two of the three voices to explore the extremes of their ranges, in a shift from the solo singing styles of pop music in the 1950s that typically placed the female voice squarely in the middle of its range.[17]

Given producer Richard Barrett's background as a manager/producer of groups like the Valentines and Frankie Lymon and the Teenagers, it is hardly surprising that the Chantels were commonly billed as a female doo wop group. Doo wop was a predominantly male genre of ensemble singing that flourished specifically in urban communities in the mid- to late 1950s. Indeed, with the exception of Zola Taylor's backing vocals on the Platters' "Only You," "Maybe" is the only instance of female voices heard on Rhino Records' five-CD *Doo Wop Box*. The doo wop world was made up of gangs of adolescent boys roaming inner-city neighborhoods and claiming particular street corners as territory. Singing was an important way of bonding and of guarding turf. In this public sphere as in the realm of the Chantels singing together, teenagers made use of the musical means at their disposal; the voice is an entirely portable, versatile medium of expressivity, and vocal music can be developed and created without extensive tutelage. Doo wop syllables, one of the hallmarks of the genre, filled out songs by replacing instrumental sounds, and the wide compass of vocal ranges in male doo wop performances together with the variety of individual vocal timbres created a rich musical texture that teens could produce at the drop of a hat.[18]

Soul singer Ben E. King recalls the role of doo wop in his 1950s Harlem adolescence:

> My buddies and I would walk from a Hundred Sixteenth to maybe a Hundred Twenty-ninth. And on those blocks you'd find anywhere from three to five groups. We'd stop and listen, and if we felt that we were better, we would challenge them. It was territorial, you know, and you'd have to go out looking for the competition. You'd stand around and check it out; they'd have a crowd anyhow. And their girls, of course.... We'd learn from the records, like everybody did. The group to get you over the best would be somebody like the Moonglows. If you could sing Moonglows, you could *kill* the neighborhood. They had great harmonies, the Moonglows.[19]

The idea of doo wop's tight harmonies, sweet falsetto voices, slow tempi, and sentimental lyrics functioning in the context of marauding and swaggering is fascinatingly incongruous, but this is not the place to unpack the complexities of masculinity described in this account.[20]

Simon Reynolds and Joy Press have analyzed the role of the street in male adolescence, citing songs such as Dion's "The Wanderer," Chuck Berry's "No Particular Place to Go," and Bruce Springsteen's "Born to Run" in their discussion of male restlessness and rebellion against the confines of domestic space. They argue that wanderlust is inextricably linked with detachment from women and that the "wanderer" type is invariably a brooding male.[21] Certainly, this issue is connected to the projects of canon formation in popular music studies I discussed in the introduction to this book; as numerous scholars have argued, histories of rock'n'roll have aggrandized the male teenage experience to the point of obscuring all others.[22]

A Culture of Containment

I want to draw attention to the contrast between Ben E. King's reminiscences of wandering the streets of Harlem looking for a vocal "duel" and Arlene Smith's recollections of sitting patiently and singing with friends during basketball practice. This juxtaposition demonstrates that the thrills of running with street gangs—even ones that fought with voices and not fists—were generally off limits to young girls at mid-century. Indeed, the association of girls with closed spaces and boys with the vast outdoors was hardly new in the 1950s, and it continues to dominate hegemonic understandings of gender roles today. As scholars following Gayle Rubin's famous essay on the traffic in women point out, most societies place a cultural imperative on keeping girls and women contained in order to protect their sexual purity and worth on the marriage market.[23] Females who defy these strictures are usually punished to maintain social order. Elaine Tyler May argues that the impetus for females to be housebound was particularly strong during the 1950s. She suggests that the desirability of this containment was emphasized by a generation of new parents who had lived through the disruptions and uncertainties of the Depression and the Second World War, and who witnessed the beginnings of the Cold War as a dangerous threat to their newfound prosperity and to the safety of their children. May shows that the suburban nuclear family was a new construction that arose at mid-century, "the first whole-hearted effort to create a home that would fulfill virtually all its members' personal needs" rather than the last examplar of "traditional" values.[24]

More specifically, Wini Breines considers the effects of containment on white, middle-class girls, providing ample statistical evidence and analysis of the contradictions of girls' experience in the 1950s. During this decade, a girl was more likely than ever to be confined at home and kept under the watchful eye of a mother intent on preserving her daughter's respectability and marriageability. While unprecedented affluence and opportunity surrounded them, these girls, as well as girls from families with middle class aspirations, were increasingly restricted by conservative values from pursuing independent lives and were directed instead to aspire toward wifedom, motherhood, and isolation in suburban homes. Precisely because of this containment, Breines argues, many white girls from suburban backgrounds rejected their privileges and aligned themselves with marginalized cultures. Breines recalls that:

> "I longed to get my ears pierced, which was unheard of in my suburban high school (it was probably too close to the immigrant pasts we, and especially our parents, were determinedly shedding)."[25]

Fifties mores for "good" girls were unrelentingly repressive:

> "Like the undergarments that constricted our bodies…the 'rubber coffins' that were girdles, the breasts squeezed out and up—the culture constricted our minds and spirits."[26]

These values made it important for girls from respectable families to be confined to a safe, domestic sphere, while their brothers were directed just as sternly toward risk-taking and exploration. As I shall argue in the third section of this book, music with a "girl" aesthetic tends—in the 60s and afterwards—to emphasize its provenance in the recording studio and to make use of sounds and effects that could not exist in concert settings. In this and other ways, it differs sharply from music that aspires toward a "live" concert aesthetic and attempts to conceal any "produced," prefabricated sound. These different priorities are closely connected to the ways in which girls and boys are educated musically. Boys interested in rock'n'roll, jazz, or other vernacular genres are often able to follow musicians that they admire, watching them play, copying their style, and perhaps earning their support through building personal relationships with them. Learning from recordings, as Ben E. King did, is another important method that is arguably more available to boys, who are more likely to spend disposable income on recordings and record-playing equipment, whereas girls may be encouraged to spend any available funds on makeup, hair, and clothing.[27] Music training for girls, on the other hand, usually involves a regimen of lessons and solitary practice in a domestic space—conversely, those girls who do follow musicians are often considered "groupies" more enchanted with the glamour and sex appeal of rock stars than with their music.

Girls' musicking, like girl culture in a larger sense, has generally not revolved around the culture of the street or the call of the road. Females on the road are rare with good reason; this life is generally closed to them, fraught as it is with physical dangers and the risk of losing respectability. Furthermore, parents—particularly parents in 1950s USA, a moment of both unprecedented affluence and paranoia—tend to be more careful about protecting daughters than sons, often believing that boys need to take risks in order to grow to manhood, while girls must be kept safe and tame. Thus, while upwardly mobile African American city boys in the 1950s were able to form doo wop groups and roam the streets in search of adventure, their sisters were more likely to sing in the school choir and to harmonize behind closed doors at home.

Safely sheltered here, girls were free to experiment with different kinds of vocal personae and relationships. Through singing, girls can "try on" the voices and stances of different kinds of femininity, in much the same way that they might try on clothes, makeup, and hairstyles. These kinds of pastimes are, to many minds, the very stuff of girlness: film and television depictions of girl teens from the 50s to the present abound with pajama parties where mudpacks and makeovers are the main activities. Furthermore, these are interests that self-respecting adult women tend to look back on with a mixture of embarrassment and fondness; such frivolous pursuits seem to have little value for females being socialized to take their places in a post-feminist world. And even in the midst of their girlish pleasures, teenage females may believe that giving one another makeup tips and conferring about what to wear to school are less important adolescent behaviors than missing curfew and sneaking into bars underage. Dressing up, writing in diaries, and daydreaming are dismissed as trite activities when compared to more serious experiences of teenage rebellion and angst.

Singing into her hairbrush, and strutting and pouting in front of the bedroom mirror while listening to a record about the thrills of love and the perils of heartbreak may indeed have been playacting for the sexually inexperienced girl at mid-century. To dismiss a musical event because it does not stem from lived personal experience, however, ignores one of the most valuable functions of music. Listeners can turn to music to seek access to their inner selves and find new ways of experiencing emotion through rehearsing the passions of others, whether through listening or otherwise participating in music. The histrionics of songs about boyfriends killed in motorcycle accidents (as in the Shangri-Las' monumental 1965 "Leader of the Pack") can resonate with the heightened emotional state that typifies adolescent fantasy life, even if the actual events narrated seem far-fetched and melodramatic. To be sure, these kinds of fantasies are predicated on the power of "the Guy" as the determinant of a girl's worth, suggesting that only through being recognized as special by a boy can a girl achieve self-actualization. Daydreaming can be dismissed as a reactionary and even destructive activity for girls' self-esteem, but Angela McRobbie makes a case for "forms of fantasy, daydreaming and 'abandon' to be interpreted as part of a strategy of resistance or opposition; that is, as marking out one of those areas which cannot be totally colonised."[28]

Singing in particular is a highly self-conscious and staged medium for "abandon" and expressing one's innermost sentiments; there is something inherently artificial about bursting into song at a moment of intense passion. In a discussion of vocal performance in recording, noted singer and scholar John Potter goes so far as to argue that

> [t]here is little actual emotion expressed within the "performances" of a song on record, whether it is classical or popular, and the singer can be quite detached from his or her own rhetoric.…It is the rhetorical formula which enables the singer to concentrate on the technical aspects of

> delivery: accuracy of intonation, management of breath, remembering words. . . . Singers are not normally moved by their own performances: the aim of the recording is to write the blueprint from which others may construct their own meanings from the rhetorical framework provided by the performers.[29]

Confined as they are to restrictive spaces and prefabricated emotional experiences, and with little support for taking up the study of instrumental music, many girls are understandably attracted to singing and other forms of playacting as they drill themselves in preparation for public life. Thus, from a musical vocabulary based on their church repertoire and the close-knit, predominantly male genres of barbershop and doo wop singing, the Chantels whiled away their boredom by piecing together girls' narratives of abject devotion, and they created songs that other girls could recognize as representative of female experience, whether or not they stemmed from actual events. Arlene Smith admits sheepishly that much of the passion performed in the Chantels' songs was a result of playacting: "I was singing about a kind of love I didn't know: I loved my *parents*."[30]

Vocal Range and Singing Style

Smith recalls that "I was singing in a range that was considered unrecordable, that people supposedly wouldn't listen to. Everyone else was singing mid-range to low—I came out screechy and high."[31] To a reader familiar with formally trained voices, this assertion may be mystifying: Smith's range scarcely compares to that of an operatic soprano. Her remarks make more sense in the context of 1950s mainstream, adult pop artists like Rosemary Clooney or Debbie Reynolds, or even their contemporary R&B singers such as Ruth Brown. These performers sang most effectively in a low middle range and with the chest voice, not significantly higher than light baritone/tenor male singers like Bing Crosby or Frank Sinatra. Indeed, many duets between male and female pop singers included voice crossing, where the woman sang in a lower range than the man, as in Sinatra's 1967 duet with his daughter Nancy, "Something Stupid." Record buyers comfortable with women's singing at conversational pitch were understandably surprised and intrigued by Smith's novel sound.[32]

Repertoire designed for the Chantels' high voices would ultimately circulate among other girl groups, but when the Shangri-Las recorded "Maybe" in 1965, they lowered the key by a third, from B-flat to G major.[33] In 1963, however, the Crystals recorded "Look in My Eyes," a song that had reached #14 when performed by the Chantels in 1961. The Crystals' version lowers the key by only a half step, so that the bright, high sound of the Chantels is approximated in a departure from the Crystals' customary style. Another unusually high voice appeared in the girl group soundscape in 1960, when a San Diego group called Rosie and the Originals released "Angel Baby," a #5 hit that featured 15-year-old Rosie Hamlin's striking vocals. Latina Hamlin had written the song herself, drawing on the lilting guitar arpeggios and slow 12/8 meter of many doo wop ballads, and she sang with a nasal, breathy soprano that often extended above the staff. Although Hamlin's career as a pop vocalist was short-lived, her distinctive voice in this song was renowned; John Lennon cited her as a favorite singer, while journalist Mark Sten castigated the song as a "robot mantra" and Hamlin's voice as a "piercing, disembodied-siren vocal."[34]

The appeal of these voices was thus controversial, and certainly connected to their youthfulness, even if they did not sound especially childlike. Other girls of the same age were widely heard by radio listeners in the late 1950s, and the popularity of singers such as Brenda Lee and Connie Francis (to say nothing of their predecessor Judy Garland, who began her career in early childhood and continued playing child roles in her twenties) stemmed at least in part from their ability to sound like an adult. The Chantels' vocal training resulted in strong upper registers that distinguished them from other female pop singers of the day, and their full, developed voices are deceptively mature.

The Bobbettes

A startlingly different kind of precociously adult voice issued from Reather Dixon of the Bobbettes, a quintet from Harlem who signed a recording contract with Atlantic Records in 1957, at which time

The Bobbettes

the group members ranged in age from eleven to thirteen. They were already seasoned performers, having sung at school functions and talent shows—including Amateur Night at the Apollo—and, like the Chantels, they wrote their own songs. "Mr. Lee," their only Top 40 hit, was originally a gleefully spiteful song about their much-hated fifth-grade teacher in the style of a rollicking jump blues. This was the song that earned the Bobbettes (or the Harlem Queens, as they were originally called) the attention of their peers, a professional manager, and ultimately a recording contract. Nevertheless, at Atlantic it was felt that the song was simply too nasty to be recorded by sweet-faced little girls, and the Bobbettes were compelled to perform it instead as a perky love song. "Instead of 'He's the ugliest teacher that I ever did see,' we changed [the lyrics] to 'the handsomest sweetie that I ever did see,'" lead singer Reather Dixon later recalled.[35]

The account of this transformation is, to me, positively breathtaking: it encapsulates so many of the complexities of representing girl identity (as well as black identity) and demonstrates clearly the issues at stake with regard to female utterance. In the history of this song, we encounter fifth-grade girls devising and performing an expression of intense dislike, feelings held to be both implausible and unseemly for them; the energy and musical vocabulary of this expression is considered suitable for a love song and is twisted accordingly. In other words, it was acceptable—even adorable—for preadolescent African American girls to articulate fiery and passionate statements of love, but not anger or hate, and *the same musical language was appropriate in both cases.*[36]

Based on a blues progression, "Mr. Lee" features a boogie-woogie bass line, a honking tenor sax solo (played by legendary session musician King Curtis, who also recorded regularly with the Shirelles and other girl groups), growling lead vocals, and squeaks and shouts from the backing singers. It reached #1 on the R&B charts and #6 on the pop charts, so that the Bobbettes were able to ride on its fame for some time—indeed, they were the first female group to achieve this kind of chart success. They never again matched this feat, however, perhaps because Atlantic Records restricted them to more novelty songs, exploiting the charming juxtaposition of the girls' childlike bravado with their uncanny ability to sing like the roughest, toughest blues shouters.[37] Moving to Triple X records, the group released a follow-up single in 1959, "I Shot Mr. Lee," in which they disposed of their hero because of his unfaithfulness.[38] The cheerful vindictiveness of this song is presumably more in line with what the group had in mind with their initial composition—it follows the same tune as "Mr. Lee" and changes only the lyrics and some aspects of the instrumentation, and it has a slightly slower tempo.

The contrast between the adoration expressed in the lyrics of their first recording and the unrepentant murderousness of the second is startling, but there is an important continuity in the quality of the singers' voices—the pistol-packin' protagonist of the second song does not sound markedly different from the enthralled heroine of the first. Reather Dixon's voice is characterized by a gruffness well beyond her years, a deep, growling timbre that closely resembles the impassioned gospel sound of Sister Rosetta Tharpe. According to gospel historian Horace Clarence Boyer, the singing style nowadays known as gospel began to develop at nineteenth-century revival meetings, where "singers made no pretense of placing the voice 'in the head,' as was the practice of European singing masters, but chose the voice of those 'crying in the wilderness.'"[39] The desired vocal style in that genre was gritty and highly individual, and many aspects of the sound remained even after decades in which more refined singing was sought.[40] The great female gospel singers of the mid-twentieth century, such as Tharpe, Mahalia Jackson, Clara Ward, Sallie Martin, and even Aretha Franklin and Patti Labelle, contemporaries of the Bobbettes, are all distinctive vocalists who demonstrate both sweet and rough timbres in chest-dominated vocal technique. Reather Dixon emulates these kinds of sounds in the various versions of "Mr. Lee," while the rest of the Bobbettes maintain a straighter timbre more in the style of jubilee quartets such as the male Golden Gate Quartet or the female Meditations, a Detroit group that was immensely popular and influential in the mid- to late 1950s. The interplay between lead and backing singers in the "Mr. Lee" songs involves shouted interjections and quick exchanges, demonstrating both extensive rehearsing and attention to arrangement, as well as a familiarity with gospel's call-and-response strategies.

Girlhood, Race, and Class

The roughness of Reather Dixon's voice seems a strange sound to be issuing from the mouth of a prepubescent girl, but it can be connected to an interest in sweet little girls with rough voices and tough, womanly stances. The sound and the look of the Bobbettes were certainly in sharp contrast to the white, demure ideal of girlhood upheld in the 50s. As I shall argue in the next large section of this book, the model of blue-eyed, blond-haired, and soft-spoken femininity was (and is) a powerful image in female adolescence, with authority in many class and ethnic groups. The Bobbettes call to mind the character of Topsy, the wild, rough, pickaninny slave girl who serves as foil to angelic, blond-haired (and fatally ill) Eva St. Clare in Harriet Beecher Stowe's *Uncle Tom's Cabin*. These iconic versions of black and white girlhood were reinforced through a 1923 musical play *Topsy and Eva*, which starred the white Duncan Sisters, Rosetta and Vivian (Rosetta in blackface as Topsy) and continued to be performed into the 1950s (there was also a film version with the Duncan Sisters in 1927).[41] It is still possible today to find "Topsy and Eva" dolls; these are usually made of cloth, have a full skirt, and two heads. Held up

Apollo Theater Souvenir Pin: The Duncan Sisters as Topsy and Eva. Courtesy of John Sullivan.

one way, the doll is the sweet, saintly Eva, while impish, wild-haired Topsy lurks in her petticoats. Held up the other way, the opposite is true, so that the doll represents a version of girlhood that includes sweet and rough, good and bad, white and black.

As repressive an image of black girlhood as Topsy may be, she is a rare instance of a little black girl who is allowed to speak in U.S. culture.[42] Throughout the twentieth century at least, Western capitalist culture has been fascinated with the idea of little girls who have the characteristics of women, as Valerie Walkerdine shows in her discussion of the Depression era cartoon character Little Orphan Annie and her real-life contemporary, child star Shirley Temple. Walkerdine observes that "[Annie] is a young girl on the street, who would be innocent and child-like, but is not. This figure is precisely the one which presents the threat to the discourse of the innocent and rational child: the child who is not a child, and whom, in the case of the little girl, we may understand to be sexually precocious as well as full of street-savvy. This is the model of a little girl who becomes a popular heroine, a girl heroine of the populace, the masses."[43]

Walkerdine contrasts this model of the adorably tough working class girl with the sweet and helpless "poor girl whose main function is to charm the rich, persuade them through their love for her to love the poor and the unemployed, and to provide charity in the face of depression," a role superbly performed by Shirley Temple in many films.[44]

I suggest that the character enacted by Reather Dixon and the other Bobbettes in "Mr. Lee" appealed to listeners in much the same way as did Topsy and Little Orphan Annie.[45] Walkerdine argues that the Orphan Annie version of poor, disadvantaged girlhood serves as a kind of working class hero(ine), and that the precocious knowingness of this kind of child reinscribes class distinctions by presenting a foil to the archetypally innocent, protected little girl of the middle class. The Bobbettes' subaltern voices can utter—literally, and more metaphorically through the jukejoint quality of their vocal timbres—feelings that are distant from dainty middle-class mores.

At the same time, Walkerdine's theorizing allows that the success of the Bobbettes and the unrefined roughness of their sound could represent a triumph for their disenfranchised community. She contends that the differing reactions of approval and horror to the spectacle of little girls performing are "overwhelmingly a matter of class difference."[46] In an application of her theories to a discussion of African American girls, it is obvious that these different responses are connected to race as well as class. The full-throated raunchiness of preadolescent African American girl singers like the Bobbettes represented at once an attractive Other version of girlhood to white listeners and, at the same time, an opportunity for black femaleness to speak and to be heard. In the last years of the 1950s, as acts of civil disobedience were increasingly disruptive to a racist, militaristic, Cold War social order in the United States, vocal ensembles such as the Bobbettes stood at the nexus of conflicting ideas about race, class, gender, and age.

2

The Voice of the Girl

While the Chantels were studying Palestrina motets and harmonizing on the basketball bench and the Bobbettes were hollering and shouting their way into the Apollo Theater, that hallowed sanctum of R&B, a quartet of seventeen-year-old African American girls in suburban Passaic, New Jersey, was experimenting with voice parts and doo wop vocables in an effort to create a group sound. The Shirelles, as they came to be known, were inseparable friends who entertained their classmates with renditions of popular doo wop songs at school talent shows and local dances. A school friend convinced them to audition for her mother, Florence Greenberg, who ran a small record label called Tiara and would later be a record producer and owner of Scepter Records.[1] The Shirelles performed their own composition, "I Met Him On a Sunday," in Greenberg's living room, impressing her enough to sign them to her label and take them into the studio to record the piece. The song entered the pop charts in 1958, reaching a modest #49. Minimal instrumentation of drum kit, bass, and a single muted horn was added to handclaps, finger snapping, and singing, and its "do-it-yourself" aesthetic was an important part of its appeal.

The finger snaps and handclaps, audibly rendered by real hands clapping (as distinct from more stylized representations used later in more sophisticated recording studios), evoke girls' handclapping and ring games, as does the singsong melody. Indeed, it is not difficult to imagine the song evolving from these kinds of girls' activities; the structure of the song closely resembles girls' singing games that are transmitted orally from peer to peer, such as handclap games, ring games, and double dutch. Kyra Gaunt theorizes that double dutch, handclapping, and ring games function like *études* in the musical acculturation of practitioners, an arena where girls learn the dance moves, rhyming procedures, and rhythmic vocabulary that will be useful in adult music-making.[2] The call-and-response step-and-clap songs documented by Eve Harwood feature a rock-steady step-and-clap pattern under a recurring sing-song refrain, with girls improvising, in turn, short solo lines. Harwood identifies this as a rare junction in girls' emotional playscape where skillful musical improvisation is prized in an otherwise strict and conservative genre: "From such games, girls learn to fit their individual contributions within the context of an ongoing musical performance, to enter and exit at the moment defined by the gestural and metrical structure, and to develop the presence of mind requisite for many kinds of improvisation. Although it seems simple enough, in the context of play it requires considerable concentration."[3]

The notion of improvising cleverly within a strict musical structure hands me a convenient metaphor for girls' experience speaking out from within a culture that regulates them fiercely: inventiveness and ingenuity are encouraged, but the opportunities for girls to speak are so clearly defined that they actually shape the kinds of utterance possible.

The Shirelles' "I Met Him on a Sunday" describes a one-week romance that the protagonist blithely ends because the boy shows up a day late for their date—the contrast with the Chantels' self-recrimination and regret in "Maybe" could scarcely be greater. Furthermore, instead of a clear distinction of lead singer supported almost hierarchically by wordless backing vocalists, "I Met Him on a Sunday" involves shared duties as a different Shirelle sings each solo line, as in an improvised call-and-response game. The tessitura of the song is also strikingly dissimilar and fills the interval of a fourth almost exactly an octave below Arlene Smith's melody on "Maybe." The backing harmonies are clearly conceived in a linear fashion, probably devised by one girl mirroring another's part at a higher pitch as the voices move in stepwise motion through parallel triads. Smith's carefully modulated vibrato and precise diction, along with the timbral balance achieved within the Chantels' ensemble work, are noticeably countered here with the highly individuated, often unsteady voices of the Shirelles, occasional inaccuracies of intonation and diction, and their thin, chest-dominated vocal timbre. Here, in other words, we have ordinary teenage girls who sound unmistakably like ordinary teenage girls.

A notable feature of the song is the rhythmic pattern: |𝄽 ♫𝄽 ♩ |𝄽 ♫𝄽 ♩ , reminiscent of the step-clap groove of ring games and the handclapping and body-slapping of many girls' games, which typically follow a four-beat pattern with a low sound on beats 1 and 3 and a higher one on 2 and 4.[4] This heartbeat pattern characterizes so many girl group recordings that I have come to think of it as the "girl group beat"; usually, beats 2 and 4 are stressed in the melody, coinciding with the handclaps or the snare, while downbeats are held steady by bass drums. This pattern and arrangement of low- and high-pitched sounds from the drum kit is the blueprint of rock drumming, certainly shaped by clapping and stomping practices in Pentecostal churches, but also perhaps by girls' play.

While "I Met Him on a Sunday" draws on some aspects of the doo wop tradition, the predictable harmonic progression, 12/8 meter, and lyrics expressing vulnerability are entirely absent. Instead, borrowings in this song take the form of doo wop syllables sung as a refrain by all group members in the second half of four-bar phrases. Within the doo wop genre, the use of these vocables developed as a means of creating full musical textures for ensembles that had no recourse to instruments—male vocal groups could sing nonsense words to fill in bass lines and horn riffs while roaming inner-city streets. Doo wop syllables can be celebrated as a resourceful and creative strategy by itinerant musicians emulating the bands they heard on the radio, a poor man's version of a big band or rock'n'roll lineup. As the doo wop genre became more established, and as the ensembles came to have access to studio instrumentalists during recording sessions, they nevertheless retained the vocables as a distinctive and increasingly virtuosic aspect of their overall idiom. Specific patterns of syllables came to be associated with certain kinds of musical lines, so that singers could draw on a shared vocabulary of musical/linguistic gestures in creating an intricate rhetoric of doo wop singing. For example, bass lines tend to rely on full vowel sounds and hard consonants, and a phrase such as "dip dip dip dip dip doo wah" is easily understood as mapping onto a musical phrase that hits the fifth scale degree six times before dropping to the tonic:

|dip dip dip dip|dip—doo—|wah—||

Female vocal groups in the late 1950s embraced this library of vocables and musical gestures in order to address listeners already familiar with their rhetoric, but when the Shirelles sang "doo dan, dey ron dey ron dey pa pa" in "I Met Him on a Sunday," the syllables needed not be understood as references to missing instrumental lines. Instead, the stylized syllabic phrases connected the female quintet with the established doo wop genre, allowing the group to participate in this important area of youth music culture. As the girl group genre in turn became more established, ensembles began to create a specifically female version of doo wop syllables that related equally to the use of vocables in handclapping and ring games, where syllabic phrases often function as a refrain. Phrases such as "da doo ron ron" from the Crystals' eponymous hit in 1963, and "doo lang doo lang" from the Chiffons' "He's So Fine" in the same year are made up of syllable groups not typical of doo wop songs.

Both "da doo ron ron" and "doo lang doo lang" appear in songs celebrating an idealized boy, "the Guy" who is central to so much girl group music. It is possible to understand these vocables as conveying an appreciation for the Guy's charms, perhaps as ecstatic expressions of sexual longing and even fulfillment, "passing" as a charming and childish gibberish. Girl singers in the 1960s drew on childhood games and on a style that developed as a form of public male culture in order to put together a language for their own discourse about *affaires du cœur*, but in such a way as to pose no threat to accepted beliefs about propriety. While this might seem an accomplishment hardly worth celebrating, given that it reinscribed an order that confined female talk to a secret, private sphere, I nonetheless applaud it as a means by which girls could talk about desire without provoking outright censure.

Girl Talk

Nicely brought-up girls in the early 60s, after all, could scarcely use frank language to talk about these feelings, and the euphemisms of "rock and roll" were not only transparent but were also associated with an older, less urbane generation. Making use of a feminine dialect permitted girl singers and girl listeners to articulate and explore their desires with impunity, preserving their sexual innocence and respectability. Indeed, "He's So Fine" depicts a gang of girlfriends whispering about a boy who has caught their eye, practically licking their lips as they look him up and down, and the "doo lang doo lang" refrain conveys a lustful appreciation far beyond the vocabulary of the prim middle-class teens who made the song a #1 hit for four weeks in 1963. Similarly, the refrain "da doo ron ron" from the Crystals' hit functions as a suggestive ellipsis, covering explicit description of what happened after lines such as "he looked so quiet, but my oh my" and—in every verse—"yes, and when he walked me home, da doo ron ron ron, da doo ron ron."[5]

But the use of the syllable "shoop" in Betty Everett's "It's in His Kiss" (1964) is surely the pinnacle of this kind of girl code—this vocable allows Everett to break the rule of "don't kiss and tell" without condemning her to the role of shameless harlot. The "shoop shoop" refrain of Everett's "It's in His Kiss" conjured the delights of a first kiss and was so central to the song's appeal that the subtitle "the Shoop Shoop Song" was added to its name. This all-important syllable is actually never uttered by the lead singer herself; rather, backing vocalists the Blossoms, who begin by questioning Everett about how she can tell if her boyfriend loves her, take it up as a knowing refrain when words fail her. "Shoop," with its slushy initial consonant, round "oo" vowel, and plosive "p" ending, requires the singer to pucker her mouth into the shape of a kiss, in keeping with the song's theme.[6]

Since the success of Everett's recording—ten weeks in the Billboard Top Ten in 1964—"shoop" has surfaced in other girls' and women's songs as an expression of ineffable pleasure. In hip hop trio Salt-N-Pepa's 1993 "Shoop," it coyly represents a specifically feminine experience of sexuality, and it functions in much the same way in Whitney Houston's 1995 "Exhale (Shoop Shoop)." Of course, both these songs are far more explicit about sexual desire than Betty Everett or other girl group singers could have dreamt in the 1960s! In these newer contexts, "shoop" should not be understood as a sly allusion to what "nice" girls cannot say directly, but rather as a reference to girl talk about sexuality, an acknowledgement of an earlier generation's strategic language.

Another example of mysterious language in a girl group song comes from the Dixie Cups in 1965, with their impromptu recording of "Iko Iko." They were a New Orleans trio of two sisters and a cousin who had been singing together since childhood and had recorded under various names before achieving a #1 hit as the Dixie Cups with "Chapel of Love" in 1964, by which time two of the members were university students. During a break in a recording session the following year, the trio began playfully to sing a traditional Mardi Gras song, accompanying themselves only with handclaps and a complex, shifting rhythmic pattern played with drumsticks on tabletops, ashtrays, and glass bottles. Session producers Ellie Greenwich and Jeff Barry were intrigued and began recording, later adding bass and more percussion to the track, in a similar method to that employed by the producers of the Shirelles' "I Met Him on a Sunday."[7] "Iko Iko" follows a call-and-response pattern, and it features cryptic lyrics that ostensibly derive from a Native American language:

Talkin' 'bout hey now, hey now
Iko iko ah nay
Jockomo fee no ai ah nay
Jockomo fee ah nay

Charlotte Grieg notes that "with its sing-song tune and simple backing, 'Iko Iko' had the genuine feel of a group of young girls, children almost, playing games in the school yard."[8] The song reached #20 on the Billboard pop charts and became the title track on the group's only album, indicating that these young women's performance in the style of a girlish singing game resonated with fans in large numbers.[9]

Can these vocables, which express more than conventional language allows, be understood as a kind of girl language, an *écriture feminine*? In a famous essay, French theorist Hélène Cixous urges that "il faut que la femme s'écrive par son corps," positing that writing through the body can resist the language of patriarchal discourse.[10] Singers do quite literally write with their bodies and voices, bringing out utterances from deep within and through flesh, fluid, and bodily tissue. Often, corporeal effort is audible in recordings, and this physical presence is an important feature for many listeners; fans may memorize exactly where and how the singer's throat catches on a held note, or participate in an audible intake of breath.

Écriture Feminine

The heard workings of the singer's body are part of an intimacy created through interacting with recordings in private, as opposed to being one listener in a large audience and hearing a singer from the stage. This kind of relationship, whereby a listener can take part physically in recorded performances by adding her voice to what she hears, is perhaps unique to sung music. The peculiarities of an individual voice can be mimicked as the listener explores the position of the vocalist, trying (as it were) to sing from within that singer's throat. In the case of girl group music, efforts to sing with the voice of another girl provide an opportunity to experience *being* that other girl, if only for two and a half minutes. These vocal experiments are crucial to the self-fashioning of teenage girls, an important strategy in their endeavors to construct coherent but complex and layered selves to present to the world. To be sure, the unique character of any voice can only be approximated and never perfectly reproduced, as human voices are as individual as fingerprints. In attempts to sing like other singers, however, an adolescent girl in the 50s and early 60s made important strides toward finding her own voice. For example, my impression of Etta James' deep belly growl is certainly no substitute for the original, but it is valuable just the same for the way it enables me to access a particular kind of strong woman's voice in my own guts and throat.

An insistence on the singer's embodiedness defies efforts to divorce music from a sense of the body, a need to elevate language—even sung language—above its origins in the flesh. That this separation of utterance from the body is a male privilege is demonstrated by Theodor Adorno's edicts on recording technology and female voices: "Male voices can be reproduced better than female voices. The female voice easily sounds shrill…in order to become unfettered, the female voice requires the physical appearance of the body that carries it. But it is just this body that the gramophone eliminates, thereby giving every female voice a sound that is needy and incomplete…wherever [sound] requires the body as a complement—as is the case with the female voice—gramophonic reproduction becomes problematic."[11]

Adorno considers that the male self is not tied to the body—indeed, that his self is fully represented in the sound of his voice—whereas the female self can never transcend its body, and the female voice is thus never an adequate representation of the female self. In the days of acoustic recording, there were indeed many difficulties with recording women's voices; in 1898, a Columbia Records executive instructed recording engineers to ensure that a woman singer "put her head as far as it will go into the [recording] horn when she's on her very low notes, and when she soars to the heights she must draw her head quickly back and sing straight to the ceiling."[12] Adorno's discussion of recording voices acoustically via this kind of gramophone was first published in 1928, by which time electric recording using microphones was becoming increasingly available, at least in the United States. By the late 1950s in New York, polydirectional microphones even more sensitive than those crucial to the careers of Bing Crosby and Frank Sinatra were standard.[13]

Adorno's remarks about the shrillness of women's voices in recording were written thirty years earlier than the emergence of the girl group phenomenon, but they should nonetheless recall Arlene Smith's report that her voice was considered too "screechy and high" for recording purposes, as well as Mark Sten's description of Rosie Hamlin's singing as a "piercing, disembodied-siren vocal" (see chapter 1). The perception of a disjuncture between women's voices and bodies continued after Adorno's theorizing and appeared earlier in other social and historical contexts as well. In the Italian convent tradition that might have been familiar to Arlene Smith and the nuns who taught her, for example, there were edicts in the sixteenth and seventeenth centuries prohibiting nuns from appearing in public; choirs of nuns were required to sing behind a screen, so that their disembodied voices could be heard as separate from their problematically female flesh.[14] In her ethnographic work in the Lubavitcher community in New York in the early 1990s, Ellen Koskoff learned from a female informant that the sight of a woman singing was prohibited because of the stimulation it could cause to males. Thus, women in the Lubavitcher community do not sing in front of men, following rabbinical teachings, but there are two interesting exceptions that allow women's voices to be heard. Koskoff's informant states that "Live, choral performance is no problem, because you can't distinguish one voice. If it's really a good choir, even if it's a cappella, if it's like one voice and has a good conductor, and he got them to pronounce their vowels, and they're in the same pitch [i.e., singing the same notes in unison], and they're all together, then there's no problem…then there's a live performance with some kind of electronic device, like a microphone…some kind of change in her voice through the microphone, that's the next level. It's not really her voice anymore."[15] Within the Lubavitcher community, then, the threat posed by a voice issuing from a woman's body is contained if the singing woman conceals her voice among a group of singers, and the danger is also negated if the voice is separated from the body through a recording process.

The notion of *écriture feminine*, by contrast, subscribes to the necessity of connecting female utterance to the body, and writers such as Cixous celebrate the embodied nature of the voice, seeking to validate women and women's experiences by insisting that their bodies be heard in their writing. Singing—even recorded singing—is valuable for exploring these ideas, because through this medium, utterance is part and parcel of flesh. Roland Barthes' influential discussion of what he terms the "grain" of the voice, "the materiality of the body speaking its mother tongue…the body in the voice as it sings," hinges on a discussion of vocal performances. Barthes insists that the presence of the body is the most important aspect of music.[16] As well as identifying the fleshliness of singing as a form of *écriture feminine*, I consider that the use of vocables specifically associated with girls' songs (as in the case of "shoop") can be identified as a form of girlspeak, a code that signifies while refusing conventional language. The idea that girl talk is a specific language, knowable only to initiates, is borne out in countless representations of teenage girls squealing and chattering incomprehensibly in film and television programs and commercials. While this kind of representation of girls clearly intends to mock them (albeit gently and perhaps even affectionately), it identifies an aspect of girlness that has disruptive and even subversive potential. If girls have a secret language, then it is possible for them to talk about their experiences in ways that patriarchal authority cannot control.

Talking about Boys

In 1958, the Chantels, the Bobbettes, and the Shirelles were poised on the cusp of an emerging genre of pop music directed toward teenage girl listeners, a forum for discussing girlish concerns about boys, the strictness of parents, gossip, and other aspects of growing up female in North America's cities during the Cold War. Of these three vocal ensembles, the Shirelles would become the first girl group to earn a #1 pop hit—"Will You Love Me Tomorrow?" in 1960—and five more top ten hits before 1963. Why did this ensemble become so much more successful than the other girl groups I have discussed? The importance of the Shirelles to girl groups and to rock'n'roll history caused them to be inducted into the Rock and Roll Hall of Fame in 1996. The unrefined voices and precocious aggressiveness of the Bobbettes' "Mr. Lee" songs, as well as their R&B instrumentation, passed almost entirely out of favor with urban teenage girls interested in defining themselves as sophisticated and ladylike. The Chantels and the Bobbettes were less successful in the long run, but the Chantels' "Maybe" was actually a more popular song in 1958 than was the Shirelles' "I Met Him on a Sunday." Indeed, although in many respects the Chantels could be understood as a female doo wop ensemble that influenced, but was not part of, the girl group phenomenon, in some ways "Maybe" is more representative of what the girl group style came to be than the Shirelles' song.

History bears out that the Shirelles, path-breaking examples of girl singers who sounded like teenage girls, would come to be considered the first example of a girl group, but the structure of their first song would not endure. The communal lead singing of "I Met Him on a Sunday," its origins as a collaborative effort by the group members, the cheeky girl of the narrative who dismisses her love object without soul searching, and the sparse instrumentation that places girls' voices squarely at the center of the recording are all characteristics that the Shirelles would abandon by the time they recorded their breakthrough

The Shirelles performing as a trio in 1966 for a television audience. Courtesy of Photofest.

hit "Will You Love Me Tomorrow?". "Maybe," with its pitiful and demure protagonist agonizing over appropriate behavior, its grand, almost melodramatic instrumentation, and its clear demarcation of lead vocalist and backup singers, demonstrates these hallmarks of what would be called the girl group sound.

Those only casually acquainted with the girl group repertoire might believe that the genre has always been entirely dependent on (male) professional songwriters, a lovestruck or lovelorn subject position, and a sharp demarcation between roles of lead and backing singers. Accounts of the Chantels, the Bobbettes, and the Shirelles writing their own songs, of the Dixie Cups playing a complicated polyrhythmic percussion pattern on a hit record, of the Shirelles' scrupulously even distribution of vocal parts, and above all the rejection of a boy who does not meet up to the narrator's expectations will come as a surprise. It is tempting to lament the fact that this style did not endure, positing more equal relations between teenage girls and boys and greater self-respect for girls. However, the supremacy of the Boy in 1950s girl culture was in fact pervasive, to the point that girls were often encouraged to accept boys who repelled them simply for the sake of participating in dating rituals. In Queen of the Prom, a popular 1961 board game about the Mattel doll Barbie, for example, the goal of being crowned Prom Queen is hopeless without an escort, no matter what other credentials the player may have earned through the course of the game.[17] A suitably devoted male is the required proof of a girl's worthiness, and fulfillment in life is impossible without one, but the game makes the *fact* of the relationship far more important than the *nature* of the relationship or the boy himself.

"The Guy," who seems so central to the girl group repertoire often functions as a cipher, a symbol conferring prestige on the girls singing about him; such is certainly the case with the hapless Jimmy of the Shangri-Las' "Leader of the Pack." Charlotte Grieg applauds this change in the role of boys in popular song: "The rock'n'roll idol had now become the subject of the girls' songs, rather than the instigator of the music himself. The girls had him swap his guitar for a motorbike, as they took over the centre stage of pop music themselves. They relegated him to the role of the cool guy who does nothing much at all, except remain on show as a status symbol."[18]

Nevertheless, there are proper ways to treat boys in girl group songs, and the brisk dismissal of "I Met Him on a Sunday" does not correspond to the worshipful tone of most songs. In general, girl group songs treat their shadowy male characters with great reverence.[19] This sort of breathless wonder surrounding boys is arguably more enjoyable to girls daydreaming about love than warts-and-all portraits of actual boys could ever be, and it became encoded with increasing rigidity as the girl group repertoire established identifiable characteristics. The ill-mannered boy in the Shirelles' "I Met Him on a Sunday" may have been altogether too realistic to feed a girl's fantasy life, and songs with this attitude were not adopted by the majority of girl groups in the 1960s.

The peak of the girl group moment was in the first years of the 1960s, before the first North American tour of the Beatles launched what would be called the "British Invasion"; the voices of girls like Arlene Smith, Reather Dixon, and Shirley Alston spoke to and for female members of the baby boom generation. Girl group music continued to be important in teen culture even after the new British bands dominated North American charts, of course, and the girl group style was a powerful influence on bands such as the Beatles. The main audience for girl group music (and for the Beatles at that stage of their career, for that matter) was teenage girls, many of whom would grow up to become second-wave feminists. How might the girl group repertoire, with its focus on romantic fantasies and ladylike behavior, have functioned as a dialogue that prefigured the consciousness-raising groups of the 1970s Women's Liberation movement?

The established girl group ensemble singing style of the early 1960s typically follows a rhetoric of call and response, wherein a lead singer makes statements that are answered by backup singers. The response can entail encouraging remarks such as "Go ahead girl!" (in Martha and the Vandellas' "Heat Wave") or "Come on baby" (in Little Eva's "Locomotion"). Girls listening and singing along to records are free to choose between the roles of caller and responder and to imagine themselves alternately as the individual in the spotlight or as one of a group of sympathetic friends. The interactions rehearsed through call-and-response singing provide a model for relationships among girls, who can learn how to talk and listen to one another by styling their conversational skills after these performances. Girl talk at its most virtuosic involves coaxing, comforting, dissenting, and confirming remarks from friends supporting a girl's articulation of her concerns, and the different voice types I have discussed evoked different kinds of girls and different attitudes toward the whole enterprise of being a girl.

The use of specifically female doo wop syllables also contributes the backup singers' important function of representing a collective of girls responding to the lead singer/subject, "an inarticulable if not unspeakable empathy."[20] In Betty Everett's "It's in His Kiss," backup singers beg the knowledgeable Everett to share her insight into how to tell if a boy's love is true. This song is explicitly a dialogue with an opening call by Everett followed by questions from the backing vocalists that she answers. As I discussed above, the all-important "shoop" vocable is uttered only by the backing voices; the response portion of the song, then, was to provide the single most identifiable feature of the piece, causing it to be better known as "The Shoop Shoop Song" than by its actual title.

The response portion of a girl group song can also take the form of abstract, wordless harmonies, however, and this too can be understood as representing a sympathetic company of other girls. The mere presence of backing singers signifies a collective, a community of singers who agree with and support the lead singer's position (although in many cases where dialogue is represented more literally, the backup singers can contradict the soloist's statements). Backup singers conjure a sisterhood, lending their voices to strengthen the statements of an individual vocalist. In one of the first scholarly writings on girl group music, Barbara Bradby notes that "it is immediately apparent on listening to the classic girl-group numbers that the singing of the group in the form of a chorus has much greater prominence that in most other genres of rock'n'roll....If the traditional relationship of the chorus to lead singer is one of subservience, support, and sometimes apprenticeship, this is often reversed in girl-group music."[21]

In addition to the "advice song" style I will discuss in section four, an example of female solidarity represented by dialogic voices in a girl group song can be found in the Marvelettes' "Please Mr. Postman" (1961). The narrative of this song concerns a girl waiting forlornly at home for a letter from an absent boyfriend, imploring the postman to check his bags again and again for some proof that she has not been forgotten. Backing vocals here demonstrate that, although the song is explicitly the story of one girl, her anguish is shared by friends and sisters similarly fettered by social rules that keep girls waiting by the phone on Saturday nights, rather than taking the initiative in romantic relationships.

Like the other songs discussed in this and the previous chapter, "Please Mr. Postman's" genesis is a story that will surprise readers who assume that all girl group songs are constructed by professional songwriters and then taught to singers—it has a place of uneasy pride in girl group and Motown history. The Marvelettes, a quartet of girls who sang in their school's glee club, had auditioned at Motown as a result of a high school talent show; Berry Gordy politely dismissed them by asking them to come back with an original song. A songwriting acquaintance gave them a blues number called "Please Mr. Postman," which they disliked, but they rewrote the melody and some of the lyrics and promptly returned to Motown (Georgia Dobbins, the Marvelette largely responsible for recomposing the song, was astute enough to insist on a shared songwriting credit, but she left the group shortly thereafter because her father refused to cosign her contract, as was legally required in the case of a minor).[22] The group was then awarded a contract, and the song earned Motown its first #1 hit and—according to some group members—also garnered the Marvelettes the undying resentment of other Motown artists who were being meticulously groomed for this kind of success.[23]

The song opens with a distinctive spoken exclamation "Wait!" and handclaps in the rhythmic pattern heard in the Shirelles' "I Met Him on a Sunday." Lead singer Gladys Horton responds to the call by singing "Oh yes, wait a minute Mr. Postman" as though modestly agreeing with her friends' forceful request. The aggressiveness of her female friends allows Horton to assume a ladylike, sweetly woebegone attitude in her dialogue with an adult man, a tactic similar to that used in the Cookies' 1963 "Don't Say Nothin' Bad about My Baby," where tough-sounding backup singers also take the lead so that Earl-Jean McCrea never has to raise her voice above a gentle purr. In both these songs, a gang of girls gives support and strength to an individual struggling to express herself with sufficient force to alter her circumstances.

The title lyric of "Please Mr. Postman" is uttered by the backing Marvelettes before the soloist herself sings them, and the backup singers' material explains Horton's predicament before she comes to the fore in the first verse. Their voices harmonizing behind the lead singer create a sense of other girls sharing the experience, particularly since the backup singers begin by singing the call, with the soloist responding. This arrangement of voices permits the presentation of an individual who sometimes asserts herself and sometimes merely agrees with the statements of others, rather like a girl wavering between speaking out and maintaining an appropriately calm demeanor. The song is understood as the expression of one individual's feelings, with the backing vocalists—who maintain a first-person pronoun throughout—as extensions of the soloist. This musical representation of an intricate and many-voiced self suggests layers of consciousness in the subject of the song as well as in the listener. The process by which the listener makes sense of this kind of song involves recognizing and absorbing the different voices and statements as coming from a single narrator, thereby implicitly acknowledging the fragmented yet cohesive nature of one's own self.

The Voice of the Girl

This vocal texture and its construction of a complex and multifaceted individual operates differently in girl group music than in the doo wop genre, largely because female harmony vocalists tend to sing in more or less the same range. The dramatic contrasts between falsettists and deep basses that typify a doo wop classic such as the Platters' "The Great Pretender" is not a feature of girl group songs, and neither is a corresponding hierarchy based on vocal range. Instead, the voices are understood more or less as equals, and many groups shared the duties of lead singing, at least in the early days of the girl group sound. I have noted that the Shirelles shared lead vocals with exacting fairness on their first single, but this arrangement eventually gave way to a distancing between a single lead singer and the backing vocalists. The first of these recordings featured Doris Coley on lead, but beginning with 1960's "Tonight's the Night" and then that year's bigger release, "Will You Love Me Tomorrow?," Shirley Alston sang lead. Other girl groups such as the Supremes tended at first to trade solo songs among themselves, so that each had her own songs as lead singer, at least in stage performances, if not in recordings. As Berry Gordy devoted more and more of his attention to this trio, however, he put a stop to this system and increasingly groomed Diana Ross to be the group's only star.

The Marvelettes, by contrast, were unusual in that throughout their decade-long career, they featured two voices as soloists (though only once in a single song, 1963's "Locking up My Heart"). At first Gladys Horton's full texture characterized the group's sound, but beginning in 1964 with "Don't Mess with Bill," the group's main songwriter Smokey Robinson wrote increasingly for Wanda Young's voice. Young and Horton's vocal timbres have vastly different characters, and group member Katherine Anderson reflects that "we were going through the transition of going from teenagers to young adults. 'Don't Mess with Bill' was an indication of young adulthood....Wanda had the tone for whatever records [Robinson] was doing. If you think in terms of different records that Wanda led that were by Smokey, and if you think of Gladys [singing lead] on those same songs, the outcome would not have been the same."[24]

Robinson recalls that Wanda Young "had this little voice that was sexy to me, a little country kind of sexy voice."[25] These remarks illuminate Motown's shifting attitudes toward gender and voice type during the label's most influential period in the mid-60s. Gladys Horton's full, throaty contralto was set aside in favor of Young's soprano whisper for the more "grownup" songs—note also that Robinson identifies this sound as sexy. Horton continued to sing lead on almost half of the group's releases, so that the group's identity became a complex alternation of soft sweetness and robust sass.

It may be that if Berry Gordy had cared more about the Marvelettes, Gladys Horton's opportunities to sing lead would have disappeared entirely—by all accounts, Gordy took little interest in the group, perhaps because he could not entirely forgive them for achieving a #1 song without the benefit of his hit-making system. The Supremes also featured a full-throated bluesy voice and a smaller, head-dominated one in Florence Ballard and Diana Ross, and Ballard's sound was consistently muffled in favor of Ross's, as we shall see in section four. In the case of the Marvelettes, Horton's fans enthused about her voice to the extent that she continued to sing lead even after Young's more demure sound was highlighted.[26] In the case of the Supremes, by contrast, Gordy pinned his hopes on Diana Ross's distinctive nasal sound, which could cut through any orchestration, and he also recognized the singer's discipline and ambition, so that Ballard's bigger, soulful, and idiosyncratic sound was doomed.

"Please Mr. Postman" and its sequel hit "Twistin' Postman," in which the postman, the girl, and the girl's mother all celebrate the arrival of the long-awaited letter, were closely connected to the lives of teenage girls, and these songs presented narratives that could be satisfyingly incorporated into modest daydreams. The glamour of sophisticated groups like the Supremes and solo singers such as Dionne Warwick, on the other hand, could be enjoyed as fantasies of a far-off adulthood, a life that seemed impossibly distant from the mundane realities of parents, homework, and drippy boys. In both cases, however, girl listeners responded to girl group songs enthusiastically and took these texts as the basis for their own imaginings and as models for conversations. Susan Douglas is convinced that participating in this kind of discourse was an important precursor to the outspokenness of women in the 1970s Women's Liberation movement. In the concluding paragraphs of her book on the relationship of the feminist movement to the mass media, she singles out this music as a vital force, writing that "thirty years after [the girl groups] I remain convinced that singing certain songs with a group of friends at the top of your lungs sometimes helps you say things, later, at the top of your heart."[27]

In participating in these records through singing along, sometimes with the lead vocalist and sometimes with the backing voices, girls rehearsed different versions of femininity and learned ways of communicating with one another. A decade later, as Douglas attests, many of these same girls would promote the value of dialogue among women as consciousness-raising feminist forums. By responding to the call of songs featuring girls' voices, girls learned to use their own voices and later modeled an empowering women's culture in part on what they had practiced as girls singing into their hairbrushes.

PART II
A Brand New Dance Now

In a PBS documentary about Motown's importance to 60s soul music, Thomas "Beans" Bowles (saxophonist, flutist, and tour manager of the Motown Revue) recalls a 1962 stage performance by the Marvelettes, the girl group who had earned Motown's first #1 hit with "Please Mr. Postman" the previous year. He describes watching from the wings:

> Georgeanna [Tillman] walked out on stage with her eyes wide, chewing gum, and looking at all the people…country style! And I said, "It's not gonna work. We've got to have a department to groom the kids." Most of them were ghetto kids, from single parent homes, and didn't have all the cultural tactics that's needed.[1]

At that time, the Marvelettes devised their own stage choreography and presented their audiences with performances that were boisterous and energetic. Although their stagecraft was appealing to many, it did not adhere to the emerging Motown philosophy of polished, professional elegance. Motown director Berry Gordy's vision was to create African American pop stars who could integrate white America's most upscale performance venues, and the girlish enthusiasm of groups like the Marvelettes needed to be tamed and refined. Thus, Motown's Artist Development Department was conceived; at its peak, the regimen involved lessons with vocal coach Maurice King, rehearsals with choreographer Cholly Atkins, and "finishing school" with Maxine Powell. Although Motown was the only record label to require in-house schooling in the manners and graces of its performers, decorum and appearance were of crucial importance to all girl group singers. In this section I explore the ways in which a physical language of girlness coalesced in girl group performances of the early 1960s, and I consider the meanings of these ways of being a girl. Strict rules governing dress and body language can be understood as repressive and restraining, and motifs of restraint and even violence are important to many girl group songs, but I will argue that there is also room for pleasure in the masquerade of girl identity.

3

Embodying Girlness

The vocal choreography (a term usefully invented by African American dancer/choreographer Cholly Atkins to describe his work with singing groups) of Motown acts was highly sophisticated and effective, and it proved to be a crucial element of the record label's success. While all vocal groups of the period included synchronized gesture and dance steps in their performances, Atkins is generally the only choreographer to be recognized widely for his efforts in this area. His language of sophisticated movements for singers on stage required them to "*perform* their music, not by retelling a song's storyline in predictable pantomime, but by punctuating it with rhythmical dance steps, turns, and gestures drawn from the rich bedrock of American vernacular dance."[1] Atkins began choreographing singers in his late forties after a distinguished career as a jazz and tap dancer, having performed with the likes of Louis Armstrong, Count Basie, and Cab Calloway, and he derived many of his moves for singers from chorus lines of the 1940s. Before accepting a full-time position at Motown, he worked with acts such as the Cadillacs, the Shirelles, Aretha Franklin, and Gladys Knight and the Pips.

Atkins explicitly devised separate vocabularies of movement for male and female performers. Thus the Temptations, a quintet of men all over six feet tall, were noted for their striking stage walk and other bold gestures that made full use of their imposing height, while the Supremes were celebrated for statuesque stillness through the body and elegant motions with arms and hands. In a television performance of their 1964 hit "Baby Love," for example, the Supremes stand in a tight triangle formation (with Diana Ross in the middle and on a platform) and sway gently in time to the music. Ross sometimes uses both arms to make outward arcs at chest height, while Florence Ballard and Mary Wilson keep their arms carefully at their sides; at other times,

Ballard and Wilson mirror one another by bringing their inside arms up with a smooth circular motion, or by executing dainty steps out to the side and in again while Ross maintains a more statuesque posture. These gestures are carefully planned to support Ross's performance of the main melody and lyrics. The only instance of more energetic movement comes during the instrumental middle eight section, when all three singers perform a synchronized routine that involves turning in a circle, away from the audience and back again.[2]

The Supremes and Martha and the Vandellas became the most celebrated female groups at Motown, but their elegance and sophistication—the attributes that helped to solidify the characteristics of the Motown brand—differentiated them from most performers in the first years of the girl group phenomenon. The Marvelettes' performance style on stage was arguably more consistent with what other ensembles were doing. In a 1963 television performance of what was still their biggest hit, "Please Mr. Postman," for example, the Marvelettes demonstrate that their sessions in Motown's Artist Development classes (ostensibly inspired by the Marvelettes' rough-and-ready stagecraft) had indeed been "too little too late."[3] The singers move in a relaxed, lively way as they sing, arms akimbo and heads bobbing up and down as they bend from the waist, shake their hips, and dance back and forth. The television camera cuts to the audience, revealing that the Marvelettes' movements have inspired similar motions among their listeners; perhaps the group's evident imperfection was actually a part of their enormous appeal, making them more like ordinary girls.[4] Similarly, a *Shindig!* appearance by the Dixie Cups—in 1965, a year in which the Supremes were at their peak of popularity—features the three singers dressed in bulky rollneck sweaters and A-line skirts, sporting bows in their shoulder-length hair as they sing "You Should Have Seen the Way He Looked at Me," one of the last hits of their two-year career. The vocal choreography used here is very basic: rudimentary, swaying footwork, wagging fingers for the song's title line, and straightforward miming for some lyrics (for example, pointing to the head for "I remember").[5] Notably, there is no differentiation between lead and backing singers in the choreography, and the three vocalists sing in unison with some homophonic harmony passages providing contrast, but no call and response.

At the time of these television appearances, both the Marvelettes and the Dixie Cups were perceived to be in the waning phases of their careers.[6] These performances, then, suggest that while representations of imperfect, untutored girls performing simple choreographed routines were still possible in the arena of mainstream, commercial culture, they could scarcely compete with the polished style associated with Cholly Atkins's groups at Motown and elsewhere.

The Supremes' most famous move, from "Stop! In the Name of Love"—the singers stand stiffly, with right arms stretched straight forward and hands turned up arrestingly—became an almost iconic representation of the girl group genre, but it was not typical of the gestures created for them by Atkins. The dramatic thrust of the arm was contrary to the small, controlled gestures he favored for girls, and it was not, in fact, of his design. The Supremes, Berry Gordy, and the Temptations were preparing for a British television appearance on *Ready Steady Go!* hosted by Dusty Springfield when they realized the Supremes had no stage routine for their new single. All quickly collaborated to devise choreography, and they based what was to become the trio's hallmark pose on the sign language of traffic police.[7]

Atkins would certainly not have given them such an unladylike gesture so crudely representative of the song's lyrics. In his autobiography, he reflects on his aspirations for female vocal groups and the different strategies he employed in working with them:

> My work was cut out for me because some of [the girl groups] had been learning from the male groups and those cats didn't know diddly-squat about teaching females. They probably thought their approach was fine for everybody...but I worked it out, *softened them up*; the Chantels, the Crystals, the Shirelles—any group I had a chance to work with. See, the girl groups had to be more concerned with what I call physical drama. Instead of trying to move like the guys, I wanted them to use the kind of body language that was associated with women—using your eyes, hands on the hips, and so forth, but not in a macho way. *They had to really think about this approach and keep that uppermost in their minds.* And naturally, they were doing a lot of love tunes. If I demonstrated a feminine move that they thought was basically an affectation, they called it camping,

> which was the street term used at the time. When I was growing up, my mother and aunts used to call it putting on airs or being proper.[8]

I find these remarks revealing about the function of movement in performing gender identity and also about the processes of learning that are an inevitable part of being a girl. As I showed in the previous chapter, early girl groups drew on the vocables and musical vocabulary of doo wop (among other musical styles) in creating their own specifically girl-oriented dialect. In much the same way, singers in girl groups prepared for stage performances by basing their acts on the choreography of male groups, until they were taken in hand and trained in "appropriate" movements.

Atkins had very specific notions about what constituted correct body language for girls, and he did not base his ideas on observation of their natural gestures. Rather, he recognized that proper feminine comportment was something that girls had to work hard at and, in his words, keep uppermost in their minds at all times. In the famous BBC television series and subsequent book *Ways of Seeing*, John Berger observed that

> A woman must continually watch herself. She is almost continually accompanied by her own image of herself....From earliest childhood she has been taught and persuaded to survey herself continually. And so she comes to consider the *surveyor* and the *surveyed* within her as two constituent yet always distinct elements of her identity as a woman.[9]

The constant self-monitoring and obligation to work at being properly feminine described here are exaggerated in the vocal choreography of Atkins' groups, but the regimen he imposed was not wholly alien to a conventional experience of femininity. Nor is this experience specific to females of any single racial or class group: Susan Bordo observes that "the discipline and normalization of the female body [is] perhaps the only gender oppression that exercises itself, although to different degrees and in different forms, across age, race, class, and sexual orientation."[10]

It is clear, to be sure, that many of the girl singers who worked with Atkins resisted his strict regulation of their bodies. Some singers found his ideas about gesture foreign and artificial, possibly even ridiculous (I will return to the idea of "camping" in girl culture in Chapter 5). Nevertheless, his code of body language connected to broader social notions of how girls ought to move, and his choreography helped to solidify a particular kind of embodiment that continues to feel "right" for girls and women forty years later.

The physical attributes of feminine appearance have always required degrees of bodily constraint, from the corsets that were *de rigueur* for respectable Western women in the nineteenth century to the taut, aerobicized midriffs of the late twentieth century. In their social contexts, these kinds of practices are generally accepted as normal responsibilities of femaleness, and they are readily taken on by girls and women who wish to appear presentable and attractive, but they should nonetheless be considered forms of repressing the female body. In much the same way, by forcing young girls into corporeal experiences of femininity that sprang from the opinions of a middle-aged man, Cholly Atkins trained his cooperative pupils to conform to artificial sensations of their bodies and selves.

Although learning Atkins' choreography was not a painful experience (though it often was at least arduous and exhausting), to accept his physical constraints was to be complicit in regulating the young female body. When singers displayed their bodies for spectators through stage and television performances and publicity shots, they communicated particular ways of being girls to their audience members, who could copy their stances and train their own bodies in turn. Bordo notes that

> With the advent of movies and television, the rules for femininity have come to be culturally transmitted more and more through standardized visual images.... We are no longer given verbal descriptions or exemplars of what a lady is or of what femininity consists. Rather, we learn the rules directly through bodily discourse: through images that tell us what clothes, body shape, facial expression, movements and behavior are required.[11]

The stylized performances of girlness involved in girl group music had far-reaching consequences, and they effectively wrote an embodied gender script for the girls who watched them.

This kind of strictness is an inevitable part of social experience, and males as well as females tend to accept it willingly. Most cultures, for example, prescribe different ways of sitting for men and women, and they pass on the "correct" postures orally and gesturally until they become automatic, although never consciously learned. Girls in Western society are usually instructed to "sit like a lady," with knees together and ankles crossed to shield the genitals, and this mermaid-like posture contrasts with the more aggressive pose of knees apart, feet firmly on the floor, that is customary for men.[12] As North American girls in the early 1960s "tried on" various performances of girlhood by singing along with records in front of the mirror, their rehearsals involved not just emulating the voices and words of their favorite singers, but also emulating the postures modeled in publicity shots and television appearances. Their bodies were engaged in specific ways of "feeling like girls," so that Atkins' efforts to teach performers a correct language of femininity had far-reaching effects.

The Locomotion

That girl group music was often explicitly concerned with teaching this kind of physical experience is borne out by a consideration of Little Eva's 1962 hit "The Locomotion," in which the singer coaxes listeners to move their bodies in a new dance style. The song is based on movements actually developed by seventeen-year-old Eve Boyd (Little Eva) and codified by songwriters Carole King and Gerry Goffin. Boyd babysat the children of King and Goffin (recommended for the job by Earl-Jean McCrea of the Cookies, a trio of studio singers who worked closely with Goffin and King), and the songwriting couple was struck by her cheerfulness and high energy, comparing her to a locomotive train as she danced while they tried out new material on the piano. The contemporary vogue for dance crazes (e.g., the Twist, the Stomp, the Jerk) inspired the three to formalize Boyd's up-and-down gestures into a dance and to write a song based on it; when the time came to record a demo, it was only logical that Boyd herself be the singer of what was, in large part, her song. Boyd's vocals are characterized by a clean, chest-dominated timbre with little vibrato; short, rhythmically straightforward phrasing; and flat, nasal vowels. The effect is of a pert, cheerful personality encouraging listeners to try the new dance. The demo—a recording created quickly and cheaply for the purpose of being marketed to established professional singers—was offered to singer Dee Dee Sharp, whose manager declined it. Don Kirschner considered the demo recording appealing enough to be marketed with only minor refinements under the name of Little Eva, launching a number one hit for twelve weeks and four more Top 40 hits over the course of a year.

In "The Locomotion," Little Eva exhorts listeners to swing their hips, jump back and forth, and form a chain with other dancers, and she makes encouraging remarks about how easy and fun the dance can be. Susan Douglas refers to the locomotion as she notes that dancing in North American culture at the turn of the 60s was a newly emancipated forum for girls, a departure from the traditional partner dancing of the pre-war era.

> Girl group music had emerged at the same time as all these new dance crazes that redefined how boys and girls did—or, more accurately, did not—dance with each other. Chubby Checker's 1960 hit "The Twist" revolutionized teenage dancing, because it meant that boys and girls didn't have to hold hands anymore, boys didn't have to lead and girls didn't have to follow, so girls had a lot more autonomy and control as they danced. Plus, dancing was one of the things that girls usually did much better than boys. As the twist gave way to the locomotion…the dances urged us to loosen up our chests and our butts, and learn how to shimmy, grind and thrust.[13]

In Chapter 1, I noted that the voices of African American working-class girls like the Bobbettes were able to speak in ways that other voices could not, and that singing along with girl group records could enable white middle-class girls to adopt their disruptive power. Douglas's reminiscence of freeing her body through the locomotion indicates that the dance performances of girl groups were also crucial in permitting girls like her to explore their physicality and sensuality through experimenting with the stances and movements of artists such as Little Eva.

Dance historian Judith Lynne Hanna explores the notion of dance as a medium for teaching, arguing that dance gestures are often used purposefully to communicate specific ideas and information. She examines a ritual that marks the transformation of adolescent girls to womanhood among the Vai people of Liberia. The dance "communicates symbolic gender meaning, punctuates phrases of the acquisition of gender knowledge, instills discipline, develops women's muscles that aid in childbirth, builds up endurance, provides recreation, and reflects the personality and physical talents of the individual. Dance may metaphorically enact status transformation from childhood to adulthood [and] may actually bring about a transformation and new gender script."[14]

Hanna observes that the dance gestures of preadolescent and adolescent girls in this community and among the Ubakala in Nigeria focus on changing areas of the body. She writes that "the shimmy movements of the upper torso highlight the girl's developing mammary glands… [dancers] symbolize fertility with the stylization of female movement: undulations and hip shifts and rotations."[15] Thus, girls' dancing permits the pleasurable exploration of those body parts that will be important in sexual activities, and it allows girls safely to rehearse the movements and sensations of seduction, coition, and childbirth.

"The Locomotion" and its accompanying dance can also be understood as an exercise in enacting female sexuality. Little Eva requires that "You've got to swing your hips now" and points out that the locomotion is so easy that "My little baby sister can do it with me," intimating that this is, above all, a dance for girls. Throughout the song, she lavishes praise on her listeners/students, with encouraging remarks such as "You're doing fine," "I think you've got the knack," "That's right!" and "You're looking good," echoing the kinds of statements girls hope to hear from teachers and parents. Easy harmonic movement between the home key of E-flat major and its subdominant A-flat, as well as a steady four beats to a bar laid out by snare drum, contribute to the appealing and accessible feel, while saxophones sustain blaring open fifths, evoking the sound of a train whistle. The snare drum solo that opens the song recalls a militaristic march, suggesting an authority to be taken seriously, but not—as the other instruments quickly demonstrate—to be feared. Handclaps foster a sense of community, and prominent backing vocals urge the listener to "Come on! Do the locomotion!" Little Eva's vocals and genial manner promote a sense of her as a kind and affable older sister (as the lyrics suggest), the perfect unthreatening teacher for this drill in female sexuality. Many older sisters do, indeed, give their younger sisters lessons in femininity (mine certainly did), ranging from makeup instructions and dating etiquette to hygiene tips and even kissing lessons. These corporeal aspects of girlness are crucial, and they do not stem from some innate knowledge, but rather must be learned.

Eve Boyd, "Little Eva." Courtesy of Photofest.

Femininity and Self-Control

Dancing to "The Locomotion" is an enjoyable, even liberating experience, as Susan Douglas attests above. The gestures called for in the song derived from Eve Boyd's own improvised dance steps, so that it is appropriate to celebrate the song as inspired by the spontaneous physicality of a girl's response to music. Nevertheless, just as Boyd's dance steps were based on the vocabulary of movement she had been learning since infancy, the song also participates in reinforcing cultural assumptions about how girls are supposed to move. Training the body into an age-appropriate version of femininity is an ongoing experience for girls and women; indeed, the cultivation of "proper" femininity is a never-ending project, demanding tireless vigilance and self-policing, although no successful completion is ever achieved. In Foucault's theories of the docile body, control over bodies becomes an end in itself—bodies are tamed and taught to be self-regulating merely for the sake of discipline and order.[16]

Sandra Lee Bartky analyzes bodily discipline in the experience of women, arguing that "The disciplinary project of femininity is a 'set-up': it requires such radical and extensive measures of bodily transformation that virtually every woman who gives herself to it is destined in some degree to fail. Thus, a measure of shame is added to a woman's sense that the body she inhabits is deficient."[17]

Bartky also itemizes specific ways in which female bodies are rendered docile, reporting that the correct posture for women and girls involves pulling the stomach and buttocks in and protruding the chest to "display her bosom to maximum advantage," and that an appropriately feminine walk involves a gentle rolling of the hips (although to overdo this is to disrupt decorum and invite censure). She summarizes women's magazine advice on "the proper way of getting in and out of cars…a woman must not allow her arms and legs to flail about in all directions; she must try to manage her movements with the appearance of grace—no small feat when one is climbing out of the back seat of a Fiat—and she is well advised to use the opportunity for a certain display of leg."[18]

Describing her tutelage under the formidable Maxine Powell at Motown's finishing school, Mary Wilson recalls being taught how to climb in and out of a car exactly as Bartky describes. Wilson reports that lessons like these became ingrained into her habitual way of moving and thinking about her body: "I can remember feeling [Powell's] eyes upon me as I walked around.…Were my shoulders straight? Was my posture good?"[19]

In short, girls are not born knowing how to be girls—they must study the physical language of femininity and practice it constantly. The importance of proper deportment for females is such that, forty years after girl singers were schooled at Motown, male transsexuals preparing for surgery are coached in how to walk, sit, and gesture like women. Note also the existence in the early twenty-first century of organizations such as Bully Broads, a California company that trains women executives perceived to be too aggressive by their employers. Companies can pay as much as $18,000 to have their "bully broad" workers taught to speak more softly and use self-deprecating humor in order to be less resented by male colleagues.[20] Similarly, Britain's RDF Media, the company responsible for such reality television programs as *Wife Swap* and *Rock School*, introduced the reality television show *Ladette to Lady* in 2005; in this program, ten hard-drinking, rough-edged young women abandon their hedonistic lifestyle in order to submit to a finishing school training that includes etiquette, elocution, Cordon Bleu cooking, deportment, and wardrobe education.[21]

The function of this kind of discipline and training is accepted as an essential element of the girl group phenomenon, and often the genre is disdained for imposing choreographed and prefabricated ways of being on the bodies of girl singers—and, by extension, on girl listeners who emulate the stances of their idols. This kind of reaction hinges on a belief that other forms of popular music do not involve careful staging or rehearsed body language, and it also assumes that there is such a thing as a natural, authentic body—a point disputed by Bartky and other scholars following the work of Foucault. I want to argue that all forms of popular music involve deliberate representations of gender identities and that the swaggering of Led Zeppelin's Robert Plant is no less self-conscious and rehearsed than the simpering of Little Eva. Marjorie Garber asserts that the version of manhood offered by Elvis Presley intersects in many ways with the masculinity of Liberace, most obviously in the two men's Las Vegas performances. Although our contemporary understanding of Elvis (promoted aggressively by his widow through a late-1990s television series dramatizing his early years) as an authentic, virile working-class youth seems diametrically opposed to the campy, glitzy artifice of Liberace and his middle-aged women fans, Garber points out that even in his youth, Elvis carefully constructed his hoodlum persona by putting on dyed hair, padded trousers, and a famously curled lip.[22]

Nevertheless, the steps that Elvis took to appear sexy and dangerous did not involve the same degree of self-denial and discipline that girl singers needed to seem demure and feminine, and an analysis of girl group music requires an examination of motifs of physical restraint, both self- and other-inflicted, as these are themes that undergird the experience of being a girl. What is more, explicit references to physical restraint and even violence are a recurring motif through several important songs: Claudine Clark's 1962 "Party Lights" articulates the frustration of being held against her will at home while other teens are free to attend a party; the narrator of Ginny Arnell's 1963 "Dumb Head" berates herself harshly for mishandling an opportunity with a nice boy; the Cookies' 1963 "Don't Say Nothin' Bad about My Baby" is an iron fist in a velvet glove, gently but pointedly threatening a girl who has the temerity to criticize the protagonist's boyfriend; Lesley Gore's "It's My Party" and followup "Judy's Turn to Cry," both from 1963, assert that girls are helpless in the face of male inconstancy, and that concealing anger is the proper course of action when faced with betrayal; the Shirelles decry the double standard for boys' and girls' behavior in romantic relationships in 1963's "What Does a Girl Do?"; and the Crystals' 1963 "Then He Kissed Me" outlines the meek, passive behavior that is necessary to earn a marriage proposal. Furthermore, the Crystals' "He Hit Me (and It Felt Like a Kiss)" and the Cookies' "Chains" describe being a girl in love as physically punishing, in ways that are not always metaphorical, as we shall see in the next chapter.

4

Restraint and Violence

The Crystals emerged in 1961, the creation of former big band musician-turned-manager Benny Wells, who had handpicked the group's members from girls he knew in Brooklyn (of these, Barbara Alston was his niece and Dee Dee Kennibrew was the daughter of a friend). While the group was rehearsing in the Manhattan publishing offices of Hill and Range, novice record producer Phil Spector overheard them and offered them a recording deal with his new label Philles (formed in partnership with Lester Sill).

The Crystals' first release was successful, but soon the group members began to feel oppressed by their overbearing producer. Dee Dee Kennibrew reports that "We were never allowed any say in what we did at all. We were very young, of course, but we were teenagers making

The Crystals. Courtesy of Photofest.

teenage music, and we would have liked, you know, some input. But no way! There was nothing we could do: Phil Spector was our record company, our producer, our everything; I don't think our manager at that time had the experience to keep up with what was going on."[1]

The frustrations that Kennibrew describes grew steadily worse for the group—they would eventually find themselves in the ignominious position of having singles attributed to them that they had not recorded. Session singers the Blossoms (with Darlene Love on lead) provided the vocal tracks for the Crystals' biggest hit, "He's a Rebel" in 1962, as well as 1963's "He's Sure the Boy I Love." I will explore the politics of record production further in Chapter 6.

The most successful Crystals release that involved the original singers (as well as an unquantifiable number of session singers) was 1963's "Then He Kissed Me," which "officially established the 'wall of sound,' using more echo than any previous Spector effort…horns and strings were painted across a brilliant canvas of teen rock sound, with galloping castanets, maracas, and bass drums that sounded like kettle drums. Only the power of LaLa [Brooks]'s voice survived the symphonic onslaught."[2]

The song is indeed a monumental construction that quite dwarfs early girl group records such as the Shirelles' simple "I Met Him on a Sunday" or even the Marvelettes song "Please Mr. Postman." The grand scale of the piece is an apt metaphor for the drama and intensity of first love, and the "galloping" percussion and sense of vastness created by the use of echo contribute to this heady fervor. The lyrics outline the story of fairytale teen romance recounted by a girl who can scarcely believe her luck: a boy asks her to dance, walks her home, kisses her, invites her home to meet his parents, and then proposes. The only time that the girl narrator initiates any action is to whisper "I love you" when her feelings have grown overwhelmingly strong—her boldness is rewarded by the boy's declaration of reciprocating love and another kiss. This song is a musical primer on how girls and boys ought to behave in their courtship rituals, teaching girl listeners that starry-eyed meek behavior is the key to earning the all-important engagement ring.

The Crystals are also notorious, however, for a song that made no chart impact at all—1962's "He Hit Me (and It Felt Like a Kiss)," written by Carole King and Gerry Goffin. This chilling song presents a girl who excuses her boyfriend's act of violence as proof of his love: "If he didn't care for me, I could have never made him mad, so when he hit me I was glad." Gillian Gaar reports that King and Goffin based the song on Little Eva's explanation of a black eye bestowed by her boyfriend, and Alan Betrock wonders whether the song's producer, Phil Spector, was deliberately seeking to release a flop in order to get out of an unsatisfying business partnership with Lester Sill (Philles Records).[3] The theory that the song was a throwaway is undermined somewhat by its inclusion in the box set *Back to Mono 1958–1969*, one of only sixty songs intended to showcase the best of Phil Spector's entire œuvre as a record producer during an eleven-year period. Nevertheless, Lester Sill has been blunt in his assessment of the piece, calling it "a terrible fucking song,"[4] and Barbara Alston, who sang lead on "He Hit Me," has complained that "we didn't like that one. After we cut it, we absolutely hated it. Still do. Phil was so particular about the arrangement and sound that we had a terrible session. What made it worse was that after a few weeks had gone by and the record was issued and started selling, the kids at school started singing it and their teachers heard them. They didn't like the title and the lyrics, so the P.T.A. got it banned."[5]

These critics of the song are reluctant to address the source of parents' and teachers' outrage, and they skirt around the song's message that seems to condone and even celebrate male violence against women in ostensibly loving relationships. Alston's distaste for it stems from the fact that it was not a pretty song and that it came about through an arduous recording session. She seems not to have felt revulsion for enacting this kind of dutiful acceptance of abuse or for promoting an understanding of beatings as loving through her performance. Lyricist Gerry Goffin admits ruefully that "the song's blatant masochism was 'a little radical for those times,'" but he does not appear to consider its message to be a dangerous courtship model.[6]

The song begins with a solo ostinato figure in the double bass that outlines a G-major triad, accompanied only by a single triangle chime on the downbeats. The voice enters after four measures with the words "he hit me," and although G major has tried to establish itself as the tonal center, lead singer Barbara Alston's melody is unmistakably in B minor—the rest of the song enacts an uneasy struggle between these keys. Thus, Alston's C-sharp on the word "hit" is an uncomfortable tritone away from the bass foundation we have accepted, and it creates an ugly dissonance that is every bit as troubling as the words, which are foregrounded in the mix in a production style that is unusual for Phil Spector. Furthermore, the voices of the Crystals have a wooden quality on this recording that is entirely unlike their passionate performances on songs such as their first hit, 1961's "There's No Other Like My Baby" or their 1963 triumphs, "Da Doo Ron Ron" and "Then He Kissed Me"—here, they sound almost robotic as they plod through the stiff, awkward melody.[7]

"He Hit Me (and It Felt Like a Kiss)": Opening

The vocal melody insists on B minor, repeating its stepwise descent to the tonic, over a relentless G major bass line that is soon bolstered by other instruments doubling it, before the song's first harmonic move to D major (after ten slow measures). The instrumental forces build inexorably through a process of accretion, with first guitar, then organ, and finally strings adding to the plodding figure initiated in the bass. Percussive sounds also expand to include a bass drum performing—sickeningly—the girl group beat, an allusion to the perky insouciance of songs like "I Met Him on a Sunday" that sounds in this context like a painful heart thumping. At the second chorus, a high, nagging rattle enters with incessant sixteenth notes, and shrill backing vocals are also eerily high.

Over the course of the song, the backup singers and the strings enact a dialogue with the lead voice, at first echoing either her line

"He Hit Me (and It Felt Like a Kiss)" opening.

or the bass line and then departing into melodic figures of increasing complexity. During the middle eight section, screeching violins utter the main melody in a jarring D major, a third higher than Alston's statement, but she returns in B minor and the strings perform an approving counterpoint to her singing. Thus, the sound of string orchestra, long understood as a syrupy soundtrack to fairytale romance, is complicit in helping the song's protagonist accept physical abuse as a testament of love. Furthermore, the quasi-operatic gestures of the backup singers—who often stand in for a community of supportive female friends, as I showed in the previous section—also confirm the rightness of the damaging relationship by moving ever upwards to a climactic F# on the top of the staff. I interpret the string section and backup singers to represent cultural forces that can pressure women to accept dysfunctional relationships as normal. The conventions of romance ideology tend to valorize passionate intensity that can explode into violence, and many victims of domestic abuse are encouraged to stay by female friends promoting the oppressive notion that love will redeem suffering.

The harmonic language also works to bring about resolution; as the first verse draws to a close, the singer's B minor and the bass line's G major collude together to resolve on a shimmering B major chord. This shift is a relief after the dissonant struggles of the song, and it undergirds the final word of the lyrics "If he didn't care for me, I could have never made him mad, so when he hit me, I was glad." The two irreconcilable keys of the song achieve B major through movement that sidesteps the conventions of pop music's harmonic writing—the happy climax, welcome as it is, is not based on rational thinking. In my analysis, the musical language of the song enacts a virtuosic rationalization of wife- or girlfriend-battering, as disparate tonal centers come together in a transcendent moment. "He Hit Me (and It Felt Like a Kiss)" can perhaps be understood as an articulation of the thought processes of denial and rationalization that enable women to endure beatings from their partners. Thus, a song that appears at the level of lyrics to be a straightforward celebration of physical violence as a loving corrective can also be read as an attempt to speak from the position of a girl in this kind of situation, a compassionate performance of the unhealthy logic that makes abuse tolerable.

In King and Goffin's songwriting partnership, Gerry Goffin usually wrote melody and lyrics and his wife Carole King created the harmonies and instrumental arrangement of their songs, so it is tempting—particularly in light of her post-60s career as self-assured, independent earth mother—to consider that King was trying to problematize "He Hit Me's" words with deliberately ugly, unsettling sounds and harmonies. In a climate where violence against women is discussed openly in public discourse, it is, of course, impossible to respond to "He Hit Me" as we might have in 1962. The twisted connections between romance, obsession, and violence were not yet of general psychological interest to a society that laughed when Ralph Kramden alluded to hitting his wife in the 1950s television series *The Honeymooners*.

Even so, the song was advertised in *Billboard* magazine at the time as "a serious ballad with a telling message," and it was condemned early on for its lyrics.[8] It never entered the realm of stage or television performances that would have required rehearsed dance steps from the singers, presenting a tantalizing though appalling line of thought: how might such a song have been choreographed? A literal pantomime that acted out the events described would of course be impossible, horrifying on conservative prime-time television variety shows such as *American Bandstand*, *Shindig!* or *Hullabaloo*—venues where the Crystals and most other girl groups performed regularly. But a more stylized choreography, along the lines of Cholly Atkins' work, would surely strike viewers as an equally outrageous violation of a song that is so straightforward in the presentation of its subject matter.

Pleasures in Objectification

Ultimately, "He Hit Me" could never be danced to by performers or listeners—its stark lyrics and dirge-like musical language do not inspire that kind of bodily response. In this important way, the song is entirely unlike other, more acceptable pop songs that present images of violence but are nonetheless enjoyed by mainstream audiences. A contemporary example of this kind of song is the Cookies' "Chains," a 12-bar blues number with a steady groove that was a Top 40 hit for eight weeks in 1962 (the same year as "He Hit Me"); the Beatles' 1963 version of the song renewed interest in the Cookies' original recording. Lyrics in this song recount the feelings of a girl who seems to enjoy being a prisoner of love, and who regretfully informs a new boy she has met that she is not free to pursue him. Although the music contradicts the oppressive words, as we shall see, the lyrics themselves are complex—they imply that the girl in the song looks at boys and might well behave assertively if she were not already otherwise committed.

The Cookies were a trio of versatile African American singers whose main recording output was as a backing ensemble on New York–based records, including Mel Torme's 1962 "Comin' Home Baby" (his only Top 40 hit), Little Eva's "The Locomotion" from the same year, and many recordings by Chuck Jackson, Joe Turner, Tony Orlando, and Ben E. King. An earlier lineup of the Cookies had worked with Ray Charles as the Raeletts during the 1950s—of this trio, only Earl-Jean McCrea was a member of the 1960s group. Even during the Cookies' career as a headlining ensemble and studio group, McCrea had a minor solo career, releasing "I'm into Something Good" under the name of Earl-Jean in 1964, a song recorded with greater success by British band Herman's Hermits.[9] Between 1962 and 1964, the Cookies had three hits under their own name, beginning with King and Goffin's "Chains."

Given the group's renown as a backing trio, it is not surprising that "Chains" makes much of their ensemble sound, to the extent that the solo vocals seem almost an aside. The song's structure features a repeated refrain made up of two stanzas that contrast with verses a mere four measures long (half the length of the refrain). The refrain opens the song and features all singers in three-part harmony, with each vocal line distinctly audible and melodically appealing in its own right. While the girl group sound tended usually to feature a single voice on the song's main tune, with vocal harmonies providing depth and amplification only once the main melody had been established, the Cookies' considerable vocal skills made it possible to present an inversion of this style. Vocal characters in the group ranged from Earl-Jean McCrea's husky purr on the bottom to a brighter, more ringing tone at the top, and these different vocal qualities also participated in articulating both an individual self with complex layers and also a sisterhood of other girls.[10]

The song moves from an opening featuring a three-voiced subject, implying that the feelings discussed are shared by many, to the articulation of one individual's experience. The voices are stacked to outline the intervals of major sixths and thirds, and they move in homophonic parallel motion through major chords, making the lyrics easy to understand and sing along with. This vocal arrangement is key to normalizing the subject matter of the lyrics, and it contributes greatly to making the song less chilling than the Crystals' "He Hit Me," where one voice begins abject and alone and is then affirmed and reinforced by the voices of others. In "Chains," by contrast, we begin with the premise of community and the implication that the song's message describes common emotions and ordinary behavior. The vocal arrangement thus makes the song's lyrics palatable in a way that "He Hit Me" could not be, although there are striking similarities between the themes expressed in the lyrics of both songs.

The Cookies sing about invisible chains that bind the girl in the song to the lover who has locked her up, chains of love that she cannot break and that restrict her movement. This description of being imprisoned is expressed with a cheerful arrangement of rhythm guitar, saxophones, drums, and handclaps, presenting an infectious groove and melody over a blues progression in D major. The familiar girl group beat is swung, contributing further to the danceability of the song; Alan Betrock identifies this "smooth shuffle beat" as unique to the Cookies' sound.[11] The song's perky energy, rich vocal arrangement, and appealing melody contrast with lyrics that would undoubtedly seem dark and troubling in another musical setting—this is hardly the sound of victimhood. The R&B-inflected guitar and horns, steady groove, and blues progression might recall the style of women blues shouters slightly older than the Cookies; singers like Ruth Brown, LaVern Baker, Etta James, and Willie Mae "Big Mama" Thornton presented a sassy, gruff version of black femininity that spoke out about problems in relationships.

The tension created by juxtaposing an upbeat musical character with brooding lyrics about oppression and imprisonment is crucial to the song's enduring appeal. In its two and a half minutes, "Chains" articulates the thrills of playing with objectification, exploring the feelings of a girl who can enjoy being looked at and feel pleased that her boyfriend is possessive of her charms. Being forced into the position of object, something to be looked at and possessed, girls and women may indeed learn "not the desire for the other, but the desire to be desired," and it is a shame that the female experience of sexuality emphasizes being sexually attractive to men as more important than experiencing desire and sexual excitement.[12] In a culture where girls habitually learn to see themselves as though through the eyes of an appraising lover, however, it seems doubly shameful to deny them the pleasures they might find there.

In Western culture, most girls come to understand that they are to be looked at and possessed, and songs like "Chains" reinforce this kind of message. Girls are also taught not to enjoy being a spectacle, as this kind of attention-seeking opposes the virtues of modesty and shyness that are prized in girls. The girl who grows up striving to be pretty and good is discouraged from crowing "Look at me!" and inviting others to celebrate her self-satisfaction. She learns how to position herself to best advantage for inspection, but must do so without revealing the thrill she may feel when she has been judged pretty or sexy, because to divulge this would be vain and "not nice" (in my own mother's admonishing phrase). And so the exhilaration of being considered desirable is concealed and becomes a delightful secret that a girl can know but never speak of. A song such as "Chains" is provocative, even liberating, because it boasts "Look at me—I know that I am desired and I enjoy it."

The idea that a male gaze can only demean women and girls by positioning them as objects disallows for the possibility of finding this kind of delight and even power in such an experience. This theory is set forth in Laura Mulvey's classic essay "Visual Pleasure and Narrative in Cinema," in which Mulvey argues that the medium of film is predicated on the assumption of a man's gaze beholding and controlling objects (notably, women's bodies).[13] In another landmark essay, however, Angela McRobbie makes an important case for dancing as an emancipatory experience for girls precisely *because* it requires conforming physically to stereotyped and repressive postures of femininity. McRobbie acknowledges that dance is a permitted form of female self-expression because it involves performing (hetero)sexuality for the approval of a presumed male gaze, but she argues that dance's link to fantasy life connects it to a liberating arena of resistance "which cannot be totally colonised...[dance and music] are associated with being temporarily out of control, or out of the reaches of controlling forces."[14]

McRobbie is, of course, referring to social dancing, where dancers are watched only casually, even surreptitiously, as opposed to the preplanned dance performances of girl groups, where an audience is formally distinct from dancers. However, I consider that her observations are also true for girls dancing explicitly for the eyes of others, as girl groups working with choreographers did. Indeed, dancing for television cameras is perhaps not so very different, in girls' experience, from dancing in front of the mirror for imagined viewers. In her recent study of the play of preadolescent girls in the United States, Sharon Lamb echoes John Berger's thinking about females being at once surveyors and surveyed, when she asserts that

> Today we might assume, as many feminists do, that makeup and heels are a male invention to make women objects for their viewing, to make them ridiculous and powerless. Regardless, many girls see these items as having special power. Why else would their mothers forbid their wearing them? Why else would highly made up, fashionable women get so much attention?...There are two kinds of power in being an object. In one sense, the power is in the gaze of the other...but in another sense, when girls dress up and dance in front of the mirror, as they do, they also become the looker, the one with the eyes, the one desiring and approving of themselves.[15]

The delight of being looked at that Lamb describes is a part of a fantasy of performing and being adored that Valerie Walkerdine has identified as central to girlhood, as I showed in the previous section.[16] As the passive recipients of boys' approving gazes, girls can find confirmation of their attractiveness in a way that does not disrupt their positions as demure and modest. This accords with the ideology of romance and proper female reserve, wherein being the docile object of a man's flaming desire enables females to have sexual experiences without instigating them. In this kind of scenario, a girl need not take responsibility for her sexual feelings and can still be a "good girl"—I will have more to say about the issue of respectability in girl culture in the chapters of Part 4.

Girls can feel that it is imperative to be sexually attractive but at the same time not sexually active, that it is proper to receive attention from boys, but not to seek it. Under these circumstances, the pleasures of being looked at are cherished, and to be looked at desirously without having actively sought out this attention is the greatest delight. Such is the position articulated in the Dixie Cups' 1964 "You Should Have Seen the Way He Looked at Me," the song whose corresponding television performance was mentioned earlier in Chapter 3. In this song, a girl narrator brags about the adoring looks her boyfriend gives her and emphasizes her own inertia in soliciting his gaze. With lines like "I just stood there," "Before I knew it, he put his arms around me," "He asked me for a kiss, and I just had to do it," and the recurring title line, the girl distances herself as much as possible from any agency in the romance. In a nice touch, though, the song begins with the girl's own act of looking; she spies the boy at a party, and when their eyes lock, he bestows a special gaze that confirms her worth, and she instantly dispenses with any active role in their ensuing relationship. As in the Dixie Cups' biggest hit, 1964's "Chapel of Love," this song culminates in a wedding as the girl finds herself dressed in something old, something new, something borrowed, and something blue in the final verse, continually amazed at the way her lover looks at her.

5

Uniformity and Masquerade

In the relationship described in "You Should Have Seen the Way He Looked at Me," the girl celebrates above all the fact that her boyfriend is pleased with the way she looks—as in so many girl group songs, we learn nothing about the boy's character or his own powers of attraction. What is important about him is the way that he looks at her and that he has selected her as the prettiest girl, and his approval is worth all the more because the girl has done nothing out of the ordinary to elicit his love-struck gaze. Still, a girl listener impressed by the narrator's achievement would know the hard work that went into being so (apparently) unselfconsciously adorable, because she herself would carry it out and accept it as a normal part of being a girl. This disingenuous façade is as much a part of the veil of girlness as any of the other bodily practices I have discussed. An equally important aspect of this mask in girl group performances is the matching costumes worn by singers as they enacted the approved gestures and stances of girlhood and sang of its experiences.

The matching dresses worn by members of girl groups are like uniforms, erasing elements of individuality and humanity as they explicitly proclaim the wearer's membership in a group and discourage seeing her as unique. In her elegant meditation on the language of clothes, Alison Lurie considers that "to put on such livery is to give up one's right to act as an individual—in terms of speech, to be partially or wholly censored. What one does, as well as what one wears, will be determined by external authorities."[1] The idea of being censored or erased by dressing in uniform or moving uniformly with a group is intriguing, and we can understand this as another kind of violence enacted upon members of girl groups.

The look of the Supremes, for example, was considered an essential element of the trio's work: upon casting about for a replacement for

Florence Ballard in 1967, Motown was concerned above all with the importance of finding a singer who would fit into Ballard's gowns. New Supreme Cindy Birdsong could wear the dresses, and even looked uncannily like her predecessor, but she had a different vocal range than Ballard, so that the Supremes had to reorganize their vocal arrangements.[2] Motown had made a significant financial investment in the clothing of its star female group and considered the wardrobe to be more valuable than the sound of the Supremes, for all that the group had, by 1967, earned the label many successes.

This anecdote demonstrates that individual members of girl groups—and male vocal groups, to be sure—were considered by many record producers to be replaceable as long as the look of the group was maintained more or less intact. In this regard, wardrobe was key; most girl groups performed in matching dresses and wigs and many were defined by the kinds of clothes they wore. For example, the stiletto heels and satin sheath dresses of the Ronettes marked the trio as sexy, just as the boots and tight pants of the Shangri-Las presented a tough, dangerous image even before they sang. In both of these groups, as in the Supremes, members came and went but the listening public's relationship to the ensembles was largely undisturbed: Cindy Birdsong supplanted Florence Ballard in the Supremes, and the group's next change came when Diana Ross departed for a solo career and was replaced by Jean Terrell. During the 1970s, the trio would include Lynda Lawrence, Sherrie Payne, Susaye Green, and Karen Jackson, as well as stalwart Mary Wilson; the Ronettes sometimes toured with a cousin filling in for lead singer Ronnie; and the Shangri-Las were a group that performed most commonly as a trio, although there were four group members (lead singer Mary Weiss was the only constant).

The interchangeability of bodies in girl groups corresponds to bell hooks' remarks about black models in fashion magazines: "The black female is the best medium for the showing of clothes because her image does not detract from the outfit; it is subordinated."[3] In much the same way, even in ensembles that gain fame and success from singing, the voices and bodies are subordinated to the outfits. The valorization of gown over gown-wearer may represent a callous disregard for the girls and women who sang in girl groups, a reducing of human beings to the status of mannequins. However, an insistence on uniformity of appearance for girl group singers made each group represent more than the sum of its parts, thus creating interesting possibilities for listeners' relationships to them. Whereas the Beatles were famously marketed as four distinct young men, so that even casual fans could name all group members and identify their faces, girl groups stressed the importance of the ensemble by de-emphasizing the singers' individual identities. This made interchangeability among performers possible—and this was often necessary, given that many girl group singers took leaves of absence for school or family commitments and had to be replaced for prolonged periods. Before embarking on her own solo career, for example, Dionne Warwick performed with Scepter label-mates the Shirelles, without causing dismay among the group's fans, when Shirley Owens and Doris Coley both married in 1962, and again when Owens took maternity leave.[4] Similarly, a cousin of the Ronettes filled in for lead singer Ronnie Bennett when her romance with producer Phil Spector made it difficult for him to let her go on tour with Dick Clark's Cavalcade of Stars in 1963.[5]

The girl group uniforms also helped to project a notion of inclusiveness to girl listeners. Cynthia Cyrus has observed that

> If there is little to distinguish one group member from another, then one has only to don the attributes of the group to belong to it. The newspaper stories in which new singers are suddenly discovered to fill the vacancies of an established group entice the reader into imagining or even believing that she too might find a place within the group she idolises. In short, the urge to dress and look alike which so heavily affected girl-group self-presentation mimics more generalised fads; both embody the adolescent desire for acceptance and belonging....[T]he girl groups were carefully positioned to communicate their message of belonging: all the girls (in the group) are the same, all the girls (in the audience) are the same.[6]

Thus, the phenomenon of girl group members dressing in uniform is interpreted as an extension of stereotypically girlish endeavors such as planning to dress alike at school, in order to confirm a feeling of connection to one's closest friends. Signalling membership in a group of friends by wearing coordinated outfits can be reassuring and gratifying in the midst of adolescent insecurities. Analysis of the uniform of female adolescents pervades social commentary throughout the twentieth century; in particular, the "bobby-soxer" of the 1940s was a recognized American stereotype whose saddle shoes and socks were *de rigueur*, and though this emblem of girl identity was typically constructed as white and middle class, it influenced the style and behavior of girls in other race and class groups—even Japanese American girls in internment camps.[7] The legacy of the bobby-soxer to teen culture in the 1960s was such that Phil Spector produced records credited to a group called Bob B. Sox and the Blue Jeans, session singers Bobby Sheen, Fanita James, and Darlene Love. I will have more to say about the influence of white middle-class ideals of girlhood in the next section of this book.

The stiff elegance of the Supremes' matching dresses signalled their identity as group members as distinct from highly individual singers, and they marked the trio as refined and adult, in contrast to the vulgar frills and girlish bows favored by groups like the Dixie Cups but prohibited by middle-class tastes. As Carolyn Kay Steedman recalls in her study of femininity and class in post-war Britain, "The material stepping stones of our escape [from the working class] were clothes, shoes, make-up."[8] Thus, appropriate dress and comportment are essential to the enterprise of becoming an "ideal" girl and woman, and tastes must be cultivated just as discomfort must be endured. What is more, proper dress and comportment can actually mask a working-class body, enabling admission to higher class groups for girls and women. Accessing this social world was an explicit and important goal for all performers at Motown Records, and other girl groups whose members were marked as ethnically different were able to assimilate by virtue of their self-presentation, just as Steedman describes. Some girl groups, of course, chose instead to reject conventional middle-class ideals, and the versions of girlhood presented by these groups are examined in Part 5.

Minstrelsy and Camp Strategies

Berry Gordy's oft-stated goal for his Motown stars was for them to gain access to mainstream pop audiences and be accepted in supper clubs such as the upscale Copacabana in New York and the best stages in Las Vegas, predominantly middle-class white venues that would eventually welcome performers such as black gospel and soul singer Sam Cooke and poor white rock'n'roller Elvis Presley. Innumerable African American performers have shared Gordy's dream of crossing over, and the tactics employed by persevering black musicians involved complex representations of blackness that would be exciting to white audiences. In the post–Civil War era, when blackface minstrelsy was still in its heyday as mainstream popular entertainment in the United States, black performers "blacked up" just like white ones, taking on the burnt cork face paint, exaggerated large lips, mugging facial gestures, and cartoonish physical comedy routines that were conventional. The public personae of vaudeville legend Bert Williams, jazz great Louis Armstrong, jump blues bandleader Louis Jordan, and comedians Flip Wilson and Martin Lawrence can all be interpreted as latter-day examples of black men donning minstrel masks.[9] Black women singers have also had to bow to stereotypes of black femininity: Billie Holiday was required to sing in blackface with Count Basie's band in Detroit in 1937, and Josephine Baker's performance career through the 1920s has been analyzed as a series of provocative and daring experimentations with stereotypes of black female sexuality.[10]

In some of these cases, it can be argued that the importance of reaching a mass audience compelled musicians to accommodate demeaning conditions, and that the other means of making a living available to them were significantly less attractive. Tina Turner, for example, has explained that she became a performer largely because she hated picking cotton.[11] Analysts of the minstrelsy tradition, however, insist on a more complex understanding of the mask, arguing that blackface minstrelsy performances could satirize social hierarchies and unsettle racist thinking.[12] If "the liberatory power of the minstrel show" lies in presenting black characters as cunning and sexually powerful,[13] then the spectacle of Smokey and the Miracles wearing monkey masks to perform their closing number "Mickey's Monkey" and coax their audience into a dancing frenzy can be seen as an example of black performers employing racist imagery to direct the bodies of their audiences into a physical experience of blackness.[14] Equally, the mask offers a disguise behind which performers can laugh at their audiences. Rachel Rubin argues compellingly for an understanding of country star Buck Owens as a wearer of "hillbilly-face," adopting the embarrassing role of hick buffoon on his television show *Hee Haw*, but collecting a check for $200,000 after every taping.[15]

The uniform and mask of girlness can subsume the individuality of a girl while promoting her identity as belonging to a specific type, and this function can be both stifling and, paradoxically, liberating. One of the arguments made in favor of school uniforms for girls is that they free students from the pressures of the fashion wars; girls from wealthy families are unable to flaunt their designer clothes and humiliate their less well-off peers. Even the head-to-toe veil mandated for women in strict Islamist culture might present emancipatory possibilities; an eighteenth-century Englishwoman in Turkey observed that the "'perpetual masquerade' of the Turkish ladies makes sexual indiscretion not only possible, but undetectable."[16] The uniform of femininity in this context made it impossible to distinguish between a lady and her maid, and women could appear as they wished under the veil.

I want to argue that there is room for negotiation, play, and even subversive power in the veil of girlhood. In the introduction to this book, I defined girlness as a set of characteristics and behaviors that signify "girl" and that may be self-consciously rehearsed and put on by girls. Girlness is distinct from girlhood; it is not a phase of the female life cycle that is passed through between childhood and womanhood. Rather, girlness is always available to girls and women (though it is certainly most common during one's teenage years) as a subject position associated with frivolity, self-absorption, and fun. In Chapter 3, I hinted at the possibility of understanding girlness as a form of camp—a term used, in fact, by the girl singers tutored by Cholly Atkins. I am intrigued by the idea of girls performing masquerade, following a carnival of stereotypes enacted by girl groups and accepting conventional stances and behaviors that could be a useful disguise.

Esther Newton asserts that

> Camp is style. Importance tends to shift from what a thing is to how it *looks*, from *what* is done to *how* it is done…the emphasis on style goes further than this in that camp is also exaggerated, consciously "stagey,"

specifically theatrical...camp is suffused with the perception of "being as playing a role" and "life as theatre."[17]

Mark Booth explains camp thus:

> *To be camp is to present oneself as being committed to the marginal with a commitment greater than the marginal merits....*The primary type of the marginal in society is the traditionally feminine, which camp parodies in an exhibition of stylised effeminacy. In the extent of its commitment, such parody informs the camp person's whole personality, throwing an ironical light not only on the abstract concept of the sexual stereotype, but also on the parodist him' or herself.[18]

Pamela Robertson complicates Booth's understanding of camp as a male practice that both parodies femininity and excludes (for the most part) female participation, suggesting that females are capable of playing with camp in ways that parallel the strategies of black performers adopting blackface. Robertson argues for a notion of feminist camp whose pleasures can be ends in themselves:

> I want to avoid reifying pleasure as wholly resistant. I would like to claim camp as a kind of parodic play between subject and object in which the subject laughs at and plays with her own image—in other words, to imagine her distancing herself from her own image by making fun of, and out of, that image—without losing sight of the real power that image has over her.[19]

These and other discussants of camp agree that camp is "stagey," parodic, fun, and that it interacts with and comments on conventions of gender identity.[20] In the arena of girl culture, girls' performative explorations of female stereotypes can be understood as camp devices that permit safe experimentation with the otherwise serious and daunting prospect of becoming women. Dabbling with the trappings of what society demands of girls, girls can alleviate some of the pressure of being a "good girl," have fun, and perhaps reassure themselves that it is all a masquerade.

In this way, the exaggerated gestures and postures taught by Cholly Atkins to girl singers, associated by them with an artificial sense of a prim femininity, but copied nonetheless by their audience, could become part of a girl's disguise, and this charade of femininity could protect an interior sense of self that remained secret and precious. Patricia Juliana Smith considers that Dusty Springfield "paradoxically expressed and disguised her own 'unspeakable' lesbianism through an elaborate camp masquerade that metaphorically and artistically transformed a nice white girl into a black woman and femme gay man, often simultaneously."[21] Springfield's connection to girl groups in the United States is significant; her first North American hit as a solo artist was in early 1964 (making her the second success of the British Invasion), and she was an exact contemporary of the Crystals, the Marvelettes, and all the rest. Indeed, what Smith identifies as Springfield's "parodic femme" style of bouffant hair, "panda" eye shadow (reportedly rendered with shoe polish), and frosted pink lipstick was deliberately and self-consciously copied from American singers such as the Ronettes.[22] Furthermore, Springfield's emulation of American girl groups in her early solo recordings was an impressive feat of vocal cross-dressing for a middle-class, suburban English girl of Irish Catholic descent, and her affinity for African American musical aesthetics ultimately earned her the title "Queen of Blue-Eyed Soul."

Springfield's use of an über-girl disguise to conceal her unacceptable queer identity was also deployed by her New Jersey counterpart, Lesley Gore, as we shall see in Part 4. A veil of exaggerated girlness attributes and behaviors functioned like a coat of armor protecting the person inside. In both these cases, the girl in question had good reason to fear the consequences of revealing her lesbianism in a climate where homosexual activity was actually criminal.[23] This strategy accords with Joan Rivière's 1929 suggestion that "women who wish for masculinity may put on a mask of womanliness to avert anxiety and the retribution feared from men."[24]

Rivière is writing primarily about gay women (whom she understands as wishing for masculinity), but she also asserts: "The reader may now ask how I define womanliness or where I draw the line between genuine womanliness and the 'masquerade.' My suggestion is not, however, that there is any such difference; whether radical or superficial, they are the same thing."[25]

Camp strategies of girlness can create a protective shield for any girl as she struggles to make sense of her changing body and notion of gender and generation identities. To fling oneself wholeheartedly into the most banal, despised aspects of girly behavior—pink ruffles and lace, incessant giggling, self-absorption, and high-pitched chatter about boys and clothes—is to play the part of the girl to the hilt. Indeed, the most campy elements of feminine experience can be irresistibly attractive to young girls:

> In the sixth grade Marilyn took a walk down Bourbon Street in the city of New Orleans. There the strippers and prostitutes hung out on the streets, waving and smiling at the little girls. They had long feather boas and high heels. Their dresses were long and studded with thousands of sequins. Her mother said to her as they passed these women, "I want you to promise me you won't do that when you grow up." So of course, said Marilyn, she used to pretend to be a stripper for hours at a time, prancing around her room with a boa and high heels.[26]

In this informant's story, tawdry and sexualized accessories of femaleness were fodder for secret girlish fantasies of glamour. Note also that in her account, Lamb's informant recalls that the strippers and prostitutes were directly addressing little girls, inviting them to enjoy their parade of exuberant womanly excess.

This episode has a carnivalesque quality to it—strippers and prostitutes, women marginalized by legitimate society, appear to be resplendent and powerful, and they inspire the games and daydreams of middle-class girls. Just so, there is a carnivalesque inversion in the phenomenon of African American girls from working-class urban backgrounds posing in matching dresses, wigs, and exaggerated gestures of demure girlhood in order to serve as role models and icons of teen femininity to prudish suburban America. As bell hooks writes with regard to women's bodies in Spike Lee's film *School Daze*, "They are not a silenced body. Displayed as playful cultural nationalist resistance, they challenge assumptions that the black body, its skin color and shape, is a mark of shame."[27] Susan Douglas, a middle-class white woman who came of age during the early 1960s, asserts that "of utmost importance was the role Diana Ross played in making African American beauty enviable to white girls....The Supremes made it perfectly normal for white girls to idolize and want to emulate their black sisters."[28] Recall that the heyday of African American girl groups was concurrent with the most visible acts of the Civil Rights movement;

it is a fairly astonishing fact that the persona of the teenage girl occupied such a prominent place in popular consciousness during these turbulent years, and that it contributed to the rapprochement of black and white America. The camp elements of girlness became a forceful statement in a society that tended to brush over girl culture as trivial, foolish, and inconsequential.

Flaunting this kind of highly self-conscious, artificial presentation of girlhood can, in fact, be a provocative and bold gesture. Embracing the most superficial and despised aspects of teen femininity—excessively demure posture, coy clothing, and trivial subjects of conversation—girl groups insisted on those aspects of girl culture that society tends to despise, or at least dismiss. To understand girl group performances of what girls were expected to be as reactionary, misguided, or even complicit in a misogynist agenda is to misunderstand the complexities of their cultural importance. More dangerously, it is to misunderstand girls and their strategies for negotiating a sexist culture as they leave childhood and, willingly or no, begin to take on the burdens and stigma of womanhood.

Mary Russo writes that

> For a woman to dress, act, or position herself in discourse as a man is easily understandable and culturally compelling. To "act like a woman" beyond narcissism and masochism is, for psychoanalytic theory, trickier. That is the critical and hopeful power of the masquerade. Deliberately assumed and foregrounded, femininity as a mask, for a man, is a take-it-or-leave-it proposition; for a woman, a similar flaunting of the feminine is a take-it-*and*-leave-it *possibility*. To put on femininity with a vengeance suggests the power of taking it off.[29]

When girl group singers and their fans willingly took on the restricted movements, prissy postures, and elaborate makeup foisted on them, they put on girlness with a vengeance and thereby could undermine assumptions about what is natural and appropriate for girls. This kind of performance of girl identity is recognizably artificial and can thus be scorned by those invested in notions of authenticity; girl group music has been correspondingly maligned as unoriginal, reactionary, and trite by histories of popular music that wish to uphold 60s rock'n'roll as genuine, dangerous, and rebellious.

Transgressive gender performances are easy to identify as rebellious, but the parodic gestures of girlness embodied by girl groups can be understood as a disguise, whereby girls dissemble pert frivolity and compliance. Girl groups could signify all the stereotypes of girlness writ large, showing their audience how to play with these clichés. The appeal of participating in girl group music as a performer or a listener resides at least partly in this fun. If adolescence "disposes girls to see the cultural framework, and girls' and women's subordinate place in it, for the first time," and if their response to this awakening often involves frustration and anger, as Lyn Mikel Brown asserts, then the camp strategies of girlness seem invaluable.[30] The possibility of irreverence and playfulness at this crucial juncture may alleviate the pressures of incipient womanhood, and the opportunity to rehearse some of the darker themes of femininity in songs about restraint and violence may diminish their power to terrify. The giggly, deliberately superficial chatter of girls dressed self-consciously in the fashions of teenage uniformity can serve as a shield, a defense strategy against too-adult responsibilities, and playing at being a girl with a vengeance can actually point to the artifice of behaviors believed to be natural and inevitable.

PART III

He Makes Me Say Things I Don't Want to Say[1]

In the midst of 1999's millennial fever, Rhino Records issued a lavish box set called *RESPECT: A Century of Women in Music*. The collection was inspired by feminist artist Judy Chicago's watershed *Dinner Party* installation piece (1974–9), and it aimed to resurrect the lost music of female artists through the age of recording. The five-CD set is a rare compilation of tracks by such past luminaries as Sophie Tucker, the Carter Family, and Marian Anderson, as well as hits from the 1990s by PJ Harvey, Ani DiFranco, and Liz Phair, and it traces a chronology of female music-making from oppressive beginnings to ascendancy in the present day.

According to the liner notes, the girl groups of the 1960s represent something of a roadblock in the history of women in music recording because their "male-producer-driven style…relied on the legendary Brill Building for material and favored songs about boyfriend problems.…[A] classic girl group, the Shirelles had little creative control over their music, which was sculpted by male producers for teen listeners. In other words, the Shirelles sang exclusively about The Boy, that mysterious dreamboat who has it in his power to make life heaven on earth."[2]

The writer seems to consider songs about heterosexual teenage love reactionary, and she also implies that girl groups like the Shirelles were frustrated by the constraints limiting them to mere singing (and singing trite material at that), implying that all musicians aspire to have complete control over their creative output. (The writer also overlooks the fact that the Shirelles did write some of their material and that they were signed to a record label run by a woman, Florence Greenberg's Scepter.)

That this kind of discussion should appear in an explicitly feminist project celebrating the travails and triumphs of women in the music industry goes to the heart of my thesis. In identifying the arena of producers and songwriters as the most important locus of creativity, the *RESPECT* team belittles the work of singers who breathe life into songs, and it reinscribes (no doubt unwittingly) a code of musical values that regards singing and dancing as activities that "come naturally" to females and thus deserve scant respect. In the next few chapters, I want to consider how this ideology affects our understanding of girl groups; close readings of key songs will enable me to address the politics of record production and to propose an understanding of recording processes from the standpoint of the singer. When the creation of a song involves many people, whom should we identify as the speaker? When a song exists in listeners' ears largely because of the vocal performance that brings it to life, how much importance should we ascribe to producers and songwriters? Finally, why have these issues been seen to devalue pop music like the 1960s girl group repertoire, but not the work of artists such as Elvis Presley, who likewise wrote none of his songs but is nonetheless generally considered the author of his music?

The hierarchy that places producers and songwriters at the head of the musical enterprise—followed at some distance by lyricists, sound engineers, and ultimately by musicians in their various ranks, beginning with lead guitarists and keyboard players and continuing downward, until drummers and rhythm guitarists emerge only slightly ahead of singers at the bottom of the ladder—became well established during the 1960s. Paradoxically, the rise of artists who wrote, arranged, engineered, performed, and produced their records during this period did not lead to the demise of record producers;

instead, it led to the phenomenon of "star" producers who were often as famous as the performers they worked with. Phil Spector, Berry Gordy, George Martin, Andrew Loog Oldham, and Quincy Jones were among the first generation of record producers who had public personae as young, chic figures, credited as "the creative genius behind" the musicians who recorded with them, and they helped to make the role of the producer far more prominent than had previously been customary. The fact that the *RESPECT* collection subscribes to this understanding of the importance of the producer underscores the extent to which it has come to govern our conception of how music gets made.

To be sure, many talented male singers as well as female ones suffer when measured against this yardstick, but women's reliance on producers is more emphasized and contemptible in many eyes. Of course, women who flourish in the music industry are almost always suspected of having traded on their personal relationships to established figures, as the cases of Courtney Love, Mariah Carey, and Shania Twain—to say nothing of Fanny Mendelssohn, Clara Schumann, Barbara Strozzi, and Francesca Caccini—demonstrate. At various times, all of these women have had to contend with suggestions that their lovers, brothers, or fathers were the true architects of their successes. And indeed, it is highly unusual for a woman to secure entry into the world of professional musicianship without the support of a man already savvy in the ways of the industry. (For example, David Crosby famously agreed to act as "producer" on Joni Mitchell's first record in 1968, but actually he stayed out of her way altogether. Lending his name to the project was his way of ensuring Mitchell would be able to create the record she wanted.) We might better interpret the scarcity of independent women musicians as an indication of the ways in which females are denied access to musical training than as an indictment of the few who do succeed.[3]

6

Record Producers and the Politics of Production

Much recent scholarship on record making argues that records are produced through a collaborative process, and that trying to discern who devised which pleasing effect in the studio is "like who does what to whom in bed....Nobody knows what goes on at a record session unless you're sitting there."[1] There are indeed many producers who think of themselves as collaborators on the records they make—George Martin, to take a well-known example, considers that he was part of a production or composition team that created Beatles records.[2] It is noticeable that producers who worked predominantly with girl groups and other girl singers, on the other hand, tended to insist on more hierarchical roles in their work. Phil Spector, George "Shadow" Morton, and Berry Gordy became famous as much for their eccentricities and hot tempers as for their excellent musical instincts, and they often made sure that their names eclipsed the names of performers on their records. In 1960, for example, Berry Gordy advertised a new single by the Miracles (featuring Smokey Robinson on lead vocals) with a picture of himself and a write-up describing his achievements at Motown.[3] Similarly, Rolling Stones manager/producer Andrew Loog Oldham "took out a congratulatory ad in *Melody Maker* touting the Righteous Brothers' recording of Barry Mann/Cynthia Weil song 'You've Lost that Lovin' Feelin" as 'the great new PHIL SPECTOR record.'"[4]

It is notable that both of these anecdotes, singled out as striking instances where the record producer overshadows the performer, involve male singers. When the group or solo singer was female, it seems, the producer's self-aggrandizing was less remarkable; certainly, there is no shortage of instances where a girl group is thought of primarily as the creation of its producer. The malleability of adolescent female singers was attractive to young male producers seeking to establish themselves in the music business, as was the ingénue quality that many of these singers possessed in their teens. Berry Gordy, for example, perceived that his ambitions to break black artists into mainstream culture would be best served by a girl singer:

> Gordy intended from the beginning to cross over with a woman because he felt that black women were less threatening and, in some ways, more comforting to the white public than a black man would be, especially with the intense sexuality and sensuality that the "new" popular music of Rhythm and Blues and Rock and Roll suggested. The fate of Diana Ross and the Supremes reveals how Gordy saw women as both necessary and expendable.[5]

Gordy's sense of black women as unthreatening and comforting in comparison to black men corresponds to a prevalent stereotype of black woman as mammy. The function of controlling stereotypes like this one is explored further in Chapter 9.

Whether the producer considers himself (and I use a male pronoun advisedly) to be a collaborator or an auteur, he is generally believed to contribute usefully to a recording session in light of his ability to hear the record as a whole because of his greater distance from the music-making. This detachment, impossible for musicians to achieve, purportedly allows for a more sophisticated understanding of how best to prioritize sonic elements and fit the various parts together.[6] In a Marxist feminist analysis, however, the person occupying this role is far removed from the actual production of music. An examination of the material conditions of recording shows the musicians making the sounds documented in the recording process as the producers, whereas those running the recording session are in positions analogous to overseers in factories, or patriarchs whose wives' bodies are "instruments of production in pregnancy, giving birth or lactation."[7] Marx argued that the closer the connection between labor and the body, the more abject the worker, and feminists invested in historical materialism have compared this phenomenon to the debasement of the female body and the ways in which cultural practices seek to elevate the products of female labor above their fleshly origins. These observations are useful in the arena of music recording, where the work of singers is most clearly a product of bodily effort and is correspondingly dismissed by instrumentalists, record producers, and engineers who manipulate external apparatuses in order to make music.

The trivializing of singers and their cultural work is so widespread as to be practically endemic to the fields of musicology and media studies. The dramatic shift in the creative paradigms of popular music heralded by the self-contained bands of the British Invasion in the mid-1960s meant that "the autonomous band of singer/instrumentalist/songwriters as an institution largely supplanted the practice of entrusting composing, arranging, instrumental performance, and singing to separate individuals."[8] While this may be an overstatement (I have already pointed out the rise of celebrity producers in this period, and many British Invasion bands at the time relied on the studio system which continues to thrive until the present day), it is true that the necessity of performing self-written material became central to rock ideology in the mid-60s and after. Music that stemmed from other practices came to be seen as inferior to the supposedly unmediated expressions of pure feeling emanating from the new bands. Ironically, mastery of an instrument became a badge of musical truth, while bringing music out from within the body itself was dismissed as facile and "inauthentic." With this system of values firmly in place, it is hardly surprising that the *RESPECT* team mentioned above heaps praise on Paula Cole, the first woman to be nominated for a Grammy award in the producer category (in 1996), while it pours shame on the exploitative system that kept Little Eva off the mixing board.

But in fact, the sonic aesthetics and production values of girl group songs seem unconcerned with the importance of technological control or of unmediated expression in music. While rock recording techniques—particularly those from the 1970s on—often aspire toward an invisible means of production, implying a concert performance that just happened to be captured on tape, girl group songs are clearly and unapologetically products of the recording studio. Many of the musical effects that characterize this music could not be created in the context of a concert; the crucial prominence of handclaps in a recording such as the Supremes' 1964 breakthrough "Baby Love" (actually not handclaps at all, as we shall see shortly) could never carry in a live performance venue. Similarly, the hollow rattle that undergirds the Shirelles' hopeless devotion in "Baby, It's You" (1962) would require a tambourine the size of a small car to be heard on stage with a band, and the slithery metallic sound heard in Martha and the Vandellas' 1965 "Nowhere to Run" was famously created by rattling the snow chains taken from someone's car, a strategy typical of Motown's resourceful house musicians, but not one that would be effective in live performances on tour. These examples of percussive sounds used in the rhythm tracks of girl group songs are among many instances of effects that are utterly dependent on a studio environment. In important ways, the production techniques of girl group records mirrors girls' experience in a culture that tries to confine them to safe, domestic spaces and hands them ready-made and obviously prefabricated experiences to make their own.

In an examination of the concept of authorship in popular music, Will Straw notes that the priorities of album-oriented rock (AOR, in industry and fan parlance) in the 1970s precipitated a shift from considering songs as part of a shared cultural system of collectively developed genres to understanding them as expressions of personal honesty that could be connected only to a specific artist's career and lived experiences. Straw describes the challenge that disco music presented to the music industry when, in the late 70s, this genre emerged from a scene wherein there had been little interest in distinguishing the faceless musicians behind extended tracks that blended on the dance floor. Disco then came to the attention of listeners who cared about "the development of long-lasting artists with distinct identities and stable careers," and who were bemused when faced with tracks (not songs).[9] The phenomenon of disco "tracks" marked a return to a system resembling the singles-based market of rock'n'roll in its heyday, which the ideology of AOR had rejected. With the rise of AOR in the late 60s and early 70s, and especially the phenomenon of "concept albums" (albums organized around a single theme that unifies the different tracks), albums began to be considered large-scale works of art, central to an emerging notion of rock (as distinct from rock'n'roll) as serious, important, and able to stand the test of time in the same way as classical music. Accordingly, the fast-paced business of making and marketing singles, which gave little thought to either career longevity or profundity, came to be associated more and more with pop music, and the records themselves understood as ephemeral, vapid, and less significant than rock albums.[10]

The puissance of this ideology seems to explain why the music of girl groups in the early 1960s is typically either dismissed as the inane chirpings of mindless puppets controlled by some behind-the-scenes Svengali or lambasted as the result of an oppressive system of misogynist opportunism. However, the rigid patriarchal structure that led to many 1960s girl group records, so often excoriated for the way it permitted adult men to impose their adult will on young girls, comprised relatively few actual middle-aged men. For example, Aldon Publishing (one of the hit song factories considered part of the Brill Building phenomenon) numbered eighteen writers on its staff in 1962, all aged between nineteen and twenty-six.[11] Phil Spector himself, that legendary tyrant who built his famous Wall of Sound with the sweat and tears of young girls like Ronnie Bennett (later Ronnie Spector) and Darlene Love, had his first number one hit at age eighteen, reached the height of his powers and earned the moniker "the tycoon of teen" at twenty-three, and announced his retirement at age twenty-five.[12] Those males apparently driving the girl group sound, then, were for the most part close in age to the girls who sang for them, and—in a significant break with the practices of professional songwriters in the late 50s—they actually listened to and cared about rock'n'roll themselves.

The Brill Building Songwriters

Consider the excitement generated in the Brill Building at this time, and what it must have been like to be part of this hive of activity and optimistic camaraderie. Between 1958 and 1970, the work of Brill Building songwriters and publishers dominated the music charts, launched several performance careers, and sustained entire genres; as well as girl group music, uptown soul depended largely on songs created in the tiny offices and even hallways and restrooms of the Brill Building. An example of the unusual, almost haphazard circumstances that gave rise to many hit songs is the case of "The Locomotion," the Little Eva hit analyzed in Chapter 3. Many of the records born in the Brill Building came to be through capricious circumstances like these, and the reminiscences of Carole King and Gerry Goffin, along with other songwriters, confirm that their collective youth was a crucial ingredient in the atmosphere of vigorous excitement that led to such successes.[13] Jerry Leiber and Mike Stoller, writers of "Hound Dog" (a hit for "Big Mama" Thornton in 1953 and again for Elvis Presley in 1956), recall the inventiveness with which they presented their material to producers and publishers: they would perform their songs with any available instruments in a cramped office and start their tour of offices at the top floor of the building because "it was easier to walk downstairs than up" as they went from door to door.[14] The youthful energy of these songwriters was infectious and inviting: in 1968, star songwriter Ellie Greenwich published a series of tips for aspiring songwriters, including advice on how to make a demo recording and addresses to send it to.[15]

It is important, then, to recognize the youthfulness of the Brill Building songwriters and also to examine critically the phenomenon represented by young women such as these. All accounts of the Brill Building girl group sound acknowledge the prolific output of female songwriters Carole King, Ellie Greenwich, and Cynthia Weil, who actually came to dominate the songwriting industry and were on par with figures such as Neil Sedaka and Burt Bacharach. Each of these women began to work as a professional songwriter in her late teens, and each came to work more or less exclusively with a partner whom she married in her teens or early twenties. Among their successes, the teams of King and Goffin, Greenwich and Barry, and Weil and Mann were responsible for many of the most popular songs in the 1960s, and their songs include "The Locomotion," "Chains," "Will You Love Me Tomorrow?," "One Fine Day" (King and Goffin); "Leader of the Pack," "Chapel of Love," "Be My Baby," "Da Doo Ron Ron" (Greenwich and Barry); "On Broadway," "You've Lost That Lovin' Feelin'," and "We Gotta Get out of This Place" (Weil and Mann). In the cases of King/Goffin and Greenwich/Barry, the men were lyricists and the women songwriters. According to industry terminology, the lyricist often writes words and melody, while the songwriter fills out harmonies, devises rhythms and grooves, and may arrange instrumental parts (though often the arranger has a separate function). The team of lyricist Cynthia Weil and her husband, songwriter Barry Mann, reversed these responsibilities, and they also were known for writing socially conscious songs like "Uptown" and "Five O'Clock World." All of these songwriting teams, like Nickolas Ashford and Valerie Simpson at Motown Records, wrote for male and female performers alike, and they were instrumental in creating the girl group sound.

Women in the Music Industry

As surprising as the activity of women songwriters may seem, an equally unlikely figure in this regard is Vicki Wickham, one of the few women to achieve international success as an artist's manager and producer in television and recording. Wickham worked with artists such as Dusty Springfield, Patti LaBelle, and, later, Morrissey, and in the 1960s she was one of the founding producers of the British television variety show *Ready Steady Go!*, a forum that was crucial to the careers of Dusty Springfield, the Rolling Stones, the Kinks, and other British acts, as well as African American artists trying to appeal to British audiences. Wickham went on to become Springfield's manager, cowriting her biggest hit, "You Don't Have to Say You Love Me" in 1966, and when *Ready Steady Go!* was cancelled the following year, she left to explore new possibilities in New York.

Finding that the American television industry was difficult to break into, she turned to artist management, and her greatest success was with Philadelphia girl group Patti LaBelle and the Bluebelles, whom she transformed from a demure teen quartet[16] into the glam, space age, funk women of Labelle: "When Patti first asked me to manage them I was reluctant. The name Patti LaBelle and the Bluebelles sounds so old. I said, 'If we're going to do this, it's a new day. You've been together sixteen years, and you can't get arrested. You can't wear those nice little frilly frocks and wigs, we've got to rethink it. You've got to make a statement, you're women, there's a lot to be said.'"[17]

Wickham thus directed the rebranding of Labelle as an adult ensemble, enabling them to be one of the very few girl groups to navigate the transition into womanhood. During the 1970s, Labelle continued to perform new material to great acclaim, with songs like 1974's "Lady Marmalade" marking a dramatic shift away from 60s' recordings such as Rodgers and Hammerstein's "You'll Never Walk Alone" (1964). Wickham's ideas about femininity were evidently crucial to her success in managing this group.

Unlike the savvy young Wickham, record producer Florence Greenberg began working in the industry because she was bored as a New Jersey housewife whose children were all in school. Although she had no background in music, she began traveling into Manhattan in order to observe publishing offices and get to know songwriters, and she eventually rented an office at 1674 Broadway, near the Brill Building (located at 1619 Broadway, with Aldon's office across the street at 1650). Her daughter, Mary Jane, pestered her classmates the Shirelles to come and sing for Greenberg, who arranged for them to record their song "I Met Him on a Sunday," as discussed in Chapter 1. Although the record was not a huge success, Greenberg felt she had learned enough from the experience to launch her own record label, Scepter. Greenberg would also run the Wand and Tiara labels (because multiple labels made promotion work easier), drawing inspiration for the labels' names by considering the attributes of regal femininity, "looking at a picture of a throne and a queen, and thinking of all the things a queen possessed: a scepter, a tiara, a mace, a royal chair."[18] These labels would record artists associated with rhythm and blues and pop alike; as well as the Shirelles, Scepter and affiliates produced records by Dionne Warwick, Chuck Jackson, the Kingsmen, and BJ Thomas. Scepter also blurred racial boundaries when Greenberg began collaborating with young African American songwriter Luther Dixon, who had written "Sixteen Candles" for doo wop group the Crests as well as numbers for Perry Como and Pat Boone and who had offices in the same building as Greenberg. The two "struck a financial arrangement; they agreed to be partners in Scepter Records with Greenberg running the record company and Dixon producing the artists and involved in the company's song publishing entities."[19] Dixon produced the majority of Scepter recordings until he left the label and moved on to Capitol Records in 1962, at which point Greenberg increased her practice of assigning production responsibilities to her son Stanley, with some credits—like the Shirelles' 1959 "Dedicated to the One I Love"—dating from when Stanley was a high school student.

Greenberg evidently carried her role as a respectable suburban mother into her professional activities, both by involving her children in her business and by trying to foster a "family" atmosphere at the record label. She remembers touring the Southern United States with the Shirelles and staying with them at YWCAs when other hotels would not accommodate a Jewish woman and four black teenage girls—her sense of matronly duty precluded the possibility of staying in separate lodgings.[20] Unfortunately, it seems that Greenberg may have been no more scrupulous than many men in the industry, and the Shirelles entered into a legal dispute with Scepter in 1964, when the singers turned twenty-one and discovered that the trust fund they had been assured of did not exist.[21]

While Greenberg's work in the music industry proved to be lucrative, most session musicians were less well remunerated and often felt compelled to take work even when it was inconvenient. Carol Kaye, a stunning California blonde who began playing guitar and bass professionally in her late teens, became the top bassist at Los Angeles recording sessions in her mid-twenties during the early 60s. Kaye was part of an elite number of session musicians sometimes known as the "Wrecking Crew," who played on records by the Beach Boys, the Mamas and the Papas, the Byrds, and groups produced by Phil Spector, as well as film and television soundtracks. Kaye recalls some of the obstacles facing a woman in this competitive industry:

> [Session singers] the Blossoms did most of [Phil Spector's] tracks (didn't matter who the group was) and [engineer Larry Levine] would shudder when we all got pregnant at the same time but kept on working.…You had to get along with people, be on time, be professional in every way. No soreheads allowed. No one held your hand or played your instrument for you either.…I remember a particular time when I had to get away, took the kids and housekeeper up to a houseboat in the [San Francisco] Bay area…just a gorgeous place for the kids. But a movie contractor found me with a well-placed phone call and insisted that I have to come back for a movie score "NOW," and that meant you had to obey.[22]

Kaye's musicality and professionalism meant she was often in demand, and she created many distinctive bass lines that enhanced popular songs. She is justifiably proud of her work on tracks like

Sonny and Cher's 1967 hit "The Beat Goes On": "About the fourth or fifth line, I came up with the line you hear today. And I do credit Sonny stopping the band and saying, 'That's it, Carol. What's that line you're playing?'... I wish you could've heard it with the original boring bass line and then heard the difference. You would know why I think the bassist is really the arranger of the band. It made the tune happen, and of course made some loot for Sonny & Cher (and a few dimes for the musicians)."[23]

The bass provides the foundation of a song, a heavy sound that supports and directs the groove of the piece; the bassist has a certain power in a recording session, as Kaye's remark suggests. Given her obvious talent, why would she choose this kind of work instead of aspiring to a career as a headlining performer, with the chance of fame and greater financial reward? It is clear that the conventions of the music industry (then as now) offered few and inflexible roles for female performers, and that a pretty young woman playing a man's instrument like the bass was considered unmarketable. Also, Kaye may have been wary of the fickle nature of a solo career, preferring the anonymity of work in the background and a (relatively) stable, if less spectacular, income. Her family responsibilities may also have encouraged her to continue working in environments that were often hostile to women; she recalls her colleagues in the studio shooting darts at pictures of naked women during breaks.[24] Kaye evidently possessed a considerable personal courage, sometimes standing up to an overbearing producer like Phil Spector when her male fellow musicians would not:

> I was playing electric 12-string while eight months pregnant and after two or three hours with no break, I had to scream at Phil to give us a break or I was going to wet my pants! He dutifully called a break and the guys later thanked me, the bums! The sessions were too long and sometimes boring but we were professionals and they paid well too.[25]

If "obeying" producers and maintaining professional composure enabled Kaye to have a successful, if difficult, career as a working musician, these tactics also helped predominantly black session singers such as Fanita James (member of L.A.-based the Blossoms) and the legendary Cissy Houston (member of New York–based session vocalists the Sweet Inspirations, and mother of Whitney Houston), as well as the Cookies (discussed in Part 2) and other female backing vocal groups such as the Andantes at Motown and the Sweethearts of Sigma Sound, who recorded during the 1970s heyday of Philadelphia Soul. On the other hand, singers who tried to make the transition from backing singer to soloist were often sorely frustrated, as the case of Darlene Love demonstrates.

Love's career as a singer who worked most commonly with Phil Spector almost literally exemplifies Marx's observations on estranged labor:

> The worker becomes all the poorer the more wealth he produces, the more his production increases in power and range. The worker becomes an ever cheaper commodity the more commodities he creates...the worker is related to the product of his labour as to an alien object...if the product of labour does not belong to the worker, if it confronts him as an alien power, this can only be because it belongs to some *other man than the worker.*[26]

All of these conditions were true for Love, a Pentecostal preacher's daughter who began singing professionally in her late teens and tellingly describes her work as a member of the trio the Blossoms as "something to fall back on; it was a job, like being a secretary."[27] Secretarial work, or "pink collar labor," has been identified as an exploitative arena where invisible female drudgery is the necessary preexisting condition of male success.[28] Love (whose very name was chosen by Phil Spector in tribute to Dorothy Love, a gospel singer he admired—her birth name is Darlene Wright) often sang lead vocals on tracks that were released as records by other groups in the Spector stable, as the producer liked to "cast and recast" singers "like actors playing roles."[29] Such was the case with girl group classics such as "He's a Rebel" (1962, credited to the Crystals), "He's Sure the Boy I Love" (1963, credited to the Crystals), and "Zip-a-Dee-Doo-Dah" (1962, credited to Bob B. Soxx and the Blue Jeans). Spector's biographer Mark Ribowsky asserts that the producer used Love and the Blossoms to record "He's a Rebel" because he felt he could not wait to bring the Crystals out from New York to Los Angeles; time was pressing because he suspected other singers would be quick to record competing versions of the song.[30] Although the record was a great success, difficulties ensued because Barbara Alston (the usual lead singer of the Crystals) had a soft, light voice that could not approximate the gospel-fueled power of Darlene Love, and Alston was unable to perform the song convincingly in stage shows. Thus, Dolores "La La" Brooks, a thirteen-year-old who had recently joined the Crystals to replace a pregnant Myrna Gerrard, was assigned the lead on this song in stage shows and sang lead on most of the group's subsequent recordings.[31] However, Spector continued to use Love when it suited him, and she provided a lead vocal for the Crystals' 1963 release "Da Doo Ron Ron." In this instance, Spector later decided that Brooks' brasher and more youthful sound (she was then fifteen, and Love was twenty-five) would be more effective, so he replaced the solo vocal track without telling Love, who was dismayed to hear a voice not her own when the record was released.[32]

Nevertheless, Love was shrewd enough to appreciate the steady work that session singing assured her and her children:

> I was nineteen when I met Phil, and I was a professional singer. That probably gave me the edge on the rest of the girls he was working with, because they were really young, about thirteen up. He always had to pay me, because as professionals, the Blossoms and I went through the union....The only money I made in those days was through sessions. After "He's a Rebel," I wanted a contract. I wanted royalties...the next thing he wanted was another record for the Crystals. I said, this time you're going to pay me a royalty, not just no $1500. But I didn't get it.[33]

Indeed, the more fame and financial reward her labor brought him, the more elaborate became Phil Spector's stratagems for keeping Love a faceless and nameless worker. His power and influence increased with every successful recording he coaxed from a singer like Love, so that he was able to overlook the wishes of those vocalists creating his achievements—to say nothing of the Crystals, who were confused and hurt at earning a number one hit they had had no part in recording. The conditions of girl groups in the music industry in the early 1960s were such that a producer could own the names of groups and could shuffle voices around from recording to recording like disembodied commodities, alienated from the human efforts that produced them.

Keeping Darlene Love and the other Blossoms invisible was not entirely feasible, however; Love, backed by Fanita James and a succession of other singers, ultimately recorded "Today I Met the Boy I'm Going to Marry" and "Wait 'Til My Bobby Gets Home" under her professional name in 1963. At the same time, the Blossoms continued to do session work for other producers in Los Angeles, and soon they became nationally known for their controversial work as the regular backing vocalists on ABC's *Shindig!* television variety show that aired from 1964 to 1966. (The show's producer, Jack Good, heard the group singing at a Jackie deShannon recording session and insisted on having them on his show, overriding ABC's concerns about having black performers appear regularly on primetime network television.)[34] On *Shindig!*, Fanita James recalls in an interview for this book, the Blossoms "had to learn thirty songs a week…and we didn't have cue cards! We had to learn them by heart, and then as we choreographed, we had to learn to do quick changes." Often their parallel career as a recording session group helped, as when Aretha Franklin appeared on *Shindig!* singing "It's in His Kiss"; James and Love had provided backing vocals on the original recording by Betty Everett (discussed in Chapter 1).[35]

Whether in the television or recording studio, the Blossoms provided backing vocals for a diverse array of artists, singing for Elvis Presley, Patty Duke, Buck Owens, Doris Day, and Tom Jones as well as Ray Charles and innumerable girl groups. While Darlene Love's powerful, gospel voice was attractive to a producer like Spector for certain recordings, the singers had to alter their sound to suit the material and style at hand, often becoming involved in complex representations of race. Fanita James reports that when the Blossoms backed white artists "The producers would tell us; they would say, you know, 'less vibrato, and sound "white."' That's exactly what they would say. That meant smoother…we would all breathe together. Isn't it pitiful to say it like this!—but this is what we thought it meant. Besides breathing together, just a softer, and more conservative sound."

In this kind of situation, the Blossoms followed directions closely and sang their parts as notated, but they were often also required to improvise their harmonies and roles in a recording session, working quickly to avoid taking up expensive studio time. A familiarity with

The Blossoms on the set of *Shindig!* Courtesy of the Fanita James Archive and Star Revue.

the aesthetics and procedures of many different styles was necessary, and the fiercely policed distinctions between black and white music tended to blur out of public view; in the same interview, James remembers singing obscure gospel songs with Elvis Presley during breaks in the making of his 1968 comeback special. She also speaks glowingly of extended improvisation in Ray Charles' *Shindig!* performance of "What'd I Say?":

> [Y]ou know how the dancers are flinging their hair and jumping around, and the song got so heated and so…how can I say it? It was at such a peak, when the director said "Cut, great, we got it" we didn't stop, we kept going and so did Ray Charles, we went on for another five minutes. Oh, I'll never forget that.[37]

Fanita James, Carol Kaye, and Vicki Wickham have fond memories of their years in the trenches of the music and television industries, in spite of the grueling work and frustrations they encountered. Kaye remembers the almost indescribable thrill of musicians locking into an interpretation of Barbra Streisand's 1973 "The Way We Were" after more than thirty takes:

> Take after take, we kept going, each take as intensive as the last one … I started to really improvise around the written part…after a few arpeggios, especially in the bridge, it felt like "the" take, I looked up and caught Ms. Streisand's fast gaze from her little soundbooth as she was holding a long note (through the glass window), our eyes locked like "wheeeee. This is it."…I remember how peaceful the world felt as I drove home that night.[38]

Likewise, Vicki Wickham recalls the bonhomie of her early career: "It was an incredible time because everybody was just starting out…it wasn't at all sophisticated; everybody just knew everybody, we all went to the same clubs and parties. We didn't realize how fantastic it was because we were just with our mates."[39] Perhaps this sense of making it up as they went along helps to explain how, at the outsets of their careers, young, inexperienced women like Wickham, Kaye, and James, as well as Carole King, Ellie Greenwich, and Cynthia Weil, could make forays into nascent industries that were to become rigidly male dominated and competitive. Florence Greenberg, older than these women, also remembers the early days of her career as a record producer wistfully: "It was such an exciting time—the birth of an industry really. You could cut a record, press it up and get it on the radio very quickly. Things weren't corporate like they are today."[40]

7

Carole King and Ellie Greenwich

Today, Carole King is certainly the best known of the women discussed in Chapter 6, largely because of her own immensely successful recording career as a singer/songwriter in the 1970s. Her landmark 1971 album *Tapestry* included performances of one of her finest girl group songs, "Will You Love Me Tomorrow?," the first number-one hit for a girl group (the Shirelles) beginning in 1960. However, King's reinvention of herself as liberated, barefoot earth mother was so successful that many fans were blithely unaware of the fact that she had ever been part of a song-writing factory, churning out tunes with titles like "Please Hurt Me" and "He Hit Me (It Felt Like a Kiss)."[1] The ease with which King negotiated these dramatic metamorphoses is not uncommon in the careers of women in pop, as the examples of Dusty Springfield, Labelle, Marianne Faithfull, and, above all, Madonna attest. Strategies of camp artifice and disguise are integral to girl music and girl culture, as I discussed in Chapter 5.

King was born Carole Klein in Brooklyn, 1942, and she demonstrated an aptitude for music and songwriting early in adolescence. Her entry into the music business was facilitated by her childhood friend Neil Sedaka, a songwriter who found her occasional jobs playing piano, singing backup, and arranging recording sessions while she attended college. While she collaborated occasionally with Sedaka, as she would with other songwriters and producers, her most significant partnership was with Gerry Goffin, a fellow student at Queens College who also wrote songs professionally. "They meshed immediately, as Carole considered herself 'a musician who wrote bad lyrics' while Gerry called his early songs 'lyrically interesting, but sung over inane melodies.'...During their first year and a half at Aldon, they provided the company with some of its biggest hits."[2]

When King became unexpectedly pregnant, she and Goffin married and dropped out of college in order to pursue careers in songwriting. Their first success was with 1960's "Will You Love Me Tomorrow?," a song that explores the conflicting feelings of a girl struggling with what is undoubtedly one of the most momentous decisions in a girl's experience: whether or not to trust her lover's promises and surrender her virginity. Obviously, this was a topic of great significance to King and Goffin at that juncture in their relationship.

"Will You Love Me Tomorrow?"

Since 1960, the song has been recorded by a diverse array of performers, including Tony Orlando, Sandy Posey, Linda Ronstadt, the Righteous Brothers, Frankie Valli and the Four Seasons, and Bryan Ferry.[3] Incredibly, Alan Betrock has reported that King and Goffin originally hoped to sell the piece to established recording artist Johnny Mathis (although they were thinking of the then-little-known Shirelles during the process of writing).[4] Luther Dixon, songwriter and Florence Greenberg's partner in Scepter Records, heard King's piano–vocal demo of "Will You Love Me Tomorrow?" while visiting the offices of Aldon Music to consider new material. He was struck with the song and took it to the Shirelles, who initially disliked it and felt that it was too far away from the sound they had established.

> The Shirelles...said it just wasn't right for them. Dixon felt otherwise and prevailed on the group to trust him, saying that when they heard his arrangement in the studio, it would be perfect for them. Dixon worked on the vocals with the group, and then had Carole [King] devise an intricate musical arrangement. At the session, things were sounding good, but Carole couldn't get the drummer to play the way she wanted, so she went in and played the kettledrums herself.[5]

Before turning to the song, I wish to unpack these statements and try to trace the genesis of the piece. "Will You Love Me Tomorrow?" is credited to Goffin and King, as are all the songs they worked on together, but Gerry Goffin seems conspicuously absent in the foregoing account. Furthermore, Dixon convinced the Shirelles that his arrangement of the objectionable song would induce them to like it, but then entrusted much of that arrangement to King. Her authority in the recording studio was evidently respected enough that she was able to take over for the drummer when he could not play what she wanted.[6] Indeed, most of the young songwriters working in the industry at this time found themselves creating musical arrangements and producing record sessions of the songs they had composed, so King was not exceptional among her colleagues in this respect. Bear in mind, however, that King at this point was eighteen years old—a year younger than the Shirelles—and working with seasoned professionals, who apparently stepped aside and deferred to her; here, clearly, was a young woman very much in charge.

The characterization of King as a woman and of the Shirelles as girls is itself a study in the artificiality of both these subject positions. Shirley Owens was a year older than King, but in 1960 her unmarried status and prominent association with other unmarried females precluded the possibility of her being viewed as an independent adult. King, by virtue both of her motherhood and relationship to Gerry Goffin, fit into the role of adult woman with all the privileges and burdens that title implied. Furthermore, King was white (since her name change, it may not even have been apparent that she was Jewish) and had been a college student, while Owens and the rest of the Shirelles were black and had only high school diplomas. The difference between "girl" and "woman" here has little to do with age and everything to do with race, class, and relationships to men.

If King was in control of the song, it emerges that Dixon was in control of the group. The Shirelles, whose first recording had been of a song they composed themselves about telling off a boy who doesn't treat girls with adequate respect (1958's "I Met Him on a Sunday"), and who were signed to a woman-run record label, deferred to the judgment of the man now producing their records. "Will You Love Me Tomorrow?" was a departure from the sassy stylings of "I Met Him on a Sunday," enacting the kind of slavish devotion to "the Guy" that came to be a hallmark of the emerging girl group style; under the tutelage of Dixon, the group moved away from pert self-assuredness and into a subject position that set the standard for other groups in the genre. With their coerced recording of "Will You Love Me Tomorrow?," a song written by a teenage girl but intended for a man to sing, the Shirelles achieved the number-one position on the charts, a first for a girl group, and consequent superstar status. It would be left to songs like "Party Lights," "You Don't Own Me," and—much later—the Spice Girls' "Wannabe," to reclaim for girl groups the stance of "I Met Him on a Sunday," one of the first girl group songs to enter the Billboard Charts.

In her insightful feminist study of American mass media from the 1950s on, Susan Douglas considers "Will You Love Me Tomorrow?" to be the girl group song par excellence, speaking most compellingly to and for girls in conflict over their developing sexuality. Douglas clearly accepts the song as a text that articulates a girl's authentic expression of sexual desire:

> "Will You Love Me Tomorrow?" was about a traditional female topic, love, but it was also about female longing and desire, including sexual desire. And, most important, it was about having a choice. For these girls [i.e., the Shirelles], the decision to have sex was now a choice, and *this* was new. This was, in fact, revolutionary...what we heard were the voices of teenage girls singing about—and dignifying—our most basic concern: how to act around boys when so much seemed up for grabs.[7]

In the end, Douglas goes so far as to claim that girl group songs like this one provided many young females in the 1960s with their first chance to express and explore their own specifically girly concerns, and she suggests that girl group music was an important precursor to the Women's movement. Certainly, the phenomenon of a "nice girl" articulating desire was novel, and the song's release in December of 1960 was timely; six months earlier, the U.S. Federal Drug Authority had approved the clinical use of oral contraceptives developed with the support of birth control activists Margaret Sanger and Katharine McCormick. Early in 1961, when "Will You Love Me Tomorrow?" was at the top of the charts, the first of many landmark cases was fought to make birth control legally available to married women in Connecticut. The question of female desire and the consequences of sexual activity were topics of heated public debate, and the Shirelles' recording participated in this discussion.

To be sure, fans like the then-teenage Douglas were doubtless unaware of—and probably uninterested in—the politics of recording sessions and enjoyed songs more or less as self-producing entities, with little relation to the tedium of labor. The power plays that had to take place before the Shirelles could provide teenage girls with a means of articulating their own feelings about sexuality and femininity took place in a closed sphere, so that it was easy to believe that the Shirelles sang straight from their own hearts. With the knowledge that King and Goffin had entered into a hasty marriage in reaction to an unplanned pregnancy just before writing the song, it is certainly possible for me to argue the song's status as a "genuine" expression of a teenage girl's anxiety over the possibility of a sexual relationship. However, I am wary of raising the totem of authenticity here because I consider that celebrating truthfulness and confessions of personal experience through song adheres to an ideology that goes against the aesthetics of girl group music; in many cases, the very artificiality of this music served as a kind of reality, and still does.

"Will You Love Me Tomorrow?" begins with a prominent C major chord on acoustic guitar over piano and a steady snare drum pattern in the girl group "heartbeat" pattern identified in Chapter 2: |𝄽 ♫𝄽 ♩ |𝄽 ♫𝄽 ♩ | The song is in a straightforward duple meter, and the harmonic framework of the piece is simple, maintaining a sense of C major with strictly conventional movement through closely related major chords such as F, G, and the relative A minor. The boldest harmonic excursion moves through E major and E7 to A minor on the refrain's "Tonight the light of love is in your eyes/But will you love me tomorrow?" This brief visit to the relative minor underscores the doubt and trepidation expressed in the lyrics, but the song returns quickly to C major when the lyrics expand further on the feelings of tenderness and sexual anticipation that are the main themes of the song.

After its opening statement, the guitar—by this point in history the signifier sine qua non of masculinity—retreats almost entirely for the rest of the song, and violins supply melodic contrast to the voices. Violins and string sections in general are featured on a great many girl group recordings, hearkening back to Tin Pan Alley conventions and distinguishing these songs from the guitar-based rock of Chuck Berry and Elvis. Here, the closely miked violins stand out from the rest of the instruments and contribute to a studio sound that bears little resemblance to the sound of a live performance. Indeed, the violins and snare have the cleanest, clearest sounds in this recording; Shirley Owens and the rest of the Shirelles seem to be much further away from the listener and might literally have been further away from their microphones. This is an entirely different sound from their first release, "I Met Him on a Sunday," which demonstrates a sparer recording aesthetic and brings the singers' voices and finger snapping much closer to the forefront.

It would be easy to conclude that King and Dixon placed the mike far away from Owens because she had a weak, dull-sounding voice and tended to sing out of tune (most spectacularly on 1962's "Baby, It's You"). Indeed, this kind of disparagement has typified much writing about girl groups, whether in reference to 60s groups like the Shirelles or more recent examples such as the Spice Girls. But Owens's voice was the sound desired on this and other recordings by the Shirelles and, in fact, she was not the original lead singer of the group. Early recordings by the quartet—apart from the unusual, democratic "I Met Him on a Sunday," discussed in Chapter 2—feature Doris Coley as soloist. Coley's voice was bigger and rougher than Owens' thin sound, powerful in stage performances but less effective in the recording studio because she had less technical control, as even cursory hearings of songs such as "Dedicated to the One I Love" (1959) and "I Saw a Tear" (1960) attest. Shortly after Luther Dixon was brought in to produce the group's recordings, Florence Greenberg asked Shirley Owens to write a song quickly for an upcoming recording session: "She said, 'Shirley, why don't you go home and write something?' And I asked, 'When?' Florence said, 'Tonight. Maybe you can do it tonight. We need it as soon as possible.' So I looked at her and said, 'Well, I guess tonight's the night!' And that's how I got the title."[8]

Owens sang lead on her song (for which she shared a songwriting credit with Luther Dixon) and on subsequent recordings; evidently Dixon, the group's new producer, felt that her small, often dull-sounding voice was the right sound for the group's studio work, although Coley continued to sing solos in stage performances. Whatever the series of events that elbowed Coley away from the microphone, the results were good, as "Tonight's the Night" became the group's first Top Forty hit, achieving a number 39 position late in 1960 and setting the stage for their number one with "Will You Love Me Tomorrow?" beginning in December of that year.

To dismiss girl groups because their members are not always technically skillful singers is to miss the point entirely. Girl group producers certainly knew accomplished singing when they heard it, and they had access to proficient and versatile singers like the Blossoms and the Cookies, and a producer such as Phil Spector certainly did not hesitate to use his preferred voices when it suited him, no matter whose record he was creating. The girl group sound was and is predicated on the unpolished voices of girls like Shirley Owens (nineteen at the time of this recording), whose passion and earnestness prevent the musically conventional and formulaic songs from being empty and insipid. Of course, acknowledging the chain of events that brought Owens into the recording studio for this song raises the possibility that her performance might have been grudging and unenthusiastic; however, the sound of her voice on the record demonstrates that she was able to give a convincing and professional interpretation. Owens' ability to throw herself into the song illustrates the ways in which girls are adept at negotiating subject positions created for them (I will have more to say about this later on).

Owens begins singing alone, backed by the other Shirelles on the line "Tonight, the light of love is in your eyes," where they vocalize an E major and then E7 chord on an "ah" vowel, joining Owens with words on the urgent question "But will you love me tomorrow?" From this point, the backup voices sing a doo-wop–inspired "sha-la-lap-shap" figure during the verses that corresponds to the snare drum heartbeat. Most girl group songs are best understood as representing a single—if often conflicted—subjectivity, wherein the interplay between lead singer and backing singers performs the struggle between different points of view that accompanies any individual's decision-making. In this song, the Shirelles as a group can represent a single point of view, with the violins providing the counterpoint. Thus, the lead vocal line, the heartbeat drum pattern, and the backing Shirelles taken together all signify trepidation and nervousness.

Were these elements the whole text of the song, the listener would not doubt that the subject/singer would end by spurning her lover's advances. But the violin line's dramatic range, soaring legato phrases, and erratic fluttering figures—especially during the middle eight section—counter this line of thinking and overwhelm it, if only by virtue of the violin's comparative loudness and closeness to the microphone and, by implication, the listener.

The rapturous violin voice, then, makes the outcome of the song indeterminate, and I contend that the ambiguity surrounding the subject/singer's momentous decision is the key to the song's import. The seeming proximity of the strings contrasts with the way Owens' voice sounds submerged, and it skillfully depicts the way passion threatens to overwhelm reason for this girl at this moment; placing the voice further forward in the mix would have produced an entirely different effect. What is more, the distance of the voice and the violins from the listener must be read as a deliberate artistic choice, one that is necessarily bound to the setting of a recording studio and could not be reproduced in a "real," live performance. Taken as a whole, the song creates a sense of an ordinary girl, heart pounding, who uses stock musical language to rehearse the questions she knows she ought to ask of her lover even as she is swept up by desires and feelings she does not yet have the words to articulate.

King and the Shirelles did extremely well with "Will You Love Me Tomorrow?"; their simulation of virginal anxiety rang true with many listeners, and the song established the foundation for all their careers, not to mention the fact that it set the standard for the girl group style. King and her partner Goffin came to be in high demand following this song and were instrumental in creating many of the finest pop songs of the 1960s. When they divorced in the late 60s, King was well known in the field, having received her share of credit for such hits as "Up on the Roof" (the Drifters, 1962), "Natural Woman" (Aretha Franklin, 1967), and "Pleasant Valley Sunday" (the Monkees, 1967), so she was able to move into the Los Angeles music scene with relative ease, collaborating with figures such as James Taylor, producer Lou Adler, and new husband, bassist Charles Larkey, on her 1971 performing breakthrough *Tapestry*. Not every songwriting woman fared as well in the Brill Building system as King, however, as the story of Ellie Greenwich and Jeff Barry demonstrates.

Ellie Greenwich

Born in 1940, Greenwich grew up in Levittown, Long Island, and attended Hofstra University, eventually securing a record deal with RCA through the owner of a record store she frequented.[9] She began dating songwriter Jeff Barry shortly after his success with "Tell Laura I Love Her," a hit for Ray Peterson in 1960, but she managed to capture the interest of veteran songwriters Lieber and Stoller without exploiting her connection to Barry and wrote her first hit, "He's Got the Power" for the Exciters, in collaboration with Tony Powers. The Exciters, a Jamaican quartet comprising a male as well as three female singers, reached only number 57 on the Billboard charts with this song in 1963 but established Greenwich as a serious talent. The two-and-a-quarter-minute song begins with a bang, as lead singer Brenda Reid utters a rowdy "Yeah! Yeah! Yeah!" that establishes a lively 4/4 meter. The lyrics tell a story of straightforward domination by a lover who dictates "his" girl's behavior, but the potential for oppressiveness is undercut both by the light-hearted buoyancy of the groove and by Reid's bluesy rasp, a vocal quality reminiscent of Willie Mae "Big Mama" Thornton. Most of all, the pointed use of solo kazoo during the middle eight, a strategy no doubt copied from Joanie Sommers's "Johnny Get Angry," a number-seven hit earlier that year, establishes a cheeky irony.[10]

After several hits for artists working with Phil Spector, providing background vocals for many artists, and even releasing records under the name "The Raindrops," Greenwich and her partner/husband Jeff Barry formed Red Bird (for pop records) and Blue Cat Records (for rhythm and blues work) in partnership with songwriting legends Jerry Leiber, Mike Stoller, and producer George Goldner (who had produced the Chantels in the late 1950s). Here, Greenwich's biggest successes were with the marvels of melodrama she created with the Shangri-Las. Unlike the demure-looking Shirelles, the Shangri-Las projected an image of sullen street urchins, unsmilingly clad in skin-tight pants and high-heeled boots (I will have more to say about the Shangri-Las' version of girl identity in Chapter 13). Correspondingly, the subject matter of their songs was much darker, even frightening to some, than bouncy dance tunes like "He's Got the Power." A song like 1964's "Leader of the Pack" (analyzed in Chapter 13) means to be listened to, and its dramatic pauses, spoken voiceover, motorcycle sound effects, and frequent changes of tempo discourage dancing and could hardly be achieved outside the recording studio. The song's tragic tale is of a misunderstood teen rebel killed in a road accident after his girlfriend breaks up with him (though only at her parents' insistence), and this maudlin story provoked controversy and an official ban on the song in England.[11] The histrionics of the piece have made it ripe for spoofs and parodies, but the song can nevertheless be taken as an earnest and meaningful exploration of the heightened emotions of teenage girls. Greenwich asserts that she and the Shangri-Las took the piece seriously and found it moving,[12] and it obviously provided an outlet for exploring anguish and torment in a highly satisfying way for many listeners.

By the time they wrote "Leader of the Pack" in 1964, Jeff Barry and Greenwich had married and decided to collaborate professionally only with one another, so she had ended her successful working relationship with Powers. Though Greenwich and Barry created many hits together, this proved the first in a series of grave errors with dire consequences for her career:

> Jeff suggested to Ellie that he should get sole credit as producer because Ellie might be having children soon and leave the business, while Jeff would have to carry on. It was important to keep his name and reputation well remembered in business, and this was the way to accomplish that. "I was a little hurt when he suggested it, because I always felt people should get credit for what they do, but I also felt it was in the best interests of our relationship and family setup—so I went along with it.… Who knew that we'd break up and I'd have to start all over again?"[13]

Barry would go on to produce such hits as "I'm a Believer" (written by Neil Diamond for the Monkees in 1966) and "Sugar Sugar" (which he himself wrote for the Archies in 1969). Greenwich pursued a career as a singer/songwriter with some success; her 1965 recording

"You Don't Know" (cowritten with Barry and Morton) had generated some interest in her as a singer, as had her more successful records as part of the Raindrops. Although her performance career would not achieve the heights of her former colleague Carole King's, Greenwich earned her living providing backing vocals for many artists and writing commercial jingles and eventually produced and starred in her own music theatre production *Leader of the Pack*.[14] Working outside the spotlight she had initially sought as a recording artist, Greenwich at least developed skills that she could take away from her personal and professional partnership, even if she did not get full credit for all of her collaborations with Jeff Barry.

8

Up against the Wall of Sound

While the negotiations and compromises worked out between Greenwich and Barry and King and Goffin took place on an interpersonal sphere that was inaudible to listeners, the blurring of individual contributions to a song in order to present a pleasing homogeneous product is sonically characteristic of the girl group records associated with Phil Spector. Identifying him as the first auteur among record producers, Evan Eisenberg asserts in his landmark study of recorded music that "in its urgent solipsism, its perfectionism, its mad *bricollage* [sic], Spector's work was perhaps the first fully self-conscious phonography in the popular field."[1] Spector's studio techniques involved reducing (for example) four separately recorded instrumental tracks to one track, then adding that to three other tracks that had been similarly mixed down, then mixing the four new tracks down to one, and then layering that with vocal tracks that had been through the same process to build his trademark Wall of Sound.

This process necessarily caused some degree of deterioration in sound quality, an effect he liked because it made all the instrumental tracks blend together in a wash of sonority. He had begun experimenting with overdubbing techniques at the age of eighteen while working on his first music-related effort, "To Know Him Is to Love Him," a number-one hit in 1958 for the Teddy Bears (Spector with high school friends Marshall Lieb and Annette Kleinbard on lead vocals). Throughout his career as a producer, Spector's overriding interest was in recording the sound of the room where the music happened and the feel of the musical energy, rather than attempting to get the cleanest possible lines from individual musicians: "a large sound that hung together in one piece, with no drops or drifts or wasted echoes. A sound that would pour out of a transistor like cake batter."[2] Marshall Lieb describes "the loss of quality in the vocals, background, bass, the big wash of the music…the transparency of the music. The Wall of Sound was a very transparent sound. People who tried to duplicate it did it wrong. They were always *adding* to make more sound. But it wasn't a lot of sound, not a lot of people playing a lot of notes. It was more air than sound."[3] Musicians who played in these sessions were often surprised at the simplicity and repetitiveness of their parts—the grandeur of Spector's sound did not originate in complex and dazzling musical language, but rather in his attention to production techniques and his feel for a groove, a space.

Beginning his career in Los Angeles and moving to the songwriting industry's heart in New York while still a teenager, Spector was disconcerted when confronted with sophisticated, state-of-the-art recording equipment during a brief (and largely unsuccessful) stint as producer at Atlantic Records:

> [T]he culture clash of [Atlantic engineer Tom] Dowd's eight-track machine made him swallow harder. "Phil was in his element with a two- or three-track, at most a four," Dowd said, "where he could allocate one track to all the rhythm, one to the backgrounds, one to the group.…[H]e had better ways available to him, but if it impaired or impeded or made him insecure, technology means nothing. Let him do what he does best and capture the genius of the work. You don't make Phil Spector a victim of technology."[4]

Spector's grandiose aspirations led him to involve many more musicians in a recording session than was customary. Returning to his beloved Goldstar Studios in Los Angeles, he would record an extravagant forty to sixty instrumentalists on the rhythm track alone—in an era when most songs made use of ten to twelve musicians in total—and he also commanded a veritable army of session singers who came in for backing tracks. His novel use of microphones was an equally important component of the Wall of Sound; he would place several of these throughout the recording studio, miking surfaces that might provide unusual sonorities. Finally, his recording engineer Larry Levine applied reverberation and echo effects generously to all tracks, so that the result is a distinctively opaque, shimmering sound in which individual contributions become difficult to discern. One exceptional moment in his recording œuvre serves to highlight the overpowering nature of the Wall of Sound: in the Ronettes' 1965 release "Paradise," a typically lavish and majestic celebration of eternal love, instruments cut away abruptly during the middle eight section, providing a chink in the wall that permits listeners to hear Ronnie Spector's voice nakedly avowing: "I would die for him, I would die for him."

Phil Spector's aesthetic vision is an apt metaphor for his worldview, in which individual will, distinct personality, and any uniqueness of character were subsumed to the overall effect. His need to control made it difficult for him to treat those around him as equals—is it mere happenstance that he preferred to work with naïve, professionally inexperienced, and usually non-white young females who were willing to follow his direction unquestioningly? His few collaborations with male artists such as the Righteous Brothers, the Beatles, and, later, the Ramones were difficult and gave rise to lurid rumors about Spector literally holding guns to heads in order to get the sounds he wanted (although he produced the first solo efforts of both John Lennon and George Harrison after his controversial work on the Beatles' swan song album *Let it Be*). He has often been described as a mad genius, and it is questionable whether this was an apt assessment or whether he tailored his behavior to match what was said about him in the press. Dee Dee Kennibrew of the Crystals comments that "he was a normal enough person, but after he began to be successful, I think he tried to be more of a star than his groups—you know, 'Without me there would be nothing.'" Former Atlantic Records business manager Miriam Abramson, on the other hand, states flatly: "I thought he was insane. I think now, in some sense, you would excuse it as 'star quality.' But at the time he did it he was no star."[5]

Megalomaniac though he may be, I emphasize again that Phil Spector (born in 1940) was a very young megalomaniac at the time of his greatest successes in the late 50s and early 60s. It was not the respect due his age, then, that compelled singers to defer to him. Rather, his talent in directing musicians in the studio, the fact of his meteoric rise to fame, and his (obviously considerable) personal charisma seem to have led all around him to bend to his will. Furthermore, his innovations in recording techniques were truly extraordinary; the Wall of Sound is an instantly recognizable style, heralded by many as the magnificent sunset of monophonic recording and emulated by Brian Wilson of the Beach Boys as well as other notable producers (Bruce Springsteen's 1975 *Born to Run* album, for example, owes a great deal to Phil Spector's aesthetic). By the mid-60s, however, the innovation of stereo recording affected youth music to the point that records were expected to make invisible the means of their production, proffering songs that sounded like concert performances unadulterated with studio effects. Thus, in 1966, Tina Turner's fabulous *River Deep, Mountain High*, which Spector considered his best-produced record, was too polished, melodramatic, and unashamedly synthetic to appeal to audiences listening to the stripped-down, five-piece rock'n'roll band sound of the Rolling Stones or the gentle acoustic style of acts such as Simon and Garfunkel, whose "Sounds of Silence" was the top-selling single in America that year.

The Ronettes

Phil Spector's most famous group was of course the Ronettes, those impossibly bad girls from Spanish Harlem, whose ambiguous ethnicity, towering hairstyles, inch-thick eyeliner, and dangerously high stiletto heels were matched by the sultry voices on their records. As resident go-go dancers at the Peppermint Lounge and dancers and backup singers in radio disc jockey Murray "the K" Kaufman's rock'n'roll revue shows, these girls were minor celebrities in New York's club scene, just looking for a reason to be famous when they signed with Phil Spector in 1963 (the trio's rise to fame is examined in Chapter 12). Twenty-year-old Ronnie Bennett (later Spector), her sister Estelle, and cousin Nedra Talley were enthralled by the eccentric young genius and the attentions he lavished on them, and they were excited by the possibility of working with successful songwriters like Ellie Greenwich and Jeff Barry. Looking back on her experiences recording with Phil Spector, Ronnie Spector writes that

> The wall of sound was really just a reflection of [Phil's] own personality, which was very extravagant. When Phil made a record, he might start out with the same basic tracks as everyone else...but then he'd always

> add in more sounds...he didn't have any use for a record unless it was at least ten times bigger than life. Everyone in the record business lived in fear of making the needle [on the recording monitor] go into the red—but not Phil. Sometimes I think he was only really happy when he was in that red zone.[6]

Piling track upon track and pushing the recording levels to the point of distortion had the effect of blurring individual sounds and creating a shimmering wash of drama, a new and highly distinctive sound for pop records that Phil Spector famously termed "little symphonies for kids."[7]

The Ronettes' first hit record was "Be My Baby," written for them by Phil Spector, Ellie Greenwich, and Jeff Barry in 1963. This song presented listeners with a dramatically different kind of girl from the one who agonized over her boyfriend's advances in "Will You Love Me Tomorrow?" Far from worrying about the dangers of sex, the girl in "Be My Baby" is practically panting for it, and the parents who put the brakes on their daughter's reckless romance with the leader of the pack are nowhere to be found.

The song opens with a striking drum phrase, the "baion" beat that Phil Spector favored on many records, beginning with Ben E. King's "Spanish Harlem" in 1961: , with the first three attacks on bass drum and the last a splash on the snare reinforced by handclaps with a flair that would be lost in the context of a live performance. Establishing E major, the piano sets up an energetic groove with repeated eighth-note chords, maintaining this steady motion throughout the song.

The baion beat, as its name suggests, originates in Latin American music traditions and was absorbed into American pop music in much the same way as the clave pattern known in rock'n'roll terminology as "the Bo Diddley beat." Apart from Phil Spector productions, the baion beat is heard in Roy Orbison's 1963 "Blue Bayou" ("bayou" and "baion" being variants of the same word), innumerable recordings by New Orleans pianist Professor Longhair, and in the guitar line of Otis Redding's posthumous "Sitting on the Dock of the Bay."[8] In "Be My Baby," the beat functions as a distinctive hook to the song and might conjure an uneven heart thumping followed by a gasp or sharply indrawn breath—a depiction of the sensations of heart-stopping love at first sight. The dramatic range in timbre between the bass drum and the snare means that the sounds resonate through the listener's body in different spaces, insisting that this disorienting physical sensation be shared by all who hear the song.

Ronnie Spector's voice enters with the words "The night we met, I knew I/Needed you so," moving to the dominant at the end of the phrase. As on all her subsequent recordings, her voice is characterized by fervent ardor and apparently guileless use of a "come hither-ish" vibrato, the ideal counterbalance to Phil Spector's Wagnerian orchestrations. Her range is contained within an octave (C# to the B above), and her leaps to the top note at the end of each verse grow more impassioned as the orchestration burgeons, threatening—but never managing—to overpower her. Ronnie Spector's fluid movement between throaty growling and clear, sweet timbres is an important element of all Ronettes' recordings and effectively represents the dualities enacted by a sexy girl–woman. Her voice, audibly pushed to extremes, threatens to break whenever she reaches for her high notes, lending credibility to her pleas and making them the more compelling.

The huge swell of backing voices that joins her at the first refrain, "be my baby," and continues with "ooh" vowels during the subsequent verses performs a very different role from that played by the backing vocals in "Leader of the Pack" (examined in Chapter 13). Only the most credulous fan could believe that this massive sound issued entirely from the two backing Ronettes, who actually did not even sing on this or many other of the group's records, as Phil Spector often imported only Ronnie Spector to Los Angeles for recording sessions.[9] In any case, the backing vocalists, whose voices blur together in the hazy Wall of Sound, do not interact with Ronnie Spector in a dialogue. Rather, they mirror her utterances as she begs and pleads with her love object, just as the Shirelles backed Shirley Owens on "Will You Love Me Tomorrow?" by echoing her words and offering no contrasting line of thought.

But "Will You Love Me Tomorrow?" did ultimately create a sense of ambivalence; the violin articulated feelings that countered the lyrics and made the outcome of the singer's decision indeterminate, while the Exciters' "He's Got the Power" undermined the ostensible message of the song in various ways, including using a kazoo during the verse after the middle eight. "Be My Baby," on the other hand, does not even have a middle eight section; the song is single-minded in its intent to persuade the listener to give in and love the singer. Nothing distracts from this goal, and the song's determination makes it irresistible.

The absence of a contrasting middle eight or bridge section is unusual for a pop song from this period, although not unheard of. Other examples include the Toys' "A Lover's Concerto" from 1965, a 4/4 love paean based on the first half of the Minuet in G from Bach's *Notebook for Anna Magdalena*; in this case, it seems that a move to a contrasting section in the relative minor key might undercut the celebratory glee of the song. Lulu's "To Sir with Love," the top American single of 1967, is a two-minute marvel, consisting only of a pair of verses with refrains and ending unexpectedly where the listener expects a harmonic move or other contrasting material (in the film *To Sir with Love*, the song is heard several times, sometimes with a third verse not included in the radio version, but there is never a middle eight). This song depicts a girl's momentous passage from childhood to adulthood, and its brevity corresponds to the ephemerality of that transition; a contrasting middle eight here would diminish the sense of something fleeting, evanescent, and unfinished.

As to why there should be no middle eight in "Be My Baby," the answer can perhaps be found in examining the relationship between Phil and Ronnie Spector at this moment. He commissioned the song for her to sing and coached her extensively as to how to beg for his love, as a way of exploring and expressing his own romantic feelings toward her. Alan Betrock ponders that "In a sharp turn, Phil's lyrics for the Ronettes were specific and in the first person. 'Then He Kissed Me' would have been 'Then You Kissed Me,' and 'He's Sure the Boy I Love' would have become 'You're Sure the Boy I Love' had Spector done them with the Ronettes. With 'Be My Baby' and 'Baby I Love You,' Phil was expressing how he felt for the first time, sending these musical love letters out to Ronnie, and perhaps gaining pleasure by hearing Ronnie sing the words directly to him."[10]

In this professional and personal relationship, then, working with an adolescent female singer made it possible for an adult male to express tenderness and vulnerability without compromising his authority and masculinity. This aspect of male–female collaboration on girl group records is echoed by songwriter Eddie Holland, who cowrote many of the most effective girl group songs from Motown: "As a lyricist I noticed that women were more interesting to write for. Women have a broader sensitivity to emotions than men, I think. We were taught coming up that you don't cry; you take it on the chin. We couldn't say we were hurt if we were hurt; we could only deal with those subjects through writing for women. That's why we liked working with girl groups so much."[11]

The circumstances of Phil and Ronnie Spector's relationship, for all that they gave rise to a stunningly successful song, were largely unknown to the listeners who reacted so enthusiastically to "Be My Baby." What fans responded to was the novel representation of a girl who seemed utterly self-assured in her desirability, acting with a great deal of aggression and using all the weapons in her sexual arsenal to conquer the boy she has chosen. Ronnie Spector's throaty vocal quality; the sinuous, chromatic melody; the deep pounding of the bass drum; the high drama of the orchestration and production effects; and the predictability of the harmonic language combine to create a sense of inexorable will. In this musical articulation of a girl's desire and efforts at enticement, a move to a contrasting harmonic area might not only detract from the focus on her goal but could also raise the possibility of different outcomes to the seduction. Instead of introducing this element of uncertainty, "Be My Baby" insists that Ronnie Spector's feelings be returned. This kind of sexual confidence could naturally be empowering for young girls experimenting with different kinds of adult personae, but at the same time it flouted conventional rules of behavior and threatened a rigid social order. Middle-class, "respectable" girls who "tried on" the attitudes of the Ronettes may not have been instantly transformed into stiletto-heeled sexpots simply by listening to "Be My Baby," but neither could they entirely return to the demure and prim stance of Patti Page or Doris Day. New possibilities had been raised; new ways of being a girl were visible and audible.

Strategies of Resistance

In the wake of a 1980s renewal of interest in 1960s pop records in film soundtracks such as *The Big Chill*, Ronnie Spector, the other former

Ronettes, and session singer Darlene Love launched a suit in 1998 against their former producer for breach of contract, loss of earnings, and ownership of their original recordings in the amount of $10 million.[12] After two years in the courts, the case was resolved in June of 2000 with a considerably lesser settlement of $2.6 million and a denial of the singers' request for ownership of the master recordings. In her ruling, Manhattan Supreme Court Judge Paula Omansky wrote that "Spector's contributions to the Ronettes' success cannot be underestimated, as composer of their songs, and as creator of the sound for which the Ronettes' recording hits became famous."[13] I contrast this with a statement of Darlene Love's, the Ronettes' cocomplainant and a veteran of many of Phil Spector's greatest successes: "The singers were nothing to Phil. He used to say it was all about 'his music.' So I'd say, 'If it's all about your music, why aren't you making instrumentals?'"[14]

Judge Omansky awarded damages to Love and the former Ronettes, though in a dramatically reduced amount, most of which would have been owed in legal fees after the two-year court battle. It is clear that she adheres to the common wisdom that voices are the least important element of pop songs and that the real "creators" of music are those who master mechanical skills and control technological devices in order to "compose" songs. Indeed, Judge Omansky's very invocation of Phil Spector as "composer" instantly reinforces the value system that made a millionaire of him but not of the women who sang for him. Phil Spector himself sought to make his name and work prominent while obscuring the efforts and identities of the girls whose voices made him famous, and hegemonic understandings of singing and dancing as pleasurable activities that come "naturally" to women make it difficult for us to identify singers as artists, much less workers. But a feminist concept of labor, as outlined by Maria Mies in *Patriarchy and Accumulation on a World Scale*, insists that labor is always a burden as well as a source of enjoyment, and Mies opposes the sharp division of labor and leisure that capitalist society has assumed. Mies and other Marxist feminist writers are concerned primarily with combating assumptions that domestic activities such as caring for children are "natural" pastimes that women must perform in order to fulfill their biological destinies, not "work" of the same order as men's remunerated toil. Mies argues that the historical "housewifization" of women's labor has been central to the growth of capitalism, providing industry with two workers for the price of one and dividing the proletariat along gender lines.[15]

This system is succinctly described in the Crystals' 1962 hit "Uptown," written by the husband-and-wife team of Barry Mann and Cynthia Weil and produced (ironically enough) by Phil Spector, in which a female narrator relates the dehumanization her boyfriend experiences at his workplace. His world of work and downtown are represented by C minor, one voice, and a lone acoustic guitar, but when the action of the song moves to uptown, the musical terrain shifts dramatically. Lead singer Barbara Alston sings gently that

He gets up each morning and he goes downtown
Where everyone's his boss, and he's lost in an angry land
He's a little man
But then, he comes uptown each evening to my tenement…

As the forlorn protagonist leaves the emasculating workplace and rejoins his devoted lover, the instrumentation swells to include strings, backing vocals, and a danceable groove performed by drum kit, maracas, and tambourine. Most significantly, the harmony underlying the final phrase moves from A-flat major through an F-minor seventh chord to a transcendent C major on the word "king," as the nurturing narrator/girlfriend soothes the damage done by C minor at the beginning of the song. This piece brilliantly encapsulates the experience of laborers' wives in a capitalist system: the girlfriend's sole function (we learn nothing about her daytime activities) is to restore the worker's manhood in the evening and make him fit to return to his drudgery the following day. What is more, the musical language of the song sympathizes only with the plight of the male worker and celebrates the work of the woman healer, ignoring the terrible trap that both are caught in. The listener understands that the man's condition is miserable but believes it to be happily balanced by the loving relationship Barbara Alston describes, thus identifying with the exploitation of male labor and overlooking the work of women.

A reading of this kind of relationship that focused on the woman as an unpaid worker would sound very different. Nancy Hartsock suggests that "the female experience not only inverts the male, but forms a basis on which to expose abstract masculinity as both partial and fundamentally perverse, as not only occupying only one side of the dualities it has constructed, but reversing the proper valuation of human activity."[16] An understanding of women's invisible and unpaid drudgery in the home as the necessary condition for men's travail in the paid workforce is useful in explicating the records produced by Phil Spector. The logic in this context is that a young female who loves to sing, and who has made little or no financial investment into formal vocal training, is not a professional musician in the same way as an instrumentalist, a composer, or a sound engineer. Most girl group singers fit this description; in general, the sound is characterized by untutored voices, and even after a distinguished 40-year career, a singer like Diana Ross is still subject to derisive remarks such as "she wouldn't know her musical keys from her car keys."[17] Just as the bourgeois woman is typically cast as the emblem of capitalist decadence in much Marxist criticism, a parasite whose life of idle luxury is dependent on the indenture of the male worker, so the singer—in particular the female singer—is often vilified as spoiled, feckless, and opportunistic in taking the glory for mere singing, while the "real" work of musicianship is carried out by others.

Darlene Love's trenchant response to Phil Spector's assertion that his musical arrangements were the most important element of his recordings cuts to the core of this prejudice against singers. As I have shown, most accounts of recording processes and the creation of songs dwell on the accomplishments and perceptions of producers, arrangers, and songwriters; the standpoint of the singer is rarely adopted. When singers do figure in these kinds of discussion, they are invariably spoken *of*, so that we tend to amass stories of how well—or badly—singers fit into the artistic vision of the real musicians. Often these stories sympathize with singers who are exploited and maligned, in the style of the *RESPECT* liner notes, but still the hierarchy of producers at the top and singers at the bottom remains intact. The notion that voices are the most important elements of a pop song sets this logic on its head and opens up an avenue for new kinds of discussion.

The Singer's Standpoint

The feminist standpoint, as theorized in the work of Dorothy Smith, Nancy Hartsock, and others, takes the work of Marx and Engels as its inspiration.[18] Standpoint theory has its origins in the writings of Hegel, who sought to explain the relations between master and slave, examining what could be seen from each position in that kinship. In *Das Kapital*, Marx and Engels applied this theoretical framework to the interdependence of bourgeois and proletariat, explicating the class system from the standpoint of the working class. Feminist standpoint theory argues that men and women negotiate the same structural relationship as master and slave, and bourgeois and proletariat, and that feminist studies of any social situation must start from the position of women's lives and experiences. Standpoint theory presents exciting possibilities for an analysis of production of girl group songs. Why, indeed, could Phil Spector not achieve commercial success with instrumentals? Judge Omansky rules that he created the sound that made the Ronettes famous, but it is equally possible to consider that they—and other singers who recorded with him—produced the sounds that made him famous.

Phil Spector had worked with many singers by the time he met Ronnie Bennett and the Ronettes, and he commanded many fine and versatile vocalists; nevertheless, he recognized her voice as the essential element that could make his musical imaginings real. She recalls that the first time she sang for him he stopped short and exclaimed, "That's it! That's the sound I've been looking for!"[19] It was precisely the untrained, often flawed, but always impassioned characteristics of young female voices vacillating between childhood and womanhood that made the girl-group sound. Little Eva's sweet-sounding voice with its slightly nasal edge is a decisive factor in the quality of "The Locomotion," as numerous inferior cover versions demonstrate.[20] As much as producers such as Phil Spector liked to demonstrate that all voices were replaceable at a moment's notice, releasing Darlene Love recordings as singles by the Crystals, the characteristics of specific voices were integral to the success or failure of records. Fans were entranced by Ronnie Bennett/Spector's indeterminate vowel at the end of the phrase "be my little baby,"[21] they colluded with Brenda

Reid's knowing growl, and experimented with Mary Weiss's tough, working-class accent and dramatic petulance. These voices and no others could perform the work of speaking to and for a generation of girls coming of age.

Carole King, who sang backup on "The Locomotion" and released a girl group–style single "It Might as Well Rain until September" in 1962, could not have sung lead on her composition "Will You Love Me Tomorrow?" to the same effect as Shirley Owens, for all that the idea for the song originated in her own intense experiences. The ideology of album-oriented rock, whereby a song must flow from the pen and the tongue of the same person in order to be "true" and compelling, cannot be applied to girl group songs. Indeed, the songs revel in their artificiality and elude being pinned down to anything so tiresome as earnestness or authenticity.

This is not to say that the songs are insincere. On the contrary, the vocal performances I have discussed are all heartfelt and enthusiastic; if they had not been, it is doubtful that these songs would have achieved the same level of commercial recognition. After all, the success of any song is predicated on the extent to which it rings true with its intended audience. The assessment of scholars such as Susan Douglas suggests that many girls embraced these songs as primers for girlish behavior and experience, so that in a way, they became truths no matter how contrived their origins may have been.

When we are burdened with AOR rock's masculinist ideology of authentic, unfiltered expression of a single individual's feelings through music, it is difficult to see how this could be. But a system of valuing songs that insists on their honesty and an absence of mediation in the circumstances of their creation cannot apply to songs by and for girls, because girl culture and girl identity are always built on foundations laid by others. Accepting the roles and images offered to them and experimenting with prefabricated identities are fundamental strategies for girls' self-fashioning and should not be dismissed as submissive and derivative. Summarizing Laura Mulvey's important writings on women as objects of a male gaze, Valerie Walkerdine understands gaze theory to mean that "[Girls'] fantasies are shaped entirely by the available representations: there are no fantasies that originate with girls, only those projected on to them."[22] Whether or not they consciously recognize it, girls are aware that so-called youth culture is actually boy culture, and that the onus is on girls to find ways of making cultural institutions and artifacts fit them. Terms such as "child," "youth," and "teenager," while nominally gender neutral, are generally assumed to be male, and female experiences of youth must always be distinguished as such with gender-specific pronouns. Entertainments and experiences created for children invariably assume male experience as the norm, so that little girls watching a film such as Disney's *Bambi* must perform a cross-gender identification in order to sympathize with the fawn and his forest friends. From an early age, girls become adept at this kind of flexible identification with role models, while boys are rarely presented with an opportunity to do so.[23] Thus, girls read *Hardy Boys* mysteries as well as *Nancy Drew* and learn to enjoy action movies as well as the "chick flicks" that make their boyfriends squirm. John Berger explores the divided identity that is naturally enacted by females:

> To be born a woman has been to be born, within an allotted and confined space, into the keeping of men. The social presence of women has developed as a result of their ingenuity in living under such tutelage within such a limited space. But this has been at the cost of a woman's self being split into two.[24]

Berger's analysis echoes W.E.B. Du Bois's observations about the experiences of black people in white culture:

> It is a peculiar sensation, this double-consciousness, this sense of always looking at one's self through the eyes of others....One ever feels this twoness—an American, a Negro; two souls, two thoughts, two unreconciled strivings, two warring ideals in one dark body, whose dogged strength alone keeps it from being torn asunder.[25]

Du Bois takes pride in the strength that enables an African American to navigate the cultural experience of twoness, and I would argue similarly that the experience of "being split in two" and learning to identify across gender boundaries may make females more agile at self-invention than men and quicker to adapt to circumstances requiring new kinds of behavior. Perhaps accepting boy culture as youth culture and inventing ways to find themselves in it empowers girls, because it requires them to learn the language and ways of boys as well as their own, making them—in essence—bicultural.

Music is a particularly valuable venue for making these kinds of translations and negotiations, because its ephemeral form does not tie it to a single meaning, but rather it takes on new meanings as it circulates. It is hardly surprising that girls should be willing to accept as their own music that makes no secret of its artificiality, or that young singers like Shirley Owens could throw themselves into songs that did not originate from their own experiences. Dismissing girl groups on the grounds that they are like windup dolls whose material is forced upon them by other, more creative minds ignores the parallels between girl music and girl identity in its largest sense. The important question, then, is not whether girls imbibe experiences fabricated for them, but how they do it, and how they make meanings from doing it. Once we see that girl group music in the 1960s involved a hierarchy of professional musicians, some of whom were male and some of whom were adults, but that the music nevertheless functioned as a valuable medium for real girls to explore and articulate their actual experiences and ideas, we can begin to consider girl music and girl culture as more than a mere and less worthy offshoot of youth culture.

PART IV
Look Here, Girls, and Take This Advice

Toni Morrison's first novel, *The Bluest Eye* (1970), gazes unflinchingly at the experiences of African American girls surrounded by reflections of white middle-class femininity in the 1930s, images that insist on the desirability of blue eyes, blonde curls, pink cheeks, and coy demureness. Pecola Breedlove, the novel's heart-wrenching eleven-year-old protagonist, prays for her eyes to turn blue so that she can transcend her ugly (to her mind) blackness and claim the right to be loved, cherished, and protected like Shirley Temple, who winningly tap dances with Bojangles while black children watch and admire her in the 1935 film *The Little Colonel.* Pecola longs to be like the daughter of the white household her mother works for and clearly prefers to her own family, or to be like Jane who plays innocently with kittens in the *Dick and Jane* book series.

Morrison examines the pernicious effects that images of glossy suburban whiteness have on impoverished and marginalized black communities, and she deplores the terrible cost African Americans can pay when they seek to ascend the social ladder. The character of the neighbor Geraldine imposes standards so rigidly genteel that her home becomes a prison for her as well as for her son and husband, and her determination to blot out unkemptness leads her to despise and mistreat the hapless Pecola. Geraldine is among those black women who learn

> [H]ow to behave. The careful development of thrift, patience, high morals, and good manners. In short, how to get rid of the funkiness. The dreadful funkiness of passion, the funkiness of nature, the funkiness of the wide range of human emotions. Wherever it erupts, the Funk, they wipe it away; where it crusts, they dissolve it; wherever it drips, flowers, or clings, they find it and battle it until it dies. They fight this battle all the way to the grave. The laugh that is a little too loud; the enunciation a little too round, the gesture a little too generous. They hold their behind in for fear of a sway too free; when they wear lipstick, they never cover the entire mouth for fear of lips too thick, and they worry, worry, worry about the edges of their hair.[1]

The racist implications of Geraldine's thinking are emphasized in a passage about her son, Junior:

> Colored people were neat and quiet; niggers were dirty and loud. He belonged to the former group: he wore white shirts and blue trousers; his hair was cut as close to his scalp as possible to avoid any suggestion of wool, the part was etched into his hair by the barber. In winter his mother put Jergens Lotion on his face to keep the skin from becoming ashen. Even though he was light-skinned, it was possible to ash. The line between colored and nigger was not always clear; subtle and telltale signs threatened to erode it, and the watch had to be constant.[2]

Morrison demonstrates that the vigilance required to be respectable is damaging to males as well as females in African American culture. However, the anxieties about sexuality that characterize Geraldine's own passage are absent in the description of her son's concerns—in this boy's efforts to rise above his station, his male sex is a non-issue. To be sure, stereotypes of black masculinity such as devious Zip Coon, the over-dressed ladykiller who was a staple of nineteenth-century minstrel shows; and cold-blooded Stagolee (sometimes known as Staggerlee, Stack-o-lee, or Stack Lee), who killed a man for the crime of touching his hat—to say nothing of the "sixty minute man," whose sexual stamina is celebrated in so many blues and R&B songs—derive much of their power from their predatory sexual menace.[3] Respectability, however, is generally deemed the province of women.

Indeed, it is a notion that has always been peculiarly consequential in female experience; whether women reject behavior deemed appropriate and fly in the face of those values or engage in the unceasing struggle to maintain propriety, it can be argued that respectability and middle-class decency are of central importance to girls and women of all classes and racial groups. The importance of respectability is particularly acute for girls of the black middle class (and for working-class girls of any ethnicity who aspire to upward mobility), for whom the risks of "uncivilized" behavior carry harsher penalties than for their white peers. In her book about vaudeville performers the Whitman Sisters, for example, Nadine George-Graves argues that African American women are especially pressured to be respectable in order to counteract assumptions that they are all morally incontinent.[4] Furthermore, Lyn Mikel Brown argues that idealized femininity in contemporary culture centers around representations of white, middle-class values. She notes that "conventionally ideal girls, perfect girls…look, speak and act in particular ways; they are white and well off, nice and kind, self-effacing, empathic, diligent, serious, generous, and compliant."[5]

My concern in the chapters that follow is to explore the ways in which girls are trained to conform to respectable roles and to speculate about the possibilities available to them in these positions. Girl group music in the 1960s played a pivotal role in girls' self-fashioning, and it provided an arena fraught with conflicting messages and rich with opportunities for negotiation. Thus, I want to consider whether music can be respectable or otherwise and examine how listening to music might shape girls' notions of respectability and morality. I wish also to explore which girl groups were most clearly governed by notions of respectability, and why this might be. Finally, I want to suggest that girl group music, while conventional and conformist on many levels, could be a source of female empowerment and resistance within a rigid social system.

9

Respectability versus Rock'n'Roll

Beverley Skeggs identifies respectability as a powerful signifier of class, one that informs how people speak, carry themselves, and relate to others. She points out that respectability is above all a female burden:

> Respectability embodies moral authority: those who are respectable have it, those who are not do not.…At the core of all articulations of the working class [at the end of the nineteenth century] was the discursive construct of the modern, that is middle-class, family in which the behaviour of women was interpreted in relation to their role as wives and mothers and based on their responsibility, their control of their sexuality, their care, protection and education of children and their capacity for the general surveillance of working-class men. Observation *and* interpretation of the sexual behaviour of working-class women on the basis of their appearance was central to the production of middle-class conceptualizations.[1]

Morality is invariably a female responsibility; among adolescents, girls are always expected to set physical boundaries and defend them vigorously, and those who fail in this important task are penalized. Aggression in boys, on the other hand, is tolerated—even encouraged—as a sign of "normal" and healthy (hetero)sexuality and male social identity more generally. This notion was promoted determinedly in Hollywood films aimed at mass audiences beginning in the 1930s, most of which drew clear distinctions between "good" (white, middle-class) girls and "bad" (non-white, working-class) ones who initiated sex and corrupted young American manhood (often causing the death or at least emasculation of the hero). In films depicting the new notion of adolescence during the 1930s and 40s, "active sexuality was equated with working-class existence and implied the inability to progress socially."[2]

These films taught, then, that upward mobility was dependent on sexual abstinence and the necessity for respectable girls to be chaste. During the early 1960s, when the function and characteristics of adolescence were still largely in flux, some challenges to this strict order began to appear, such as the Shirelles' "Will You Love Me Tomorrow?" discussed in Chapter 7. In 1961, when the Shirelles' hit was at the peak of its popularity, Elia Kazan's film *Splendor in the Grass* suggested that sexual frustration and rigid mores insisting that "nice girls don't" could actually be damaging.

Girl group music, especially music by black groups, played an important role in discourse about sexuality and respectability in adolescent culture, identifying the double standards for girls and boys and undermining racial segregation by presenting a source for girls of different class and race backgrounds to find ideas and information. In this way, girl group songs participated in theorizing along the lines suggested by Barbara Christian: "[P]eople of color have always theorized—but in forms quite different from the Western form of abstract logic…our theorizing…in narrative forms, in the stories we create.… And women, at least the women I grew up around, continuously speculated the nature of life though pithy language that unmasked the power relations of their world."[3]

The Shirelles' 1963 "What Does a Girl Do?" for example, identifies the injustice of rules for girls who wish to appear respectable and demure. The song tells us that boys are able to act on their attractions to girls by behaving assertively, but lead singer Shirley Owens betrays a passionate rasp in her voice as she leaps up an octave to ask what a girl can do in the same situation. The song itemizes the things that a girl cannot do: stand on street corners watching boys go by; ask to walk a boy home; ask for a boy's phone number. Instead, she must wait passively, hoping that he sees her worth and her feeling for him and takes the initiative to begin a relationship. The singer's frustration with this arrangement is clear, because of the dramatic jump to a higher tessitura and the anguished vocal timbre used to describe what girls cannot do, while the parts of the song discussing boys' options uses a more relaxed singing in a lower part of Owens' voice.

Tellingly, the song not only observes and analyzes the double standard of behavior for girls and boys, it also pleads with apparently heartfelt desperation for advice; the soloist seems genuinely not to know how to behave, asking for guidance from her listeners, and she is echoed, rather than answered, by the other Shirelles.

In *The Bluest Eye*, Morrison's character Geraldine is clearly based on a stereotype of black womanhood: namely, the hard and calculating Sapphire, a cold and possibly castrating matriarch who drives men away and is excessively harsh with her children, depriving them of mother-love. Patricia Hill Collins addresses the effects and significances of this and other images of African American femininity that circulate largely unquestioned in U.S. culture and contribute to the demeaning of African Americans that enables racist assumptions. Along with Sapphire, Collins examines the pervasive images of the ever patient, loyal and non-sexual Mammy, obese and stubbornly faithful as a bulldog; the lazy and feckless welfare mother, ever pregnant, whining, and incompetent; and the whorish Jezebel, sexually insatiable and always ready and willing for any act.[4] Collins suggests that these stereotypes of black women contain them in neat categories, allowing white patriarchy to assign other characteristics to white women, and—because they are largely economic stereotypes—serving to license the exploitation of black women. I would argue that the image of the black Jezebel serves as a counter to the white Prude, dour, bespectacled, economically privileged, and frigid, and that both of these caricatures support oppressive assumptions about female sexuality, race, and class (sexual frigidity being arguably the height of respectability, and of whiteness).

Ladylike Behavior and Youthful Rebellion

As Collins, Skeggs, and Morrison all demonstrate, respectability is always bound up with female sexuality and the question of how to contain it. By contrast, music, particularly popular music, and most especially the genres of popular music that emerged during the 1950s and 1960s, is explicitly charged with sexual energy and the question of how to release it. Rock music, for instance, is diametrically opposed to middle-class respectability, and it offers ways of transcending restrictive value systems. Thus, late 1960s British rockers such as Led Zeppelin, the Rolling Stones, Eric Clapton, Cream, and others (most of whom came from suburban middle-class backgrounds) can all be said to have borrowed the signs and codes of women and of African Americans in order to transgress against respectability and bring sexuality and sexual freedom to the forefront. Mick Jagger famously modeled his stagecraft on the performances of Tina Turner,[5] and the Stones had an early hit with a 1964 cover version of African American Irma Thomas's record "Time Is on My Side." Led Zeppelin drew power from the use of musical gestures and actual songs created by African American bluesmen, but the virility of singer Robert Plant can equally be seen to dabble in displays of feminine excess (indeed, rock critic Terri Sutton has playfully imagined Janis Joplin supplanting Plant as lead singer for Led Zeppelin, and rock-guitarist-turned-radio-host Randy Bachman has noted that Plant's vocal range and singing style are almost identical to those of Heart's Ann Wilson).[6] Using the language of oppressed peoples—particularly the blues—imbued these white male rockers with "authenticity" as well as tremendous power and prestige, so much so that their canon, now termed "classic rock," included only one woman and one African American (Janis Joplin and Jimi Hendrix). The signifiers of female sexuality as display and black working-class authenticity had all been appropriated by middle-class white men when they "arrogated the blues unto themselves."[7]

Earlier British Invasion beat bands presented a friendlier, more respectable version of masculinity, but they too were directly influenced by female African American performers, often girl groups. The Beatles, for example, included versions of five girl group songs on their first two albums (on 1963's *Please Please Me*, "Chains" had been recorded by the Cookies, "Baby, It's You" and "Boys" by the Shirelles; and on *With the Beatles* later that year they recorded the Marvelettes' "Please Mr. Postman" and the Donays' "[S]He's Got the Devil in His [Her] Heart"). The Beatles often performed other girl group songs in their stage shows and radio performances, and other male bands had international successes with their versions of girl group songs: Herman's Hermits's 1963 "I'm into Something Good" was originally recorded by Earl-Jean McCrea of the Cookies; Manfred Mann's 1964

"Do Wah Diddy" had been previously released by the Exciters and their "Sha La La" (also 1964) by the Shirelles. The Moody Blues launched their career in 1965 with "Go Now" only months after Bessie Banks' original recording, while the American Beach Boys recorded "Then I Kissed Her" after the Crystals' "Then He Kissed Me"—note that in this case, the Beach Boys reversed not just the gendered pronouns, but also the roles of actor and acted-upon. Indeed, Brian Wilson was so taken by the power of Ronettes' records that he aspired to create one himself; he wrote "Don't Worry, Baby" to be a follow-up for the Ronettes to "Be My Baby," but then recorded the song with his own group when Phil Spector declined to use it.[8] These young male performers were energized by the music of girl groups and female blues singers, and they borrowed the trappings of female sexuality and vulnerability in order to create versions of masculinity centered around transgressive earthiness or adorable approachability.

Girls who participate in youth culture and popular music, by contrast, find themselves in the cross section of two opposing ideologies; on the one hand, they must devise ways of struggling with respectability, and on the other, they belong to a culture that invites experimenting with sexual self-expression. Girls are expected to be pretty enough to attract male attention and societal approval, but they must also be able to suppress their own sexual desires in order to maintain a patriarchal social order. This paradox undergirds many areas of girls' experience, of course; in her thoughtful analysis of beauty pageants, Sarah Banet-Weiser observes that since 1935, the Miss America pageant has constructed itself as "an event that energetically sought the appropriate 'class of girl' to represent the nation through the most suspect and 'inappropriate' means—displaying the feminine body to the public."[9] In general, girls are encouraged to channel their longings into safe, heterosexual aspirations toward marriage—Patricia Juliana Smith has noted that expressions of desire in girl group music are not transgressive when they revolve around "going to the chapel."[10] I would add that even a song like the Dixie Cups' "Chapel of Love" is more closely allied with acceptably girlish fantasies about weddings than with any notion of real, adult marriage, and that this is spelled out by having all members of the trio sing the main melody together (as with all Dixie Cups recordings, but not typical of any other group), with no single voice emerging as an individual articulating her own wants. The effect is of hearing girls talk about fantasies wherein the trappings of the wedding far outshadow the importance of an actual groom.

Girl groups have often been considered somehow apart from important 1960s youth culture, sometimes even as tame music genres vanquished along with Paul Anka and the Singing Nun when the Beatles arrived and brought "good" music back to North America. But on their second North American tour in 1965, the Beatles were eager to meet more of the African American girl group singers whose music they admired and strove to imitate. The Ronettes had already toured with the Beatles and also with the Rolling Stones, and George Harrison had dated Ronette Estelle Bennett. A famous meeting took place between the Supremes and the Fab Four at the Warwick Hotel in New York (the Beatles were still in town after their performance at Shea Stadium, and the Supremes had arrived for an appearance on the Ed Sullivan Show).

The Supremes were excited to meet the Beatles, hoping to learn commercial strategies from the phenomenally successful quartet, whose public image at that time was every bit as clean-cut as that of the Supremes. For their part, the Beatles (whose closest personal connections to American girl groups, it should be remembered, were to the Ronettes) wanted to get closer to the gritty authenticity of soul music and black urban culture—the very experiences from which the Supremes and other upwardly mobile Motown acts sought to distance themselves. The Beatles may also have made assumptions about the easy sexuality of African American women, as Diana Ross biographer Randy Taraborrelli acidly implies: "The boys from Liverpool were amazed that three black women from Motown were so utterly square. Perhaps they expected the three of them to strip to black lace underwear and party into the night."[11] In any case, the "historic" meeting was a profound disappointment to all seven stars; the Supremes arrived, dressed in fur coats with gloves and handbags, found the Beatles stoned and grubby in T-shirts and jeans, asking incoherent questions about the mechanics of the Motown sound, and left after about twenty minutes, to the relief of all concerned.[12] In my view, this encounter neatly encapsulates the opposing but always intertwined values of rock'n'roll and pop, rebelliousness and respectability, white and black aesthetics, boy culture and girl culture.

Of course, it was possible for some girl groups to resist respectability; in the next section, we will consider the strategies and impact of groups such as the Shangri-Las, who perfected a sullen "bad girl" image through melodramatic songs that bragged about dangerous boyfriends and tempestuous teenage rebellion. The Shangri-Las and other white groups such as Reparata and the Delrons followed the first girl groups by a few years, and they cultivated bad reputations in some of the same ways that Robert Plant, Mick Jagger, and Keith Richards rejected the privileges of their middle-class upbringings. For non-white, working-class groups like the Ronettes, on the other hand, the dangers of being perceived as genuinely "bad" made them vulnerable to racist criticism, so that they had to play more carefully with the imagery of bad girls.

Subverting Respectability

In Chapter 8 I discussed the Ronettes' first and biggest hit, "Be My Baby," and I argued that Ronnie Spector's sultry vocals, the lack of a middle eight section in a contrasting harmonic area, and the dramatic enormity of the Wall of Sound combined to make this an irresistible expression of desire. I want here to examine their 1963 recording of "I Saw Mommy Kissing Santa Claus," a song whose lyrics fairly reek of suburban domesticity. It is narrated as though from the point of view of a child, spying for a glimpse of Santa Claus on Christmas Eve, and the effect of the song depends on the listener knowing that Santa is actually Daddy in a red suit. Thus, Mommy's kiss is not a flagrant betrayal of her marriage and a threat to patriarchal order, but rather an entirely proper display of wifely devotion.

But the song becomes more complicated when it is performed by the pouting, stiletto-heeled Ronettes, who suggest a dangerous undercurrent in the picture-perfect nuclear family. With their recording, the Ronettes unravel some of the most cherished assumptions about the respectable suburban world of the song. It begins demurely enough, with a slow, sentimental violin duet establishing A major behind the sounds of footsteps and a noisy kiss. This saccharine sweetness is unceremoniously pushed aside—never to return—after four measures, with Ronnie Spector's entrance on a sultry A below middle C, accompanied by a huge orchestration that includes horns, drums, xylophone, piano, and backing vocals, and that establishes a faster, danceable tempo. The beat is reminiscent of a 1950s dance style: a pattern of eighth notes in 4/4 time, with accents on one and on the upbeats to three and four, where the notes are tied to avoid any attack on the actual beats: . The rhythm recalls the Broadway-influenced overtures of Henry Mancini and similarly creates a sense of glamour, excitement, and showbiz flair that might suggest—in this unexpected context—that conventional domestic roles are comparable to stage and screen performances.

This pattern—played entirely on the snare drum, which typically provides only a backbeat in rock'n'roll styles—undergirds the whole song (with some variation) and persistently works against the steady, even rhythm of the melody. The rhythmic juxtaposition becomes most evident in the middle verse, when a large string section plays the tune without Ronnie Spector's vocals, and the melody issues with exaggeratedly straight, square adherence to the beat. During the sung verses, Ronnie Spector allows a more supple, swung beat that combines with her throaty vibrato to make the childlike lyrics seem knowing and suggestive. Over her held note at the end of the phrase "underneath the mistletoe last night," a piano comes to the forefront with a syncopated figure that winks at the singer (see Example 9.1). When this figure reappears during the instrumental verse, it seems to mock the stiff violins. Astute listeners would recognize this figure as a piano version of the backing vocalists' riff in Little Richard's "The Girl Can't Help It," the title track to the eponymous 1956 Jayne Mansfield film. Here, it calls to mind the titillating comedy of the voluptuous blonde, and it helps to subvert the homely, domestic nature of the Christmas song.

Music Example 9.1 "The Girl Can't Help It" riff.

The piece tries to end by mounting a grand cadence in half time, with a dramatic swell as backing vocalists ascend satisfyingly to the tonic. Then there is an unsettling afterthought as a twinkling, ethereal xylophone plays the beginning phrase of "Rock-a-Bye Baby"—surely the eeriest, most menacing of lullabies—trailing off uncertainly on the leading tone. Clearly, domestic bliss is not all it's cracked up to be, but this recording manages to have some fun by jabbing at the values of prim, respectable married life.

This sly humor runs through *A Christmas Gift for You from Phil Spector*, where the song is heard alongside versions of "White Christmas," "Frosty the Snowman," and "Winter Wonderland" recorded by the Crystals, Darlene Love (credited as such), and Bob B. Soxx and the Blue Jeans. The record refers to the tradition of Christmas specials and albums by such respectable, white stalwarts of 1950s American culture as Perry Como, an allusion borne out, as I have shown, by the use of rhythmic patterns and instrumentation evocative of the 1950s. The cover art features all the singers bursting out of festive Christmas packages, smiling cheerfully and clad in red and green; the Ronettes wear oversized cardigans and sport red bows pinned to the fronts of their lofty beehive hairstyles. This preppy attire seems outlandish on girls known for their fitted satin sheath dresses—the hairbows are particularly amusing, undermining the respectability of these kinds of demure, conservative clothes and the attitudes that go with them. The Ronettes, mixed-race girls from Spanish Harlem who were raised under the not-always-iron rod of their uneducated Native American grandmother during the 1950s and 60s, are keenly aware of the social mores of white middle-class America in mid-century, and—along with Phil Spector and other socially disadvantaged singers who worked with him—they lampoon the values of a social world that disdains them.

The Ronettes' provocative, tongue-in-cheek style may have been empowering to coddled suburban girls who had been trained not to think of themselves as sexual, but it also made the trio vulnerable to vicious diatribes. It became easy for critics to dismiss the singers' musical work altogether and to focus instead on what was perceived as their shamelessly sluttish appearance, comparing them to Jezebels and sniggering at their every move. In a particularly egregious passage,

Richard Farrar writes in 1968 for *Rolling Stone* that: "[The Ronettes were] tough whorish females of the lower class, female Hell's Angels who had about them the aura of brazen sex. The Ronettes were Negro Puerto Rican hooker types with long black hair and skin tight dresses revealing their well-shaped but not quite Tina Turner behinds.... Ronettes records should have been sold under the counter with girly magazines and condoms."[13]

This kind of sniggering account (note that Farrar deems the Ronettes less physically attractive than Tina Turner, thus appointing himself the arbiter of female beauty) surfaces with depressing frequency today in discussions about contemporary female pop stars and screen idols, demonstrating that the line between being deemed pretty and sluttish continues to be fine indeed. The racist overtones of this excerpt are obvious, but it is clear that race was not the only factor in determining whether or not a girl was trashy; the Shirelles, with their middle-class, suburban background, presented a more wholesome and demure version of girlness than the sexually assertive Ronettes. Furthermore, in a recent study of sexual scapegoating in adolescent culture, Emily White discovers that the phenomenon of the "school slut" is a construction almost entirely exclusive to middle-class, white high schools.[14]

The popularity of the Ronettes, though short-lived (they placed songs in the Billboard Top 40 charts only between September 1963 and November 1964), was immense, and it attests to the tremendous appeal of these coolly sexual girls-in-charge. As Charlotte Grieg relates: "If the Shirelles and the Crystals were all about teenage identification with the newly felt emotions of young love, the Ronettes were a much more dangerous proposition: they were about seduction, pure and simple...they were the first true girl pop stars to induce hysteria on a par with Elvis. In the early days of the so-called British Invasion...the Ronettes, far from being knocked out of the running by the boy groups, were a perfect female parallel to them."[15] While they may have stood outside the bounds of respectable society, the Ronettes had considerable cultural clout and exerted an important influence on the self-definition of working-class and middle-class girls alike.

With the important exception of Phil Spector's fantastical and even subversive productions, pop music—specifically, girl group music—aimed at middle-class, suburban, presumed heterosexual and respectable girls, adheres for the most part to conventional harmonic language, affords few opportunities for virtuosic excess, sticks to industry-standard lengths and structures, and almost never purports to offer a transcendental, rebellious experience. In the previous section I discussed the production and creation of the girl group sound in Marxist feminist terms and tried to offer an alternative to typical understandings of music production; I argued that locating power above all with record producers, sound engineers, and instrumentalists inevitably trivializes the work of singers and, by extension, demeans the (largely female) audiences for vocal music. This approach helped me to illuminate the similarities between music production and assembly-line production in mid-century; much like Ford Motors in Detroit (Berry Gordy's model for Motown Records), the music "industry excluded [singers] from controlling the means of production and profited from their labor."[16] This analogy is most apt in considering girl group music and is particularly relevant to an understanding of records associated with Phil Spector; the music he produced has an instantly recognizable sound that results from the subsumption of the voice to grandiose, symphonic imaginings. But other girl group records are also characterized by a distinctive sound, a slick, polished, and clean—even *respectable*—aesthetic, as we shall see in the next chapter.

10

Motown and the Politics of Crossover Success

The Motown sound is, of course, famously clean and straightforward; its creation involved a complex system of methodically checking for clarity on both state-of-the-art hi-fi speakers and cheap, tinny car radio speakers (because these latter speakers were the conduits of pop music for most teenage listeners),[1] and girl group music from Motown is arguably the most polished of all. At Motown, the beat had to be strong and steady, singers' diction impeccable, and melodic hooks prominent and catchy. Motown's resourceful house band and sound engineers made imaginative use of everyday items such as combs and ballpoint pens for percussive effects and often took over the toilets adjoining the studio for records that required echo. Earl Van Dyke, keyboard player and leader of Motown's house band, explains the origins of the backbeat on the Supremes' 1964 hit "Baby Love":

> After it became a hit, somebody wrote about the genius of handclapping on the backbeat. Said it was a new sound, revolutionized pop music. Hell, it wasn't even handclapping. Ain't no way we gonna pay twelve people session fees to clap hands. It was two by fours, man, two by fours hooked together with springs and some guy stompin' on them to make a backbeat. We knocked that song off in two takes.[2]

The relentless emphasis on the backbeat that characterizes the Motown sound has been dismissed as unsubtle and commercial by some, a pandering to white listeners' notorious inability to find a backbeat. Indeed, reaching out to white as well as black youth and making music easy for them to dance to and enjoy was the cornerstone of Berry Gordy's philosophy, and he favored those records that best fulfilled his aspirations toward a Middle of the Road

(MOR) sound. Gerald Early likens Gordy to a latter-day W.E.B. Du Bois for his success in forging an identity that was at once black and American:

> Gordy, with the music he was to create, pinpointed, as did Du Bois, the precise identity neurosis of both blacks and whites: the African-American's fear that he will be bleached into whiteness and the white's fear that he will be Africanized....Gordy managed to negotiate these neuroses by appealing to American youth through music that neither bleached nor blackened, although, of course, from the margins, throughout his career, he was accused simultaneously of doing both.[3]

Berry Gordy's first musical passion was for jazz; before founding Motown, he opened a record store that sold jazz records exclusively and promoted the kind of musical snobbery that many find typical of jazz aficionados from mid-century on. However, he found that out-of-work jazz musicians—his main clientele in the 50s—were not reliable customers, and he was forced to close the 3-D Record Mart in 1955 because of lack of sales.[4] Upon opening Motown Records, he hired many of these unemployed jazzers for his house band, naming them the Funk Brothers. The Funk Brothers prided themselves on their technical skill and musical literacy; the fact that they were able to read complex charts with ease meant that little time was "wasted" in rehearsals, and sound engineers could count on consistently similar takes in recording.[5]

This approach to music-making is often contrasted with the style of Stax Records in Memphis, where a riff-based, quasi-rehearsal style prevailed at recording sessions; Stax players were immersed in an aural tradition of music and developed many of their more exciting sounds and grooves as an ensemble jamming together.[6] Significantly, Stax is not known for girl group records, and female Stax singers tended to be soloists in the earthy, soulful style of Mavis Staples or Carla Thomas, although the Emotions, a trio of female singers who had a number-one Billboard hit with "Best of My Love" in 1977, might be understood as descendants of the girl group tradition.

Containment in Girl Culture

In considering the absence of girl groups at Stax, I venture to suggest that respectability comes again into play; the relaxed, informal world of jam/recording sessions that last until the small hours of the night is generally closed to unmarried girls, whose parents seek to protect their reputations and shield them from danger by containing them safely in domestic space. Girls who are allowed access to a musical education tend to participate in a system of structured lessons and solitary practice (often under the watchful eye of mother, a figure who looms large in girl group music, as we shall see), rather than to learn music-making from spending time with older, established musicians and copying their performance techniques. Singing, a form of expression that does not require any equipment or training, is one of the few musical activities that girls can do together in the kind of casual, improvisatory style of jam sessions, without risk of tarnishing their reputations and—by extension—their value on the marriage market. As I showed in chapter 1, singing together can be an important extension of "girl talk" for young females who are enclosed together in a domestic environment; this can partially explain the high incidence of girl groups made up of sisters. The strictures of containment extend as well to girl listeners, as Iain Chambers has noted: "With other options discouraged or barred, the girl fan was encouraged to organise her commitment [to music] around a romantic attachment to the star. The result: for the majority of girls, the sounds of pop were deeply associated with a largely hidden female 'bedroom culture' of pin-ups and a Dansette record player....It was this domestic space that was permitted rather than the public areas of streets, clubs, coffee bars and amusement arcades."[7]

Adhering to the rules of this hidden world is the safest way for a girl to maintain her respectability, though it does deny her many opportunities to explore her sexuality and experiment with adult personae. Patricia Juliana Smith nevertheless celebrates an emancipatory force in the closed world of girl group songs as "...a demotic adolescent female form of what has come to be known in critical discourse as 'homosociality.'"[8]

Of course, the realm of record players and private bedrooms that can be adorned with pictures of stars is primarily a middle-class, suburban construction, and one that really only comes into being in the mid-twentieth century. Storming up to one's room, slamming the door, and flinging oneself on the bed to burst into tears are self-indulgent activities considered typical of female teenage petulance, but they actually are only available to those girls whose parents can afford the luxury of—and see the value in—privacy for their children. These aspects of white, North American suburban life are presented as universal norms in songs like Lesley Gore's masterpieces of pouting "It's My Party" and its sequel, "Judy's Turn to Cry" (both 1963). In these songs, Lesley is confined to her house, sulking because "her" Johnny has disappeared with the morally suspect Judy on the occasion of Lesley's birthday party (though Lesley's virtue triumphs in the end when Johnny returns, leaving Judy to weep bitter tears of remorse for her cheap behavior).

A more radical, proto-feminist end to this saga might have been a third song with a title like "Get Lost, Johnny," in which Lesley and Judy join forces to tell off the two-timing cad. However, the two songs actually recorded make it clear that Lesley is a "good girl", more invested in the primacy of "the Guy" than in forging sisterly bonds to resist mistreatment at male hands. To be sure, Gore did record the anthemic "You Don't Own Me" in the same year, a song that pitted a defiant girl against an oppressive and controlling boyfriend. However, the piece stops short of depicting females working together to reject their roles as playthings, and the dramatic use of echo in the recording makes it clear that a girl insisting on independence is very much alone.

Gore's public persona involved careful photos of her playing with puppies, gossiping breathlessly about boys, and singing with her high school choir—images that were certainly frustrating to her as she questioned her sexual identity and orientation. Recalling the beginnings of her career, producer Quincy Jones reports that he had bragged about how easy it would be to produce a pop hit, only to be asked to prove it at Mercury Records (where he was vice president). Jones recalls "plowing through piles of demo tapes, listening to bad singers do awful songs" until his attention was drawn to "a sixteen-year-old kid from Long Island…[who had] a mellow distinctive voice and sang in tune, which a lot of grown-up rock'n'roll singers couldn't do."[9] Jones signed Gore to a contract and chose "It's My Party" to be her debut single; they recorded, pressed, and released the record quickly in order to compete with a another version of the song by the Crystals. Jones then pondered devising a stage name for Gore but had no time to attend to this before the record reached the number one position on the Billboard charts three weeks later.[10] Mercury's publicists devised a story about Jones "discovering" Lesley Gore singing along to records at a party (what Jones was supposed to be doing at a teenager's party in the New Jersey suburbs was never explained), and this story was widely accepted. Gore's own account of the beginning of her career corresponds to Jones's: she asserts that she was working with a New York vocal coach who encouraged her to make a demo and send it to Mercury.[11]

Lesley Gore with Ed Sullivan at her 18th birthday party, 1964. Courtesy of Photofest.

As frustrating as her public persona may have been, Gore's masquerade of heterosexuality and middle-class angst was completely successful and earned her a three-year career in pop music and film. (Indeed, Lucy O'Brien notes that "she was one of the few women of the girl-group era to be marketed as a magazine personality and role model.")[12] Girl groups like the Ronettes, on the other hand, could scarcely have contemplated whitewashing their "bad girl," mixed race, working-class image, and they stood in marked contrast to other non-white groups like the Shirelles, the Marvelettes and, above all, the Supremes, whose genteelness and uprightness was legendary. The Supremes are often held up as exemplary products of the Motown Artist Development system, a rigorous training that included deportment and dance classes by Cholly Atkins, coaching in singing and stage patter by Maurice King, and a finishing school (called a charm school by some of its students) run by the ultra-respectable Maxine Powell. Motown identified respectability as a tactic, a tool with which youth from penurious inner-city backgrounds (and—sometimes less than a generation back—rural Southern poverty) could scale the social and professional ladder and earn success according to the standards of middle-class, suburban whiteness. Thus, respectability was an integral part of the Motown philosophy, and artists who could not achieve it were not wanted on the voyage, as Florence Ballard's painful story demonstrates.

Ballard was officially expelled from the Supremes (and replaced by former Bluebelle Cindy Birdsong) in 1967 for missing a concert date at the Hollywood Bowl and a subsequent run at the Flamingo Hotel in Las Vegas, but it is clear from all accounts that her troubles with Motown had earlier origins.[13] Physically, Ballard did not conform to the image of upwardly mobile blackness that Berry Gordy preferred; she was a voluptuous woman who struggled to control her weight and could not achieve the chic slimness of Diana Ross or Martha Reeves. Possessed of a sharp tongue and a fine sense of comic timing, she famously responded—during Supremes' stage patter—to Ross's rehearsed "thin is in" line with a sassy, ad-libbed "thin may be in, but honey, fat is where it's at!" that delighted audiences.[14] Crucially, Ballard did not smile as easily or winningly as her fellow Supremes, projecting instead a sulky and—to many fans—sexy toughness, a brooding quality probably due to her troubled childhood and the violent rape she had endured in her teens.[15] Furthermore, Ballard had little patience for the ceaseless work and suburban aspirations expected of a socially ascendant Motown star. She refused to adopt the attitude of an unattainable icon that Gordy required of all the Supremes and instead continued to frequent the same bars and clubs that her peers did, to drink to excess publicly, and to be available to fans.[16] But I believe that it was Ballard's soulful, bluesy voice above all that doomed her from the start.

Ballard, like Ross and Mary Wilson, grew up in Detroit's Brewster projects, the eighth of thirteen children, with an itinerant father who taught her to sing while he played the blues.[17] Her parents were from the South, and her father evidently set great store by the myths associated with 1930s Blues Kings such as Robert Johnson and Blind Willie Johnson—he often lived as a hobo, sleeping in graveyards and traveling with nothing but a guitar.[18] When Florence Ballard, Diane Ross (as she was then known), and Mary Wilson began singing together as high school girls in 1959 (originally with a fourth singer, first Betty McGlown and then Barbara Martin, both of whom abandoned show business ambitions early on in favor of more promising, conventional paths to security through marriage), Ballard's full vocal timbre, growls, and shouts were fashionable, reminiscent of then-popular R&B women such as Ruth Brown and Etta James.

This, however, was not the sound Berry Gordy sought for Hitsville, USA; nor, indeed, was it the sound that record-buying teens in the early 60s fancied. Many Motown staffers preferred Ballard's singing to Ross' nasal, thin voice, but tellingly, most of Ballard's fans were members of a generation who perhaps enjoyed her old-fashioned, womanly sound. Born ten years earlier, Florence Ballard might have been a blues shouter in the style of LaVern Baker or Willie Mae "Big Mama" Thornton; in the early 60s, her R&B grit was no match for Ross's sleekness and precision.[19] Indeed, to upwardly mobile black urban youth in the industrialized north, her voice may well have sounded like an unfortunate relic of their parents' rural southern poverty, perhaps recalling the dated, boring, and "country" style of the blues that they eschewed in their efforts to forge a distinct generational identity.

Especially since the success of the Broadway musical *Dreamgirls*, it has become customary to lament Ballard as the truly gifted singer in the Supremes, unjustly ousted from the position of lead singer for purely political reasons when Berry Gordy, god-like, preferred Jacob to Esau and groomed the conniving and untalented Diana Ross for stardom. Ballard had sung lead on the group's first single, a novelty song called "Buttered Popcorn," which never entered the charts. Ross's voice has been described by one writer as "mosquito thin,"[20] and it is well known that Gordy coached her extensively and gave her tapes of other singers to study and emulate. To be sure, measured against the yardstick of rock authenticity and soulfulness, Ballard might indeed emerge the better singer when compared to Ross, but—as I have been arguing throughout this work—the ideology of rock always functions to demean girl group music and the fans who embrace it. Gerald Early recognizes this in a backhanded compliment to Ross: "Among Motown singers, only Diana Ross had a truly 'pop' voice, that is, an absolutely depthless, completely synthetic voice."[21]

In addition to her vocal quality and skills as a musician, Diana Ross's family background and personal ambitions helped to make her the focal point of Berry Gordy's Motown aspirations. Like her sister Supremes and many other Motown artists, she grew up in Detroit's Brewster projects, the second of six children born to hard-working and educated parents. Her parents fought for a place in the Brewster project because "the front yards had nice lawns, the housing was decent and there were courtyards. The apartment that we had had three bedrooms, a full basement, a living room, kitchen and dinette."[22] The values of determination and hard work were evidently instilled in all the Ross children; eldest daughter Barbara became a doctor and lieutenant commander in the U.S. Naval Reserve, no small achievement for an African American woman in any decade.[23] The young Diane Ross worked hard at her singing and musicianship, but equally hard at her image and wardrobe, selecting and even making clothes for the Supremes long before they encountered Motown's Artist Development Department—it is hardly surprising that Berry Gordy recognized her as the potential protégée who would flourish under his careful direction.

Motown's Artist Development

Though the Supremes in general and Ross in particular proved to be star pupils of Maxine Powell's classes, it is important to acknowledge that all Motown acts in the mid-60s submitted to her ministrations. Even Marvin Gaye—an artist who came to be regarded as an icon of authenticity and righteous political indignation as a result of his largely self-penned 1971 concept album *What's Going On*—studied with Powell and refined his act, learning from her such niceties as how to walk while on stage and to keep his eyes open while singing. Motown founder Berry Gordy (whose favorite singers, after all, were Doris Day and Barbra Streisand) did not himself aspire toward the blistering social commentary and rawness of Marvin Gaye's "What's Going On" or Stevie Wonder's "Livin' for the City," but rather took his greatest pride in bringing about performances by Gaye, the Temptations, and the Supremes in Las Vegas revues and elegant white supper clubs such as New York's Copacabana.

Because respectability falls so squarely into the domain of female concerns, however, Maxine Powell's work with male acts is minimized, and most accounts of Motown's glory days recall the finishing school as something that Gordy devised for his female artists. This understanding is supported by the fact that books and television documentaries commemorating Motown tend to interview only women on the subject. Of course, the fact that Marvin Gaye and four fifths of the original Temptations were already dead before documentaries like PBS's *Rock and Roll* were made also contributes to this gender bias in remembering Motown, but those artists who have survived invariably try to depict the finishing school as something Gordy established "for the girls." To my mind, this reflects a hegemonic willingness to accept the idea that femininity is a construction while refusing to acknowledge that masculinity is similarly artificial.

Martha Reeves recalls her lessons with Powell: "I look at how I presented myself, and the girls who didn't have Mrs. Powell, it shows. They don't know how to stand, they don't know how to walk, they don't know how to present themselves, they're not ladylike.…Berry [Gordy] did not just sit back and say: 'Oh, those girls are okay, but they're a bit raunchy, or they're a little wild.' He remedied the problem…[Mrs. Powell] had to teach us how to walk, how to dance.…I'll always be indebted to her."[24] Similarly, Mary Wilson of the Supremes fondly remembers that Powell "taught us how to be elegant, and that's what we wanted. We weren't being taught something that we didn't want;

we aspired to be the best. She used to say: 'Now, ladies…' Golly! [laughs] We used to hate her then."[25]

Clearly, both Reeves and Wilson consider that Powell's strict impositions on their bodies taught them elegance, ladylikeness, grace—crucial components of respectability—and that the advantages these lessons conferred were well worth the cost of their "authentic" ways of being. Powell herself, no doubt aware of the contradictions inherent in a finishing school for rock'n'roll acts, states in all seriousness that "Everything had to be done in a classy way. So if they were doing the shake or whatever, well, we didn't do it in a vulgar way."[26]

All of these remarks, identifying raunchiness and wildness as problems to be tamed and remedied, evoke Toni Morrison's fictional Geraldine, and they stand in marked contrast to the values of rock'n'roll as they are typically constructed. But in fact, the sounds and looks of girl groups were at the center of rock'n'roll, youth culture, and political life in the early and mid-1960s. Before achieving any international success, the beat bands of the embryonic British Invasion admired and imitated the style and songs of Motown and other girl groups. Further demonstrating the cultural importance of girl groups, Susan Douglas states that "Diana Ross is the first black woman I remember desperately wanting to look like";[27] Martha and the Vandellas' "Dancing in the Street" was identified as a summons to the infamous Detroit riots of 1967; and Oprah Winfrey has cited the surge of elation when the Supremes sang on television—the first black people to appear in such a mainstream forum in her neighborhood's collective memory.[28] I have already noted the tremendous popularity of the Ronettes in 1964, the first year of the British Invasion; what is more, the Supremes were the only North American act to offer any serious chart competition to the Beatles during these years, with eight number-one hits between 1964 and 1966, as compared to twelve number ones for the Liverpudlian band.[29] Although some contemporary nostalgia for the 60s may dismiss Ross and the Supremes as trivial when compared to white male artists like the Beatles or Bob Dylan, it is obvious that they were of great importance and that their ambitions mirrored the aspirations of their audience.

11

MOTHERS AND DAUGHTERS

What was it in girl group music that has led second-generation feminists like Susan Douglas to identify it as a crucial precursor to the Women's Liberation movement of the 1970s? Given the overwhelming preoccupation with respectability and conservative patriarchal values that I have identified as central themes in this music, locating proto-feminist strategies and messages might seem a hopeless task. When the subversiveness of the Ronettes' "I Saw Mommy Kissing Santa Claus" (discussed in Chapter 9) can be attributed largely to its titillating undertones, the recording might not qualify as a shining example of feminist activism. To be sure, the very configuration of a girl group can be interpreted as an example of female collectivity and solidarity, but when the music is so obviously governed by concerns about being a "good" girl, then how effectively could it encourage listeners to rail against the strictures of containment and domesticity?

Here I return to the writing of Barbara Christian and her project of locating theorizing within the stories that circulate among African American women—namely, the Old Wives' Tales that Tania Modleski has identified as important both to women's networks of shared wisdom and knowledge—and also to efforts to discredit and delegitimate female experience by explaining it away. Modleski endorses Christian's notion of women's "pithy language [unmasking] the power relations of their world" but she also decries Virginia Thomas's tales (in which she insisted that Anita Hill was in love with her husband, Supreme Court Justice Clarence Thomas) as a strategy of denial that preserves the patriarchal status quo and undermines feminist solidarity.[1] Like old wives' tales, girl-group songs are best understood as at once conservative and radical, creating a forum for discourse about girls' issues and experiences and imparting valuable insights without violently disrupting society's preferred understanding of girls as demure. Nowhere is this careful balance more evident than in the tradition of advice songs.

Advice Songs

Advice songs constitute a particular style within the girl group repertoire, and they can profitably be compared to the body of English folk songs that begin with a phrase such as "Come all you fair maidens" and proceed to dispense warnings through a cautionary tale (or—more rarely—to invite listeners to celebrate a happy occasion such as a marriage). Like these folk songs, girl group advice songs explicitly address themselves to female listeners and offer counsel and wisdom based on personal experiences; some advice songs begin with a spoken call such as "Look here, girls, take this advice" or "Girls, I've got something to say." The presence of backing female voices, as in all girl group songs, lends authority to the lead singer's statements and creates a sense of female solidarity as girls share their knowledge and suggest strategies for negotiating the world around them. Invariably, the advice centers around boys and how to behave with them, encouraging girls to be patient (as in the Shirelles' 1961 "Mama Said"), assertive (in the Exciters' 1962 "Tell Him"), or wary (the Chiffons' 1966 "Sweet Talkin' Guy"). Here again, the overarching—and often unacknowledged—concern is with preserving one's respectability and reputation as a "good" girl.

So when the Velvelettes warn listeners that "You better look before you leap!" there is little doubt as to what kind of leap they are talking about. The quintet's 1964 hit "Needle in a Haystack" features frequent and direct calls to the girls who are listening, advises that "Finding a good man, girls, is like finding a needle in a haystack," and urges young females to keep their heads and not fall for the pretty lies a man is likely to spin. With every statement of the refrain, the four backing vocalists sing the title line in unison; lead singer Carolyn Gill is not satisfied, and commands them (along with, implicitly, other girls listening) to repeat the phrase, thus ensuring that her lesson has been received.

The Velvelettes were a quintet of students at Western Michigan University (with the exception of lead singer Gill, who happened to be visiting her older sister at college the weekend that Mildred Gill and Bertha Barbee put the group together), and they felt set apart from other young female singers at Motown because of their educated, middle-class backgrounds and the stern expectations of their parents (the Gill sisters were preacher's daughters). Bertha Barbee recalls that "None of the groups there [at Motown] were in college. That was kind of different…I don't want to say we were refined, but—we learned a lot…not so much the streets, but the gutbucket—how do you say it in a nice way?—well, we learned a lot about life."[2] Ultimately, the Velvelettes' concern with "saying things in a nice way" and pursuing suburban respectability through education and good marriages led them to reject the unstable lifestyles of touring musicians. The group gradually fell apart in the late 1960s, but all members remained in upstate Michigan and reunited for some performances in the mid—80s, by which time their children were all grown.

Although Carolyn Gill was a high school girl when she recorded "Needle in a Haystack," her voice is deep and womanly, and it suits the "big sisterly" character of the song. Supporting her well-meaning bossiness, the other Velvelettes provide a unison refrain of "doo de lang, doo lang" that is typical of many girl group songs. As noted in my discussion in Part 1, these kinds of vocables can be understood as a girl language, with which backup singers express empathy for the soloist's situation. Here, the backing voices sing in harmony on the words "Those fellas are sly, slick, and shy/Don't let 'em catch you looking starry-eyed/They'll tell you that their love is true/Then they'll walk right over you." The breaking into different vocal parts at this moment reinforces a notion of plurality and collectivity implicit in the song's message. I consider the song's import unmistakably feminist; it repeatedly addresses girls as a distinct group who must rely on one another's support and wisdom, and warns them in no uncertain terms not to trust the slippery deceptions of crafty Lotharios. Furthermore, Carolyn Gill's scolding tone in and of itself reminds girl listeners to behave sensibly and guard their respectability.

"Needle in a Haystack" features Motown's distinctive steady, even beat, providing an energetic, no-nonsense pulse, but it is unusual among Motown recordings in that it is based on a blues form. Earlier in this section, I suggested that African American teens in the early

60s tended to shun the blues as an old-fashioned form belonging to their parents' generation. In "Needle in a Haystack," the reference to the music of elders may be a deliberate effort to lend authority to the song's message, an invocation of the bossy voices of 50s singers such as Ruth Brown and "Big Mama" Thornton, and an indirect reference to mother's golden rules.

The frequent and often explicit invocation of a mother, and to the authority of her words of wisdom, is a distinctive feature of advice songs. Songs as different as the Shirelles' "Mama Said" (1961) and the Supremes' "You Can't Hurry Love" (1966) quote "mama" as part of their message to other girl listeners. I consider this strategy an important effort at respectability; drawing attention to the existence of a mother figure who gives her daughters counsel is a subtle declaration that one comes from a solid family background with parents sufficiently invested in one's good reputation to set rules and dispense advice.

A mother or other female elder is almost always assumed to be a fierce protector of a girl's virtue and a guarantor of her good character, and the presence of an older female chaperone can sometimes allow a "nice" girl to venture safely into territory that would otherwise be dangerous. For example, in a scene in the classic 1939 film *Gone with the Wind*, the heroine Scarlett O'Hara pays a visit to Rhett Butler in prison; here, the prison guards set her apart from the strumpets and whores who are Butler's usual female visitors by virtue of the fact that Scarlett has her mammy with her. Similarly, when demure young girls enter into the sordid world of music and performance—participating in activities that have always been considered to diminish respectability—metaphorically bringing mother with them may help to preserve their good reputations and also to make them acceptable to the parents of their fans.

The presence of mother in song is a trait peculiar to the girl group style. Smokey and the Miracles' 1960 "Shop Around"—in which the male protagonist cites his mother's advice to try many girls before saddling himself with a marriage—is exceptional among men's songs and might even be understood as an effort to attract female listeners by tapping into the advice song style. Indeed, the positive invocation of a mother is unusual in most music traditions; for example, Jennifer Barnes has asked why mothers are so conspicuously absent among the stock characters of opera. She concludes that male composers, who often like to compare the intellectual creativity of writing a large-scale work with gestating, birthing, and raising a child, are reluctant to deal with real motherhood in their plots, especially when female characters so often die for the sake of narrative closure. Barnes wonders about the effects of this habitual rupturing of intergenerational female bonds in opera plots:

> [W]hen the curtain rises on so many operas, it is the young women, still living at home, but without their mother, who generate the story. These girls may grow into motherhood, but in opera it would seem a dangerous occupation. Moreover, who will be their role models?...Without their antecedents...opera heroines are free and yet at the same time lost—the world stretches out to meet them, and as they are pushed forward we say, "Go forth, but I'm afraid there is no map."[3]

Making bolder claims in her book *The Mother/Daughter Plot: Narrative, Psychoanalysis, Feminism*, Marianne Hirsch argues that mothers are absent or marginalized strictly in most of the canonical narratives of the Western literary tradition:

> [I]n conventional...plots of the European and American tradition the fantasy that controls the female family romance is the desire for the heroine's singularity based on a disidentification from the fate of other women, especially mothers....Mothers—the ones who are not singular, who did succumb to convention inasmuch as they are mothers—thereby become the targets of disidentification and the primary negative models for the daughter.[4]

Finally, in her examination of the material conditions of middle-class femininity in American culture, Joan Jacobs Brumberg has identified the effects of niche marketing in the twentieth century on the processes by which girls learn to deal with the onset of menarche, and she connects these changes to shifts in mother/daughter relationships. With the invention of disposable sanitary napkins that could be bought at the drugstore, for example, girls no longer had to rely on their mothers for their primary information and insight about their bodies, so that menstruation increasingly became "a matter of consumer decision-making, and...coming-of-age was a process to be worked out in the marketplace rather than at home."[5] Brumberg deplores the deterioration of intergenerational feminine collectivity that went hand in hand with this development and the resultant loss of a larger shared culture of women and girls, replaced with generation-specific experiences and senses of identity.

In her analysis of female adolescence in the 1950s, Wini Breines confirms the strong disidentification that teenage girls felt toward their mothers in the context of white, middle-class suburbia (and in families with aspirations toward this realm). She notes, however, that

> We find an interesting contrast when we compare these white, middle-class daughters to black women of the same generation. While the white women often had negative perceptions of their mothers' lives and rejected them as models, the black women were much more likely to celebrate their mothers and claim a link with them. In fact, some of the white mothers' traits were not dissimilar to common descriptions of self-sacrificing black mothers, represented as strong, forbearing, capable, practical....Black mothers were often the pillars of their families, and their strictness, repressiveness even, could be seen as strengths because of the burdens of racism and poverty.[6]

With advice songs, we encounter the phenomenon of black teenage girls acknowledging the wisdom of mother in songs that were embraced by black and white teenagers alike. As we shall see in the next section, when mother appears in songs performed by white girl groups, she is usually the source of guilt and self-recrimination for a girl narrator who has rejected her rules.

Advice songs, then, must be understood as resistant to cultural forces that urge the separation of mothers and daughters. These songs were one way in which girls at mid-century could—at least partially—respect the wisdom of their mothers and keep their words in circulation among members of their own age group. Although girl group music was certainly an important feature of a new sense of unique generation identity in the early and mid-60s, advice songs attempted to sustain connections to mothers as well as to sisters of all ages. Thus, calling on mother in a song was at once a way of sustaining respectability (by demonstrating that the singer was a good girl who minded her parents), of allying with antecedents, of interpolating a female listenership, and of promoting a sense of solidarity and homosociality among women and girls.

Note, however, that the mother rarely actually speaks or sings for herself in any of these songs. In a vocal ensemble, it would be easy and perhaps logical to have one singer stand in for "mama" and dispense advice directly to the lead vocalist and—by extension—to other listeners.[7] This happens in only one girl group song that I know of, 1961's "Better Tell Him No," a modest success for Chicago's Starlets. In this gospel-influenced recording, a sweet-voiced soloist asks her mama what to say to a boy who tells her he loves her and wants to hold her tight. Another soloist, the gritty, womanly sounding Maxine Edwards, takes the part of mother and dispenses unequivocal, no-nonsense advice with phrases like "Tell him keep his hands off the merchandise!" The Starlets, factory workers in their late teens, achieved only the number 38 position on the pop charts with this song, and they never had another chart entry in their name.[8]

With this exception, the mother's pearls of wisdom in an advice song are invariably mediated through the lead singer, who prefaces them with a statement like "My mother once told me" or simply "Mama said." It may be that for members of a new, urban generation of black youth in the industrial North of the United States, parental authority was best considered at second hand. Mother's rural Southern accent, unfashionable clothes, and work-worn body might detract from the import of her message to teenage girls concerned with presenting themselves as sophisticated and upwardly mobile. The blight that un unkempt and vulgar mother can cause for her daughter's social advancement is made heart-breakingly explicit in the classic 1937 film *Stella Dallas*, in which the title character (played by Barbara Stanwyck) takes the extraordinary step of removing herself entirely from her beloved daughter's life in order that the girl might have no hindrance in gaining access to her father's upper-class milieu. The tension between valuing mother's love and deploring her embarrassing ways (arguably familiar to all daughters) is also the crux of the Supremes' devastating 1969 "I'm Livin' in Shame" (to which I shall return).

Mothers and Daughters

The Marvelettes' "Too Many Fish in the Sea," a Top-40 hit for two months in 1964, is one of many songs in which colead singer Gladys Horton[9] shares mother's advice with listeners. In a cruel irony, Horton had been given up by her own mother as an infant. She recalls: "I can remember once when I was a very little girl, my parents came and took me home for a weekend. But I never knew them at all really. I was on the move all the time, from foster home to foster home; that's the way my life has been.…I never had a mother or father telling me what to do."[10]

In spite of Horton's independent, nomadic life and lack of experience being a daughter, she refers to home and to mother's authority in an extraordinary number of songs, including "Twistin' Postman" (1961), "Playboy" (1962), "Little Girl Blue" (1963), and "He's a Good Guy (Yes He Is)" (1964). In 1963's "My Daddy Knows Best," Horton primly instructs her boyfriend to get a job because her father has advised her that "romance without finance can be a nuisance"; however, this unsubtle plug for doing things father's way (whose authorship is credited entirely to patriarch Berry Gordy) met with little response from fans and reached only number 67 on the pop charts.

"Too Many Fish in the Sea," on the other hand, was and has continued to be an important and popular song in the girl group canon. Like the Velvelettes' cynical "Needle in a Haystack," the song revolves around a folk proverb, but it differs importantly in that its message is positive and affirmative, instructing girls not to waste time or energy on less-than-ideal boys because there are plenty more to be had. In the end, it can even be understood as a celebration of female independence from men, as I will show.

The song begins with a syncopated descending figure in the brass, a fanfare announcing a stirring spoken declaration from Horton: "Look here, girls, take this advice" over a spare accompaniment of congas and actual or simulated finger snaps. Motown house band musician James Jamerson's bass is minimal, consisting here and throughout the song only of sustained notes on downbeats that are approached each time with a sliding appoggiatura from the lower pitch. Signaling the start of the song proper, Horton sings: "Into each heart some tears must fall/Though you've loved and lost, you must stand tall," backed by a full accompaniment of brass, piano, snare drum, and tambourine. Wordless female voices, heard faintly in the background, come forward confidently to sing the song's title line during refrains. Adhering to the Motown philosophy of a foregrounded and hard-to-miss beat, the snare provides a rock-steady, hip-swinging backbeat on beats two and four, while the tambourine allows for faster, more frenetic movement at the level of sixteenth notes.

A short piano riff emerges at the end of sung phrases, bouncing between the home key of C major and the subdominant F major, lending a quasi-gospel flavor to the song, thus bolstering both its affirmative mood and—perhaps—its connection to a music tradition associated with parents. In the second verse, Horton invokes parental authority directly, sharing her mother's maxim (of which "every word is true") that it is a waste of time to love someone who does not love in return, and she commands listeners: "Do without him!" At this point, her fellow Marvelettes appear as distinct individuals, listing in turn the many kinds of men out there for the choosing; the conversation among solo voices furthers the sense of collectivity and camaraderie of females offering encouragement and sensible advice to a girl listener. Indeed, a listener can be forgiven for ignoring the boy-winning strategies that are ostensibly central to the song's message and coming away from it instead feeling that female solidarity and individual fortitude are what is most important.

With the exception of these brief solos, backing vocalists for the most part sing the song's title line in answer to the lead singer's utterances, much in the style of a gospel song's call and response (a style examined in Chapter 1). Toward the end of the song, the repeated phrase "too many fish in the sea" seems to impel Horton to improvise statements of increasing independence and autonomy:

I don't want nobody that don't want me
There's too many fish in the sea!
Ain't gonna love no one that don't love me, now
There's too many fish in the sea!
I don't need nobody that don't need me
There's too many fish in the sea!

Ain't gonna want nobody that don't want me, now
There's too many fish in the sea!

Horton's sassy declarations of independence, which are based in her mother's teachings and earn the approval of the other Marvelettes, are in marked contrast to the abject piteousness of the group's 1963 "Little Girl Blue." In this song, mother is absent, though nevertheless the idea of home and safety in domesticity prevails. Atypically, it begins with backing vocalists, calling on their sad friend to give up waiting forlornly for an errant boyfriend to return and to come out instead with them. The friends are not above reminding Little Girl Blue that they had warned her the romance would end in betrayal and heartbreak, and they gently but firmly disabuse her of her hopes, singing "You're only dreaming" when she suggests (upon her entry in the second verse) that he might phone while she is away. Nevertheless, the song ends with Horton refusing to leave the safe confines of home or to give up waiting for love to come back.

As well as its atypical reversal of the roles of lead and backing singers, the song is also unusual in its instrumentation and harmonic language. It features a finger-picked "country" guitar and grim baritone saxophone rocking relentlessly between the home key of E-flat major and C minor. The close relationship between these two chords, based on the fact that they have two out of three tones in common, means that the harmonic area based on the sixth degree (C minor in this case) can sound deceptively like the home key. This musical language is hardly typical of Motown or other girl group recordings, which generally stick to conventional movement between tonic and dominant in major keys. In this song, the swinging between these two tonal areas suggests a vacillating, timid character who cannot overcome her mournful mood in spite of the danceable groove.

The wide range of styles and affects in the Marvelettes' repertoire is largely due to the fact that they did not work consistently with a single song-writing team, as, for example, the Supremes tended to do with Holland, Dozier, and Holland. Instead, the Marvelettes performed songs that they themselves cowrote with non-Motown writers ("Please Mr. Postman") as well as songs by Marvin Gaye ("Beechwood 4-5789"), Motown engineer William "Mickey" Stevenson ("Twistin'

Postman"), William "Smokey" Robinson ("You're My Remedy"), Nickolas Ashford and Valerie Simpson ("Destination: Anywhere"), and Berry Gordy ("My Daddy Knows Best"). The Marvelettes attribute this diversity to the fact that Motown never invested in them as a group to the point that they were assigned to a consistent writing team. All accounts of the Marvelettes describe them as small-town "hicks" (from the Detroit suburb of Inkster) who earned the undying resentment of other Motown artists when they created the record company's first number-one hit with a song that they had brought in to the company with them (The song "Please Mr. Postman" is discussed in Chapter 2). Furthermore, the Inkster group tended at first to create their own choreography for performances, and they did not begin to benefit from the lessons of Maxine Powell or Cholly Atkins until the mid-60s; thus, they were never considered Motown products of the same order as the Supremes. Gladys Horton recalls that "We weren't pretty city girls from the projects like Motown's other girl group, the Supremes, with nice clothes and make up on and long nails…we were just naïve little country girls…we had no idea how to behave, we didn't know what to wear, we didn't even know how to put on make up!"[11]

The urbane sophistication and ambitions of the Supremes made the trio (and particularly lead singer Diana Ross) vulnerable to criticisms that they were hard-edged women who did not care whom they stepped on in their efforts to get to the top. This kind of characterization made Ross's interpretation of "I'm Livin' in Shame" in 1969 utterly convincing. Fans were quite ready to believe that Ross (who seems, in reality, to have been an appropriately dutiful daughter and sister) could abandon her impoverished, disadvantaged family and denounce her mother, in spite of her earlier invocation of mother's advice in 1966's "You Can't Hurry Love." "I'm Livin' in Shame," then, demonstrates the dark side of efforts at respectability and can be understood as a warning against female aspirations toward social betterment.

The song is not properly an advice song, but should rather be considered a cautionary tale that is closely tied to the advice song style, and its narrative bears a striking resemblance to the guilt-suffused monuments to mother performed by white girl group the Shangri-Las at mid-decade (particularly 1965's "I Can Never Go Home Anymore," in which the girl acknowledges that her rebellious ways caused her mother to die of heartbreak). "I'm Livin' in Shame" is the harrowing confession of a woman who despises her working-class mother for her sloppy ways, ignorance, and poverty; the narrator describes how she found a new identity at college, married well, and pretended her mother had died while vacationing in Europe. Most shameful of all, the singer bears a son but never shows him to her mother, clinging desperately instead to her luxurious life that is built on lies and deception. One day a telegram arrives, informing her that her mother has died while slaving over the hot stove she was tied to throughout her life, and that she cried for her ingrate daughter with her last breath. The narrator is overcome with remorse as she is forced to confront the unforgivable injury she did her long-suffering mother. The song obviously owes a great deal to the 1959 Douglas Sirk film *Imitation of Life* (a remake of the 1934 film of the same name) in which a light-skinned black girl denies her saintly, selfless mother in order to pass as white, only to reappear at her mother's funeral in time to fling herself on the casket in an ecstasy of grief and self-flagellation.

Both the song and the film posit a mother's martyrdom as ennobling and elevating, and they make this point more effective by contrasting the long-suffering mother with the callous, greedy ambitions of her selfish daughter. Also, both provide an opportunity for pleasurably beholding the heartless daughter collapse in shame and self-recrimination as she realizes—too late—the consequences of her dreadful ambitions. "I'm Livin' in Shame," equipped with all the lavish melodrama of late-1960s Motown recordings, functions as a morality tale warning girls not to get too far ahead of themselves. Respectability and suburban comfort are worthy goals when they are accompanied by a husband sanctioned by parental approval, but woe betide any daughter who thinks she can earn these things by turning her back on her filial obligations.

All the songs I have discussed were products of the Motown label, but I do not wish to give the impression that this record company had a monopoly on advice songs. However, Motown's goal of creating MOR pop songs that would appeal to the most sheltered, suburban white teens—giving them a sense of generational identity that transgressed class and race barriers, while never adopting an explicitly defiant tone that might offend—lends itself well to the advice song style, and it cannot be coincidence that their first number one–earning group was assigned so many songs of this type. This genre, like the lore of old wives' tales, is best understood as at once conservative and radical. Like old wives' tales, advice songs dispense wisdom that, on one level, works against rebellious 60s cultural values of free love, the defying of authority, and the primacy of individual expression, but also constructs a valuable, even crucial, forum for females to connect with one another and promote the value of female collectivity. Some songs, like "Too Many Fish in the Sea," go farther than this and propose that girls might be able to survive perfectly well without boyfriends.

Furthermore, it is instructive to consider which girls did and which girls did not sing advice songs; for example, none of the groups who recorded with Phil Spector sang them. It may be that the cheeky "bad girl" image fostered by the Ronettes, for instance, was incompatible with giving big-sisterly advice—I might also argue that Phil Spector was far too controlling to allow his singers to promote any notion of a support network. None of the white girl groups, such as the Shangri-Las, or the Angels sang advice songs either (we will examine these groups further in the next section). Even at Motown, the queens of girl groups themselves, the Supremes, recorded only one piece that can properly qualify as an advice song. "You Can't Hurry Love," a number-one hit in 1966, quotes Mama's tenets only a year after "Back in My Arms Again," in which Diana Ross celebrates having rejected her friends' advice and returned to a boyfriend everyone said was no good. In a really shocking betrayal, she actually goes so far as to call out the other Supremes by name (the only moment in the Supremes' recorded œuvre when Ballard and Wilson are brought to the fore as individuals) and to explain why their advice was so useless.

The advice song style was also co-opted for other reactionary messages, as in soul singer Betty Wright's 1968 "Girls Can't Do What the Guys Do." In terms of lyrics and in its use of backing female voices, this piece has all the features of an advice song, but its lesson teaches that freedom along the lines of masculine experience is incompatible with respectability. Wright was fifteen at the time of this recording, and her ability to perform the role of motherly advisor is astonishing; her full, gritty voice sounds positively jaded. Like Gladys Horton enacting the role of dutiful daughter, Carolyn Gill playing at being big sister, or Diana Ross performing the ruthless social climber, Wright is trying on a role she has not experienced firsthand. These kinds of performances point to an important aspect of girl culture—experimenting with different adult personae is not unlike trying on mother's clothes and makeup, and these activities highlight the performative nature of female subject positions.

Thus, the invocation of the mother in girl group advice songs is complex; if songs such as "Too Many Fish in the Sea" can empower girls to be self-reliant and to respect themselves above all, "I'm Livin' in Shame" warns not to get above one's station. Nevertheless, I consider that the advice song style serves overall as an outlet for girls to voice their concerns and share their knowledge and can therefore be understood as a proto-feminist forum. The features of advice songs—the direct address; the explicit assumption of girls as listeners; the references to mother, family, and home; the strong presence of backing female voices lending support to the lead singer's statements—have characterized songs aimed at female listeners from music traditions quite separate from the genre of girl group music, as in Betty Wright's cautionary "Girls Can't Do What the Guys Do," but also in soul singer Laura Lee's 1970 "Wedlock Is a Padlock," which warns girls (identified as such) not to leap into marriage.

Moreover, Lee's 1971 anthem "Women's Love Rights" begins with the phrase "Hear me girls!" and urges listeners to stand up and fight for consideration from men. Aretha Franklin's famous cover version of Otis Redding's "RESPECT" responds tartly to his misogynist complaint, and the supporting female voices provided by backing vocal group the Sweet Inspirations are central to the power of Franklin's recording. Sister Sledge's 1979 hit "We Are Family" celebrates the bonds between women and promotes the idea of a universal sisterhood. Madonna's 1989 "Express Yourself" calls out explicitly to girls, in a spoken introduction like that to "Too Many Fish in the Sea," and advises listeners to be assertive and maintain high standards and self-respect in relationships with men. These and other songs make use of the musical vocabulary of girl groups to promote songs celebrating female solidarity, mutual helpfulness, and strength.

PART V
OUT IN THE STREETS

In the introduction to this book, I shared an anecdote about my childhood, recounting my realization as a nine-year-old Brownie that boys and girls are socialized differently and that cultural expectations of girls emphasize the importance of being supportive, whereas boys are directed toward individual excellence. Reflecting back on my prepubescent epiphany and attendant feelings of outrage at the differing messages of the Brownie motto "Lend a Hand" and the Cub Scout motto "Do Your Best," I asked readers to consider the importance of childhood training in gender-appropriate demeanor and the socialization process that leads us to accept certain characteristics and behaviors as natural. More recently, however, I have begun to reconsider my nine-year-old self's analytical skills; why, I wonder now, did I instantly assume that "Lend a Hand" meant "Lend a hand to boys, whose goals are more important than yours"? Why could I not rejoice in the knowledge that I was being trained to be a generous member of a female collective, instead of being goaded into rugged individualism and eventual isolation from my peers?

My childish assumption that female helpfulness and supportiveness could serve only male ambition parallels in interesting ways a tendency in contemporary popular thinking to denounce these stereotypically feminine traits without considering their positive implications for feminist activism. Indeed, in a culture that understands all struggles toward empowerment as individual efforts toward success in a dog-eat-dog world, feminine kindness and supportiveness can even be considered antithetical to feminism. Thus, Florence Greenberg, the housewife-turned-record-producer whose company, Scepter Records, was one of the top labels of the 1960s, reflects in the early 1980s on her experiences in a male-dominated industry: "You had a lot of help in those days, and I think I had more help as a woman. I don't know if I really believe in Women's Lib, because I enjoyed having people help me."[1] Greenberg obviously believes that the goals of the Women's Liberation movement are incompatible with relying on the help of a network of friends, and she distances herself from the stereotype of the shrill, angry feminist by emphasizing her willingness to accept help graciously.

And who can blame Greenberg for her assumptions, when so many female role models are venerated largely for their ability to go it alone, without recourse to a network of support? Within the sphere of popular music history, "women in rock" such as Janis Joplin are more likely to be held up as examples of feminist achievement than are any of the singers I have discussed, although Joplin's achievements undoubtedly reinforced the values of virtuosity, authenticity, and individualism established by male rockers (to say nothing of the fact that the life she chose killed her at 27). More recently, solitary female musicians such as Tori Amos, who demonstrate skill as instrumentalists, songwriters, and producers, are more likely to be celebrated by many subscribing to feminist ideals—particularly if they communicate emotions of anger, cynicism, and angst—than are the cheerful groups of singers and dancers I examine in this book.[2]

Recent studies of female adolescence identify the crippling problems that girls encounter in trying to maintain a sense of self in their teen years; it has been argued that teenage and preteen girls are so in thrall to the ideal of the "nice girl" that they are unable to express anger or indignation for fear of being perceived as selfish and "not nice." In their pivotal 1992 *Meeting at the Crossroads*, for example, Lyn Mikel Brown and Carol Gilligan describe the struggles of a successful girl who does well at school and is admired by her peers: "To stay with herself—to attend to her complex thoughts and feelings—is to risk being called 'bad' or 'mad,' in both senses of the word, or more simply 'selfish.' To stay with others, [the girl] chooses in effect to bury herself."[3] The idea that girls' friendships are so duplicitous and fragile that girls learn to suppress their own opinions and values in order to remain part of the group is taken up by other analysts of girl culture, such as Mary Pipher and Rachel Simmons, whose ethnographic study of female adolescence inspired the 2004 Hollywood film *Mean Girls*, starring contemporary teen idol Lindsay Lohan in a tale of wealthy, attractive, white girls tormenting one another.[4]

By contrast, scholars of girlhood such as Meda Chesney-Lind and Katherine Irwin critique the spate of media attention to this kind of girls' bullying that appeared in the first years of the twenty-first century for its implication that, in this arena at least, girls somehow gain equality with boys by virtue of their capacity for cruelty. Chesney-Lind and Irwin note that "alternative aggressions are, fundamentally, weapons of the weak. As such, they are as reflective of girls' powerlessness as they are of girls' meanness."[5] Furthermore, it is important to note that the landmark 1992 report of the American Association of University Women so often cited in studies of girls' bullying concludes that "African American girls hold on to their overall self-esteem more than white or Latina girls during the transition to adolescence," a conclusion also borne out in Peggy Orenstein's year-long investigative study of middle-school girls in Northern California.[6] Thus, generalizations about girls' poisonous friendships and frail senses of self may offer a distorted, racially shaped view of a crisis in contemporary girl culture. Analysis of the travails of girls trying to develop coherent, self-respecting senses of themselves as individuals has been invaluable to my own study of female adolescence, but in this section I want to explore the possibility that belonging to a group of girls could provide a means of empowerment to girl group singers and their fans in the 1960s.

12

Group Identity and Public Space

It is a truism of adolescent cultures that the importance of peer relationships often eclipses that of familial ones and that preteens and teens adhere more closely to the values and priorities of their friends than those of their parents; hence, the clichéd rejoinder of exasperated parents: "If all your friends jumped off a cliff, would you do it too?" In an analysis of the enduring popularity of Noel Streatfield's 1936 novel for girls, *Ballet Shoes*, Angela McRobbie considers the value of peer groups to girls and the appeal of stories about a trio of orphan girls who forge close bonds and emerge from poverty and insecurity to triumph. McRobbie notes that the book has been continuously in print since its original publication and that its popularity among girls in the 10 to 12 age range is neither race nor class specific. She concludes that

> *Ballet Shoes* works as a text of transition and development. It simultaneously allows its readers to fantasise a family space unencumbered by sibling rivalry and parental dictate (a state of affairs experienced negatively in one way or another by boys and girls of all ages and social backgrounds) and to contemplate a future state of being which promises reward, recognition and happiness. The narrative also works through, in fictional form, the kind of psychic material which in itself is a product of the difficulty girls face in moving towards achieving a feminine identity.[1]

Thus, the prospect of peer group membership represents, for girls, an opportunity to experiment with facets of identity and self-definition not available in a family context, and the phenomenon of girls bonding together as a group of equals is valuable in the process of navigating adolescence and incipient womanhood.

Similarly, in a study of values of personal identity and self-esteem among adolescent girls in two northeastern U.S. high schools in the mid-1990s, researchers confirmed that girls are generally trained to develop their senses of identity in relation to others—at school, at home, at church, in their communities—in contrast to masculinist strategies of self-direction, autonomy, differentiation and self-reliance that are assumed to be cultural norms for men and women. Data indicated that girls who prized cooperation ahead of competition, preferred emotional expressiveness to emotional restraint, and thought of themselves in relation to friends and family rather than as individuals first and foremost identified themselves as having "traditional" values. The study's important conclusion, however, supports McRobbie's analysis in stating that "rather than a process of active seeking and individuation, the girls' interviews suggest that the losing of oneself and one's boundaries in a group identity…may be [an] alternative [route] to integrating one's personal identity."[2] Thus, the fact that belonging to a group is so crucially important to many adolescent girls need not be interpreted as detrimental to their self-development, and group membership can even be identified as a positive and important aspect of female adolescence.

The girl group phenomenon of the 1960s created a network of young females who were visible and audible in the public sphere in unprecedented ways, and girl groups who toured and made appearances on television presented a bold, self-assured kind of behavior that chipped away at the repressive containment and rigid gender roles of Cold War culture. In the late 1950s and early 60s, girl groups made manifest the phenomenon of girls bonding together and traversing boundaries that purported to keep them safely corralled in domesticity. As I will show, the "bad girl" images carefully cultivated by some girl groups even signaled new possibilities of rebelliousness and collective power to their middle-class fans.

Group Identity and Sisterhood

According to a popular slogan of the 1970s' Women's Liberation movement "sisterhood is powerful." Through the movement, many women who had grown up listening to records by the Shirelles, the Marvelettes, and the Shangri-Las developed the phenomenon of consciousness-raising groups, in which women talked together and shared their personal experiences and insights in an effort to analyze women's position in society. I suggest that these conversation groups may have been modeled, deliberately or not, on the dialogues presented in girl group records a decade earlier, and that the notion of sisterhood promoted in 1970s' feminist thought may have been partly inspired by the relationships among girl group singers. Susan Douglas makes this link explicitly in her analysis of the feminist protests to the 1968 Miss America Pageant: "[T]he sense of cultural and social collectivity many young women felt when they sang along together with the Shirelles…was about to be extended into a political movement that would change America."[3]

Many of the adolescent girl group fans who, like Douglas, grew up to become second-wave feminists, may not have realized that in the cases of several important girl groups from the 1960s, the members genuinely were sisters. Examples include the Ronettes (two sisters and a cousin), the Dixie Cups (two sisters and a cousin), the Angels (two sisters and a friend), and the Shangri-Las (two sets of sisters, including the identical Ganser twins). In the 1940s, the Boswell Sisters, the McGuire Sisters, the Fontane Sisters, and the Andrews Sisters were popular vocal ensembles that prefigured some aspects of the girl group genre, while 70s groups like Sister Sledge, the Pointer Sisters, and the Emotions (three sisters) can be understood as descendants of the style.

I consider that the preponderance of sibling relationships in girl groups is directly related to the circumstances of girls' music-making and to broader issues that necessitated keeping girls safe and tame. Ronnie Bennett (later Ronnie Spector) relates that the Ronettes formed as a singing ensemble when—following an incident in which a man exposed himself to them on the way to their Spanish Harlem neighborhood candy store—she, sister Estelle, and cousin Nedra Talley were confined to their grandmother's house every day after school (and before their mothers returned from work).[4] Bored, the three girls listened to the radio, sang along, and rehearsed dance routines in preparation for performances at larger family gatherings. Eventually

The Ronettes. Courtesy of Photofest.

their talent and enthusiasm led the family to sign them up for singing lessons and then performances at bar mitzvahs and similar events. Thus, the perceived need to protect preadolescent girls by removing them from the dangers of public life like little Rapunzels led, in this case, to the formation of one of the most successful performing ensembles of the decade.

The fact that the Ronettes were related was an important component of their success. For one thing, the girls had a distinctive appearance and looked very much alike, so that they were a visually striking trio.[5] Under the guidance of their mothers and aunts, they cultivated a unique look, with teased-up hair, dramatic makeup, and matching clothes. One fateful evening in 1961, the high school girls took these efforts as far as they could in order to try and gain admission to the legendary Peppermint Lounge, a chic nightclub patronized by rock'n'roll stars and other celebrities. Standing in line outside the club in their stuffed bras, mountainous beehive hairstyles, and identical tight yellow dresses, they were mistaken for the professional dancers expected that night and herded into the club to take the stage. Ronnie Bennett (as she was then known) recalls that they were astute enough to play along, so the three soon found themselves dancing on stage to the accompaniment of a band, Joey and the Starliters. When the band began playing a song the girls knew, Ray Charles' "What'd I Say?" sixteen-year-old Ronnie managed to take the microphone and steal the spotlight altogether. By this time, the club manager knew he had been fooled, but he was sufficiently impressed by the trio's appeal to offer them a steady job as house dancers who would occasionally sing.[6] Their position at the nightclub led to them being sent to Miami to open the new branch of the Peppermint Lounge; here, they were spotted by radio DJ Murray "the K" Kaufman, who invited them to perform at one of his popular rock'n'roll revues at the Fox Theatre in Brooklyn in 1962. Not until a year later would the Ronettes (as they eventually named themselves) meet record producer Phil Spector and have their first major hit with "Be My Baby."

This account—and indeed, most aspects of the Ronettes' career—flies in the face of the middle-class values of respectability discussed in the previous section of this book. In a culture in which parents concerned about preserving their daughters' reputations kept them confined at home, the Ronettes' mothers—working-class, mixed race women who worked as coffee shop waitresses—actually encouraged their girls to venture unchaperoned into the legally off-limits world of nightclubs. In her memoirs, Ronnie Spector demonstrates some ambivalence about her mother's role in teaching her to use makeup and pad her bra: "It's funny, but as protective as they were in most ways, Mom and my aunts didn't seem to mind grooming us to get through the doors of New York's steamiest nightclub. I guess they knew it was for the good of our careers.…Mom and her sisters helped doll us up until they were sure we could pass for at least twenty-three."[7]

With this rationalization of her mother's actions, Bennett/Spector indicates the extent to which she herself is bound by the ideology of respectability and middle-class decency. Recognizing that some readers might disapprove of the role her female elders played in pushing her into a dangerous, adult sphere, she deflects criticism of her mother by insisting that these efforts were all in the service of the trio's career ambitions.

I consider, however, that the girls' mothers felt a certain confidence in sending their disguised underage daughters into a notorious nightclub simply because they were a *group*. Dressing them outrageously meant (in this case, at least) also dressing them identically, and their uniforms that night, provocative though they seem to have been, also marked them powerfully and instantly as belonging together and may have made it difficult for any adult to prey on them individually. Furthermore, the mothers and aunts almost certainly would have instructed the girls to stick together and would have relied upon the strong bonds between Ronnie, Estelle, and Nedra to sustain them through their exploration of an off-limits world. In this way, the outing that became the Ronettes' rock'n'roll début fits into the phenomenon of the "girls' night out," when women of a comparable age and social background band together in groups to invade public spaces such as bars and restaurants. These excursions are understood to provide relief from the responsibilities of domestic containment through nostalgic recreations of girlish insouciance, and stereotypes of the girls' night out involve "girls" making spectacles of themselves and taking delight in being looked at, all the while emphasizing their unavailability to men. The phenomenon of being part of what is obviously a group gives women on a girls' night out license to behave in an unladylike way with carefree abandon.

The Ronettes' shared genes and upbringing helped them to project an aura of provocative sultriness but also untouchability, and throughout their brief but spectacular career, their distinctive "look" was a crucial part of their identity as a group. I have noted in Chapter 5 that for some of the trio's performances, another cousin from their clan assumed the duties of lead singer Ronnie Bennett/Spector, and that fans of the group did not object to the substitution. Evidently, the fact that the replacement singer looked and sounded like a Ronette was sufficient; the importance of group identity was of paramount significance to fans. How much more thrilling in this regard, then, was the look of the Shangri-Las, whose members included the identical Ganser twins, Mary Ann and Margie.

13

Rebellion and Girldom

The Shangri-Las were a group of suburbanites from Queens who began singing together when they met at public high school in 1963. Although the group was officially a quartet, right from the beginning it was common for only three singers to participate in many performances and recording sessions, usually Mary Ann and Margie Ganser and Mary Weiss, whose older sister Betty was also a group member. Likewise, publicity shots for the group throughout its career sometimes show all four singers, sometimes only Mary Weiss and the Gansers, and sometimes one of the Gansers and the two Weiss sisters. Mary Weiss, who sang lead on all the best-known recordings, provides continuity through the various incarnations of the group, and the most typical publicity shots of the Shangri-Las depict her flanked by the Gansers, who cultivated their resemblance with identical hairstyles and a tendency to pose in mirror image to one another. The balanced effect is a pleasing one, clearly identifying Mary Weiss as a leader supported by matching bookends. In performance, of course, this arrangement changed so that the Gansers stood together, slightly apart from the lead singer, in order better to hear one another as they provided backing harmonies.

The Shangri-Las' ethnic backgrounds are significant, for they are the first group examined in my study who were not (at least in part) African American; both the Weiss sisters and the Ganser twins were raised in Roman Catholic families of European descent, and all four singers grew up in difficult economic circumstances in a working-class Long Island suburb. Like the Chantels, discussed in Chapter 1, the Gansers as young girls learned to sing harmony by participating in school choirs led by nuns, and the Weiss sisters sang in a church choir.

In their early publicity shots, which coincided with the peak of the main girl group craze in 1963, the Shangri-Las present an image of

An early shot of the Shangri-Las as "good girls." Courtesy of Mary Wells.

demure suburban girlhood, with tidy upswept hairstyles, knee-length skirts, and friendly smiles. This was not a style that they liked, and their appearance would undergo a radical transformation in response to the enormous success of their song "Leader of the Pack" in late 1964. Since this song narrated the experience of a girl whose boyfriend is a notorious bad boy, the group and their new label, Red Bird, shrewdly reinvented the Shangri-Las as tough, "don't mess with me" rebel girls.[1] The Shangri-Las' whiteness afforded them greater freedom to play with this version of girl identity than was available to groups like the Ronettes, as we have seen. Nevertheless, the slacks, white shirts, and vests that the singers chose to wear were generally considered provocative, and Mary Weiss recalls raising eyebrows by shopping for the pants she preferred in men's clothing stores.[2]

By contemporary standards, it may be difficult to understand the Shangri-Las' image as genuinely dangerous and subversive; the juxtaposition of their fresh faces and sulky pouts is reminiscent of a fluffy

The Shangri-Las' *Leader of the Pack* album cover. Red Bird is a registered trademark of Red Bird Entertainment Inc. Courtesy of John J. Grecco for Red Bird Entertainment Inc.

kitten puffing itself up with rage—it seems there is no real threat, and so the anger is adorable. Certainly, the singers' 1965 roles as spokespersons in radio "Good Taste Tips" sponsored by the makers of the soft drink 7-Up (to say nothing of commercials for Revlon and Breck shampoo) presented them urging girl listeners to uphold conventional middle-class gender roles. In one of these announcements, for example, Mary Weiss recommends that girls who are "smart" let their dates know they expect doors to be held open and chairs pulled out for them: "He'll love it and think you are a lady, and in return it will flatter his masculine ego."[3] In spite of this prim advice, the Shangri-Las were generally perceived as tough and rebellious, an important instance of white girls adopting a defiant stance in a society that was still more inclined to associating unladylike, "bad girl" behavior with non-white teens.

Indeed, as I noted in Chapter 8, "Leader of the Pack," surely the group's most notorious song, was actually banned in Britain because of the dark themes in its content. It begins with spoken dialogue in unpolished Long Island accents between identical twins Marge and Mary Ganser and lead singer Mary Weiss[4] in some unspecified female space, probably the "Ladies' Room" that is so often the site of important female conversations and girl talk. Over a descent of stark octaves in the piano on C, then A, G, and F, and the rhythmic pattern of the girl group beat sounding slowly and portentously in the bass drum (as opposed to the snare drum that normally presents it), Weiss hums to herself and adopts a nonchalant tone when the twins ask her about her mysterious and dangerous boyfriend, Jimmy, but then literally bursts into song as she describes how they met and what he represents to her. The timeline of events in the song is ambiguous; are we to understand that the tragedy of Jimmy's death is something that has occurred before the beginning of the song (in which case, it is difficult to imagine that the Ganser sisters have not already heard about the ghastly accident)? Or should the listener believe, rather, that the song begins and ends at different points in the story, so that the opening discussion sets the stage for the dramatic events that will ensue? Either way, the whiny quality of Weiss's voice, strained near the top of her vocal range, perfectly evokes the slightly smug, spoiled girl who enjoys impressing her friends with the drama and status her glamorous, dangerous, rebel boyfriend confers on her. The backup singers respond, alternately begging for more information and retreating to wordless lines as she drifts into spoken reminiscence during a middle eight section in the related minor key.

A different outcome to the tragedy of the scenario in "Leader of the Pack" is imagined in the Shangri-Las' 1965 release "Out in the Streets" (which never entered the Top Forty). In this song, the narrator recognizes that her rebel boyfriend has reformed his wild ways in order to be considered respectable enough to date her. The backing vocalists sing softly about how he has turned away from his gang of friends and rejected his life in the street, and Mary Weiss acknowledges that he has made this sacrifice for her sake. Sorrowfully, she notes that he does not smile anymore and accepts that she must prove her love for him by releasing him from their relationship and letting him return to what we assume is his natural state of being. The song supports the view that love that defies class barriers is doomed, but, unlike "Leader of the Pack," it ends with all characters alive and well, if chastened by the futility of love across social boundaries. Both of these songs, then, make clear that the girl's affections are transgressive, that loving a boy from the wrong side of the tracks is a serious offense against the norms of propriety.

"Out in the Streets," like "Leader of the Pack" and most Shangri-Las recordings, was produced by George "Shadow" Morton, who earned his nickname because of his tendency to appear and disappear without warning. Morton was a former high school classmate of well-known songwriter Ellie Greenwich's, and he traded on this connection in bringing the Shangri-Las to the Red Bird record label. Morton's production style involved using echo and reverberation on a scale comparable to Phil Spector, and he also used sound effects to heighten dramatic impact; in the case of "Leader of the Pack," he imported the sounds of a motorcycle revving its engine and even simulated the sounds of a crash for the tragic climax. Morton's use of sound effects was a departure from Spector's style, as Spector preferred to create drama through musical suggestion rather than direct quotations of specific sounds (his 1964 record for the Ronettes, "Walking in the Rain," is exceptional in that it features the sound of rain falling).

In "Leader of the Pack," as in other songs by the Shangri-Las, the girl's rebellion against middle-class norms takes the form of partnering a boy who is conspicuously bad. Note that, as in songs discussed in Part 1, "the Boy" in "Leader of the Pack" and "Out in the Streets" is constituted for us only through Weiss's description of him; she and the Gansers exist in a sort of girldom, where "Jimmy's" only function is to give them something to talk about. This procedure of constructing a shadowy male figure whose purpose is simply to heighten the drama between the more interesting female characters is a strategy common to soap opera writing, as Bonnie Dow and other feminist television critics have noted, taking up an idea proposed by Dorothy Smith.[5] Drawing on Gayle Rubin's important work on the "traffic in women," Patricia Juliana Smith identifies this strategy as fetishizing the boyfriend into

"the Apparitional Boy, a simulacrum…the object of the female fantasy gaze, the token of exchange among girls."[6] Thanks to Morton's strategic use of sound effects, the lyrics to "Leader of the Pack" never have to spell out that Jimmy is a motorcyclist, presenting an elegant economy even in the midst of angst-ridden, high melodrama.

For melodrama is undoubtedly the most apt term I could use to describe the œuvre of the Shangri-Las. Even their first release with Red Bird, 1964's "Remember (Walkin' in the Sand)" relates the anguish of a girl recalling a romance that ended against her will, and the intensity of her stormy emotions is heightened by the sound of waves crashing on the beach and a veritable army of seagulls crying overhead. Much of their repertoire presents apocalyptic narratives of teenage love and rebellion leading to death; in addition to "Leader of the Pack," this motif also generates "Give Us Your Blessings" (in which a teenage couple is killed in a car crash while trying to elope) and "I Can Never Go Home Anymore" (in which a girl's mother dies, broken-hearted over her daughter's failure to conform to conventional family life), both from 1965. By the time the group had recorded their last single with Red Bird, 1966's "Past, Present and Future," they had earned the moniker "myrmidons of melodrama," and this final song consists solely of a portentous spoken monologue about suffering in love and trepidation about future romances over a piano part borrowing heavily from the well-known first movement of Beethoven's "Moonlight" Sonata (only Mary Weiss's voice is heard in this recording). From the cryptic clues given in the lyrics, the listener can construe that romance with a rebel has led to heartbreak and anguish, but it is clear that the girl's melancholy has actually added to her allure with other suitors, and that the attractions of other bad boys may—despite her protestations—eventually tempt her out of her grief.

Bad Boys and Rebel Girls

The theme of romance with irresistible, forbidden boys is not unique to the Shangri-Las, though. Among the many girl group songs celebrating rebel boyfriends, the Girls' "Chico's Girl" remains a cult favorite despite the fact that it made no chart impact when released in

1966, perhaps a few years too late to benefit fully from popular interest in girl group records. The song was written by the songwriting team of Barry Mann and Cynthia Weil (who also wrote material for the Shangri-Las), recorded by a quartet of sisters named Sandoval in Los Angeles, and later revived by comedienne Bernadette Peters on her eponymous 1980 album; it is the Girls' original version, however, that is included in the four-CD box set *The Brill Building Sound*, a showcase of the best recordings of this generation of songwriters and producers.[7] The song features a terse, arpeggiated bass line that serves as an ostinato underpinning sulky, half-spoken vocals and a dramatic instrumentation that includes castanets, maracas, horns, and distorted electric guitar. The story line should by now be familiar; Chico is a rebel (and advertises himself as such on the back of his jacket) who grew up in the toughest part of town, but he has a tender side that he reveals only to the narrator, Chico's girl. The soloist fairly spits out lyrics justifying Chico's gang lifestyle—"his neighborhood's a jungle, so he travels with a pack"—but she adopts a sweeter vocal timbre to rhapsodize about the secret, precious vulnerability that he allows her alone to see, and her melody is supported by high-pitched vocals from the backing singers that lean toward a choral sound.

Use of the name Chico, rather than the more generic and customary Jimmy or Johnny, signals clearly that the rebel in this case is Hispanic. The unremarkable name of the group, the Girls, meanwhile, together with the singers' unaccented American pronunciation, obscured any questions about the Sandoval sisters' ethnic background for those who interacted with them only through recordings. The Latin feel to the song, generated largely through percussion instruments such as maracas and guiro (or at least, a sharp, crisp, rattling sound that suggests a guiro or castanets), was not in itself unusual among songs written and produced by Brill Building songwriters at that time, as Ken Emerson demonstrates in *Always Magic in the Air: The Bomp and Brilliance of the Brill Building Era*. Songs such as the Drifters' "This Magic Moment" and "Sweets for My Sweet," Sam Cooke's "Everybody Likes to Cha Cha Cha" and Ben E. King's "Spanish Harlem," as well as the Ronettes' "Be My Baby" and the Crystals' "Uptown" (both discussed in Chapter 9) are among well-known songs of the early 1960s that gestured toward the enormous contemporary popularity of the mambo, the cha cha, and other Latin dance styles among non-Latin audiences, sometimes with explicitly Latin themes in the lyrics, but equally often without.[8] Considering "Chico's Girl" in the context of a vogue for Latin elements in pop music, it is possible to see that many listeners would not have assumed the singers themselves were Hispanic; the name of the song's hero makes Chico the only indisputably Latin character of the piece. The song thus offered the possibility of imagining the thrills and dangers of cross-racial romance for middle-class white teens who listened to the record a year before the controversial 1967 film *Guess Who's Coming to Dinner* tackled the topic of interracial marriage for more adult audiences.

Sociologist Donna Gaines reports that in suburban communities with middle-class values in the 1960s, teenage romance with the wrong boy "could ruin a teenage girl's chance at a good life. He could cost her her respectability, and the relationship could tarnish the class aspirations of an entire community."[9] The phenomenon of the American "juvenile delinquent" was of great public concern during the 1950s and 60s, and discourse surrounding "bad girls" differed significantly from the perceptions of male teens in trouble; the cases of girls going bad were particularly horrifying because they were generally understood to stem from a lack of fatherly authority. Indeed, Rachel Devlin provides evidence that because juvenile delinquency was so determinedly cast as a male problem, girls who transgressed legal and social codes at the time were treated informally and discreetly by police and other authorities who sought to minimize embarrassment for the parents of offending girls. While bad boys were more easily understood as individuals, responsible for their wrongdoings, bad girls at mid-century were seen as evidence of inadequate patriarchal control, and they threatened an entire social order.[10] Taking up with a bad boy was often understood as a girl's first step on a slippery slope away from father's loving control and toward a life of adolescent—and eventually adult—disrepute.

Thus, the subversions presented in girl group songs like "Leader of the Pack," "Out in the Streets," and "Chico's Girl" are real and should be taken seriously. Of course, the ideology of rock rebelliousness treats the comfort and security that steady relationships offer with profound ambivalence. Simon Reynolds and Joy Press observe that for legendary

1960s rock rebel Jim Morrison, for example, "women constituted his 'Soul Kitchen,' a nourishing hearth that provided a brief resting-place before he hit the road again."[11] As I noted in Chapter 1, Reynolds and Press identify "The Road" as male territory, and the rebellious wanderer hero as a male who resists the suffocating embrace of female domesticity. By contrast with this "authentic" and worthwhile kind of subversiveness, rock ideology has typically failed to see rebellion in girls' songs about being in love with a misunderstood rebel. Yet even when the girls in these songs seem to do little more than offer comfort and unwavering devotion to their rebel boyfriends, demonstrating conventional female behavior and loyalty, the mere fact of being a rebel's girlfriend entailed real risks and represented a dangerous, exciting fantasy marketed to girls.

Furthermore, the girls narrating the 1962 hit "He's a Rebel" (credited to the Crystals, but recorded by Darlene Love and the Blossoms) not only brag about a dangerous boyfriend, but they also go so far as to imply behavior on the protagonist's own part that is significantly more provocative than the stance of Chico's girl, who effaces herself entirely except to declare love and support to her rebel boyfriend. The girl in "He's a Rebel" sings the praise of a boy who will "never, never be any good" but nevertheless makes her proud when he holds her hand, precisely because he is bold and stands apart from the crowd. A buoyant groove centered in the bass drum lends confidence to Darlene Love's solo vocals, which begin deep in her range (with an F-sharp below the staff) then ascend more than an octave to trumpet her feelings of love alongside the full, gospel-fired singing of the other Blossoms. In the song's middle eight section, Love interrupts a saxophone solo to assert that she herself will reject respectable behavior to join her rebel boyfriend: "If they don't like him that way, they won't like me after today!" The girl in this song draws courage from her boyfriend's independence, and their relationship inspires her to dismiss the criticisms of those who condemn unorthodox behavior and actually to embrace nonconformity herself; her choices meet with unambiguous approval from the backing vocalists singing with her. From this song—which was significantly more popular than either "Out in the Streets" or "Chico's Girl," reaching the number-one position in 1962—it was only a small step to songs in which girls gleefully reported actual participation in inappropriate behavior.

The Shangri-Las' 1964 "Give Him a Great Big Kiss," for example, presents the account of a bold girl who dares to invade the male sphere and claim her boyfriend by kissing him in front of his friends, and the musical language is upbeat and infectious. The song begins with Mary Weiss's spoken "When I say I'm in love, you'd best believe I'm in love, L-U-V!" setting the tone for a sassy and delightful declaration of adolescent love on the part of a confident girl. Rhythmically energetic percussive forces soon come to the fore, with a horn section and piano providing syncopated R&B-styled riffs over a harmonic foundation that alternates jauntily between the home key and its relative minor. At various points in the song, the backing vocalists collude with the horns to provide a fanfare-like riff that descends low into their range on the syllables "da da da," a light-hearted and amusing effect contributing to a cheerful mood; toward the end of the recording, they echo this riff on an "oo" vowel, at a higher, more conventional position in the female vocal range. At the crucial chorus of the song, all instruments except percussion drop out, focusing the listener's attention on the Shangri-Las singing in unison with repeated, even eighth notes accompanied by steady handclaps: "I'm gonna walk right up to him, give him a great big kiss! MWAH!"

It is significant that this statement is sung by *all* the Shangri-Las, even though there are no individual vocal parts; the song is about one girl's romance with one boy, but the performance makes it clear that this is a fantasy all girls can share. The unison singing of this line thus supports the idea that group membership could embolden girls to express their desires and needs. Once again, the recipient of the girl's love is a bad boy, with dirty fingernails, ever-present sunglasses, and tight pants; although an affinity for motorcycles and gangs is not made explicit, the hero's similarity to "Jimmy" in "Leader of the Pack" makes this a possibility. This song, then, portrays a dangerous hoodlum positioned carefully in the street, and it celebrates the self-assured bravado of a girl, whom we can imagine marching uninvited up to her beloved in full view of his gang of friends (and hers, as the backing vocals attest) in order to mark her turf with a noisy, possessive kiss.

Other examples of girls transgressing propriety to take the lead in romantic relationships occur with the Marvelettes' 1962 "Beechwood 4-5789," in which the protagonist gently but firmly teaches a boy how to woo her and ask for her phone number; with the Shirelles' 1960 "Tonight's the Night," in which a girl breathlessly anticipates a romantic evening with a boy; and with the Chiffons' 1963 hit "He's So Fine," in which a gang of girls plots to win the affections of a particularly fine specimen of boy. This latter song introduced the vocables phrase "doo lang doo lang doo lang" into the lexicon of girl talk discussed in Chapter 2, and it is also famous for subconsciously inspiring George Harrison's first solo hit, "My Sweet Lord," in 1970.[12] The Chiffons began as a trio of thirteen- and fourteen-year-old girls who met their manager, Ronnie Mack, when he came scouting for talent at their Bronx high school. After some minor successes, the group—now bolstered with a fourth singer, Sylvia Peterson—recorded Mack's "He's So Fine," a song he had been trying to sell to more established acts for some time. With lead singer Judy Craig (now sixteen) declaring "I don't know how I'm gonna do it, but I'm gonna make him mine" and itemizing the boy's charms to her appreciative backing vocalists, the song made it clear that girls were perfectly capable of taking an aggressive lead in romance. The bold stance of "He's So Fine" garnered enough enthusiasm to earn it the number-one position on both the pop and R&B charts in early 1963.

Given the pressures of demure feminine behavior in a culture of respectable containment that I analyzed in Part 4, it is hardly surprising that songs like these represented exciting possibilities for the girls who listened to them. I do not want to suggest naïvely that these tiny insurrections signaled equality between teenage girls and boys—it has not escaped my attention that all of these bold statements revolve around heterosexual romance and that having the validation of some kind of boyfriend is the necessary prerequisite for rebellion. However, against the backdrop of an association of girls with domestic, closed spaces and an emphasis on passive, meek behavior with only the nicest boys, so strong in communities with middle-class values, it is clear that songs about outcast boyfriends, and songs wherein girls took the initiative to act on their own desires, must be understood as resistant to the rigid boundaries that confined girls.

Moreover, if breaking with the rules of home only in order to become the devoted consort in another patriarchal relationship seems a partial liberation at best, the girl group repertoire also includes songs that positioned girls standing apart from the confines of conventional heterosexual relationships. In most cases, the narratives of these songs take the end of a romance as their point of departure, portraying girls who venture outside the domestic sphere because of grief or—in the Angels' 1963 "My Boyfriend's Back"—outrage. While disappointment in romance is, in songs like this, presented as the most acceptable (perhaps the only acceptable) cause for girls' disruptive behavior, the fact remains that these songs depict girls going out into the world to try and resolve injury or injustice unfairly meted out by boys.

In the Angels' "My Boyfriend's Back," the dangerous boyfriend is invoked to restore a girl's reputation. Listeners witness a girl bursting into male territory to scold a boy who has been gossiping about her; she triumphantly reports that her boyfriend is back and that the hour of her vengeance is nigh, and backing voices quickly confirm her self-righteousness. The spoken introduction to the song indicates that the girl has been a victim of circumstances not unlike those that befell the biblical Susanna—a boy has taken advantage of her boyfriend's absence to make advances and, finding himself rebuffed, has spread malicious rumors about her infidelity.

Although the song purports to be about the beating the boyfriend will shortly bestow on the gossiping boy, and thus might suggest that only he has the power and authority to right the wrongs perpetrated, it is the strength of the girls' indignation and fury that dominates. Lead singer Peggy Santiglia and backing singers the Allbut sisters, Barbara and Phyllis, have all perfected the slightly nasal, whiny vocal sound of petulant teenage girls, even though all three singers were in their early twenties and were experienced vocalists who had performed in Broadway musicals and numerous recording sessions—Barbara Allbut studied vocal performance formally at the prestigious Juilliard School of Music until her career as an Angel demanded her full attention.[13] The main melodic figure used in this song is built around small, descending intervals of a fourth and a second, and it closely resembles the kind of sing-song whine used in childish taunting, further fostering a connection to young people and immature communication methods. Finally, the handclaps heard prominently throughout the song enact a variation of the girl group beat, helping to erase any doubt that this record should be considered part of the genre in spite of the middle-class and adult appearance of the singers.

Furthermore, in the last charting single of an eight-year career, 1968's "Destination: Anywhere," the Marvelettes presented the narrative of a girl who ventures alone into the world in flight from heartbreak. While the song can hardly be described as cheerful, it conveys determination and courage on the part of the girl, who stubbornly insists on a train ticket to "anywhere" in spite of the ticket agent's dismay. The girl's dogged efforts to get away from her painful circumstances, and her willingness to trust to fate in choosing a place to make a fresh start, evoke the romantic figure of the lone, wanderer hero who broods over mysterious injuries as he roams a melancholy landscape; such a character is encountered in (among other sources) the Band's song "The Weight," released in the same year as "Destination: Anywhere." When the Marvelettes adopted the stance of an aloof, brooding, and, above all, *masculine* archetype, they challenged assumptions about conventional gender roles and appropriate options for "nice" girls, suggesting that they too were capable of striding off alone into the sunset.

In "I'd Much Rather Be with the Girls," Donna Lynn articulates a tart response to a boy who has abandoned her, by rhapsodizing over the pleasures of going out with girlfriends. Backed by other female singers who confirm her statements, fourteen-year-old Lynn draws on her background as a Broadway singer/actress to produce an assertive, chest-dominated "belting" vocal sound that lends credibility to her stance. The song was written by Keith Richards and Rolling Stones manager Andrew Loog Oldham as "I'd Much Rather Be with the Boys," but the band decided not to release it themselves, perhaps because the unabashed celebration of homosociality seemed too risky for a group determined to assert their identity as sexually dangerous bad boys. In any case, the songwriters sold it instead to Mancunian beat band the Toggery Five.[14] The group was modestly successful with the song, and Donna Lynn subsequently transformed it into a girl's stirring declaration of independence, at once hearkening back to the Shirelles' unrepentant dismissal of a disappointing boy in their 1958 debut "I Met Him on a Sunday" (discussed in Chapter 2) and also anticipating the Spice Girls' cheeky 1996 celebration of girls' friendships, "Wannabe."

14

Girl Groups, the Road, and Public Record

Even a demure girl group song such as the Paris Sisters' dreamy 1961 "I Love How You Love Me" or the Supremes' 1964 "Baby Love" could be exciting and empowering to audiences of girls in the context of a concert. The mere fact of seeing girls on stage performing and earning the applause and approval of fans suggested the possibility of a life of glamour, adventure, and independence from the frustrations of conventional domesticity. When girl groups toured, giving concerts across North America and beyond, they presented irrefutable evidence that females could function in public space and could go boldly into new territories.

Girls on the Road

In the previous section I identified the respectability of many African American girl groups as crucial to their successes, and I want now to consider the implications of their careers as touring performers for an American society confronting its attitudes toward race in the late 50s and early 60s. The integrationist policies espoused by Civil Rights leaders such as Martin Luther King were predicated in large part on the notion of black Americans who could fit into mainstream society without disrupting its priorities. African Americans who were well spoken and well groomed, and who demonstrated their willingness to abide by established social values of hard work and clean living, were identified as figures who would inspire sympathy among whites. Thus, Southern Civil Rights activist Rosa Parks was elected to begin the famous bus boycott in Montgomery, Alabama, in 1956, because her local NAACP chapter believed that white America would sympathize most easily with a meek, soft-spoken woman with aching feet who was simply too weary to give up her seat. The perception of Parks as politically naïve was useful at the time—almost anyone could understand these actions of a poor, honest woman worn down by drudgery—but it became confining later on when Parks' agency and activism were downplayed in comparison to that of male peers such as Martin Luther King.[1]

Similarly, the polite, smiling girl groups whose voices were heard around the United States in the early 1960s were more easily accepted by conservative white, suburban parents who might have been alarmed to hear their daughters listening to records by black men.[2] Just as the six adolescent girls of the Little Rock Nine were carefully chosen by their community to integrate the Arkansas city's public high schools in 1957, becoming central in the rapprochement of black and white America, so too the voices of other African American girls participated in this work, even by singing "mere" pop songs.

And when these girl groups went on the road into the American South, they traveled through a country whose notions of the proper position of black people in society were shifting, slowly and agonizingly. In her famous autobiography *Lady Sings the Blues*, for example, jazz legend Billie Holiday describes with discomfiting candor the difficulties she experienced as a black woman touring the United States with the all-white Artie Shaw band in 1937; in addition to facing hostility and harassment from venue managers and audiences, Holiday alludes to innumerable instances in which hotels were unwilling to accommodate her and restaurants refused to serve her food except in the kitchen or alley. Although she emphasizes the supportiveness of her bandmates, she remarks wryly that "I got to the point where I hardly ever ate, slept, or went to the bathroom without having a major NAACP-type production."[3] Just so, white members of the all-female, mixed-race jazz band International Sweethearts of Rhythm frequently had to hide when police inspected their tour bus for signs of racial mixing during the 1940s.[4]

Responding to the international outrage that followed the 1955 lynching of fourteen-year-old Emmett Till in Mississippi, racist hostility toward African Americans actually intensified in many parts of the southern United States. Black performers who toured the country in the early 60s often faced grave dangers, in some cases because their tour buses, with their northern license plates, were mistaken for those of Freedom Riders agitating for voting rights. When Motown Records sent out its first touring revue in 1962, for example, their bus was shot at in Birmingham, Alabama. On this tour, Martha Reeves of Martha and the Vandellas recalls her shock at being seated on garbage cans behind restaurants to eat cold hot dogs on paper plates served through the kitchen window—raised in Detroit, she had never experienced this kind of Southern segregation.[5] Gladys Knight, a Southerner who had been performing nationally since the age of eight and was consequently a distinguished veteran before her group signed with Motown in 1966, remembers a youthful tour during which she and her colleagues were dragged from their bus and threatened by a group of white racists enraged by the black musicians' travel through their town.[6] La La Brooks of the Crystals recalls the discomforts of touring the South in the early 60s, echoing Billie Holiday's 1930s' travails with restaurants and public toilets; she also reports being barred from dressing rooms and changing into performance clothes in kitchens, shielded as much as possible from lascivious eyes by the bodies of her group members standing around her in a circle.[7]

The young girls who went on tour as members of girl groups thus ventured into a dangerous and hostile world, in which they were vulnerable to attack from both racists and sexual predators. In Chapter 1, I discussed the risks to girls of life on the road and stated that the very act of venturing out into public space could compromise a girl's respectability and generate assumptions about her sexual availability; this system of conventions, I argued, explains many of the differences between girls' and boys' musical training. The case of Georgia Dobbins, one-time lead singer of the Marvelettes who left the group before they signed with Motown, illustrates this dilemma: she recalls that her parents opposed her wish to be a performer because "by them being Christian, entertainment and nightclub life was out of the question. That was unacceptable. Back then they'd call you 'fast,' 'no good,' 'won't amount to anything.'"[8] Furthermore, since most girl group performers were high school students, going on the road often entailed jeopardizing their education, and some parents of girl group singers could not countenance allowing their daughters to tour.

Considering the risks to education, reputation, and personal safety, then, it is surprising that so many girl groups did participate in tours, such as Murray "the K" Kaufmann's revues, the 1962 Motown Revue, Dick Clark's Caravan of Stars, and others. Why would these girls and young women enter into such a difficult life? Motown solo artist Mary Wells recalls that "until Motown in Detroit, there were three big careers for a black girl: babies, the factories, or day work. Period."[9] Thus, the life of a touring entertainer, fraught as it was with risks and dangers, represented the possibility of something better for teenage girls whose other options were few, and unattractive at best. In her reflections on the experiences of women in rock, journalist Gerri Hershey identifies the lure of the road as a crucial aspect of a life in rock'n'roll, connecting its siren call with the appeal of performing, drawing attention to oneself and being heard, and hungering for a life beyond one's immediate surroundings and expectations. She ruefully acknowledges the incompatibility of this lifestyle with the conventional responsibilities of femininity, drawing on her own experiences leaving home in order to pursue an interview opportunity: "With the car service honking outside, I peered down at two small faces and announced, 'Mommy's going on the road. Listen to Daddy. I'll call and say goodnight. Okay, gotta go.'"[10]

Furthermore, the need to be heard, to raise one's voice and express one's creative self, evidently sustained many performers through experiences that were exhausting and uncomfortable at best, terrifying and life threatening at worst. Within the context of an actual performance, former Marvelette Katherine Anderson remembers the anxiety that arose from performing in front of segregated audiences, with black listeners roped off from white ones, during Motown's 1962 Revue tour when she was eighteen: "You try to do a good show but the bottom line is, your heart's racing because you don't know what is going to occur because you're in a whole, totally different area. It's like being abandoned, on your own in the middle of nowhere, and not being able to see rescuers for a good little while. We didn't feel that we were going to have that much support as far as rescuers if it came down to it. We had to try to protect ourselves."[11]

Fellow Motown alumna Annette Beard of the Vandellas recalls of the same tour that all Motown artists generally eschewed whatever dressing room accommodation was available to them when not performing, opting instead to stay at the sides of the stage where their presence provided some measure of reassuring support to those singing.[12]

The most famous instance of a girl group performance being connected to political unrest is, of course, Martha and the Vandellas' experience touring in 1967 with their hit "Dancing in the Street" (1964). As Suzanne Smith elucidates in the opening paragraphs of her examination of Motown and Detroit's cultural politics, the trio was actually in the midst of performing this and other songs at Detroit's Fox Theater in July 1967 when a stage manager interrupted with the news that riots were erupting in the city's streets. Lead singer Martha Reeves announced this shocking development as calmly as she could, advising audience members to get home quickly and safely, and the singers themselves left town immediately to continue on to their next performance engagement. Their next stop, however, was Newark, New Jersey, where rioting also broke out, and the rest of the tour was fraught with further possibilities of more danger and violence. Moreover, the group's three-year-old hit song, "Dancing in the Street," became inextricably linked with the riots in many news reports, and some commentators even identified the song as a call to uprising, suggesting that Martha and Vandellas were militant leaders along the lines of Black Nationalist Malcolm X.[13] The song's perky groove, bright instrumentation, gospel-styled call-and-response vocals, and celebratory lyrics may make this notion seem absurd to listeners today, but the episode affords us valuable insight into the brittle political climate of the United States in the mid-60s. It also demonstrates clearly that girl groups and their cheerful pop confections were implicated in the political struggles of the 1960s far more than many histories of the decade generally acknowledge, as I noted in the introduction.

The harrowing experiences of these young female performers undoubtedly educated them about racism and sexual menace in U.S. culture, and those able to endure the trials were certainly the stronger for them. If some contemporary parents can scarcely contemplate exposing their adolescent daughters to this kind of danger, Ralph Ellison's explanation of how the teenagers of the Little Rock Nine could be sent alone into angry racist mobs in 1957 serves as a blunt rebuke. As Vicky Lebeau reports in her analysis of the Little Rock

Martha and the Vandellas in 1966. Courtesy of Photofest.

episode, Ellison argued that in the case of a black child "the best form of protection may well be pain; 'the child is expected to face the terror and contain his fear and anger precisely because he is a Negro American.…It is a harsh requirement, but if he fails this basic test, his life will be even harsher.'"[14] One of the young female informants for journalist Peggy Orenstein's investigative study of girlhood in the early 1990s echoes this idea in recounting how she was forcibly restrained by a store security guard who caught her shoplifting:

> I was yelling "Let me go!" and this guy was choking me and I couldn't breathe and my pants was falling down and everyone was looking at me…and this black lady, maybe twenty-five years old, yells, "Don't cry! Don't cry! You let him choke you, but you don't cry!"…He was white, or maybe Mexican, and I'm black…and when you're black, you're supposed to be strong, so I tried to hold my tears in.[15]

The importance of remaining calm and dignified in the face of hostility and violence are central to the education of a black youth, and the parents of black girl singers who wanted to tour may well have considered these opportunities for facing this rite of passage.

Nevertheless, many parents of girl group singers, particularly those invested in middle-class ideals, would insist on chaperones on these tours, sometimes serving in this capacity themselves if no suitable alternative could be found. The presence of a parental or other chaperone on the tour bus often underscored the distance between girl singers and "real" rock'n'rollers, as Arlene Smith of the Chantels implies in her recollection of touring with Alan Freed:

> I was miserable. We had tutors and a chaperone, who happened to be my father. He was really diligent, I can tell you; but the more he cared, the more the resentment built up. There was a distance between me and the other girls because of him.... We were very well protected. People were instructed not to speak to us.[16]

Like Maxine Powell running a finishing school for Motown performers, Smith's father attempted to maintain standards of respectability for his daughter and her friends even in the midst of a rock'n'roll tour. The discomfort Arlene Smith experienced stemmed from the seemingly irreconcilable demands of keeping up with school work and adhering to her father's notion of how a "good" girl ought to behave, while at the same time participating fully in rock'n'roll youth culture and demonstrating her commitment to the life of a musician. Tellingly, Phil Spector assumed something like this protective, fatherly role when he sent the Ronettes on tour with the Rolling Stones in 1964, telegramming Stones manager Andrew Loog Oldham with explicit instructions that rock's bad boys were forbidden to fraternize with the teenage girl singers.[17]

Groups that toured without a parental chaperone were not altogether to be envied, of course. Perhaps largely because the Weisses' father had died when they were very young, the Shangri-Las went out on the road on their own, and Mary Weiss asserts that the group's reputation as tough girls was a useful defense strategy in deflecting unwelcome attention from men they encountered in their travels. She also recalls a Texas performance with James Brown in 1964, where a security guard threatened her with a gun because she had used the bathroom marked "Colored Girls" that was located at a more convenient distance from the stage than the one reserved for white girls.[18]

Because of their unprecedented chart success with "Will You Love Me Tomorrow?" in 1961, the Shirelles in particular came to be in great demand on touring revues, and they served as pioneers in this arena. Group member Beverly Lee recalls touring the so-called chitlin' circuit with appearances at such legendary vaudeville theatres as the Regal in Chicago, the Royal in Baltimore, and the Apollo in Harlem, sites where such iconic entertainers as Cab Calloway, Bert Williams, Ella Fitzgerald, and the Isley Brothers had performed, and where Sam Cooke and James Brown produced famous live recordings in 1960 and 1961, respectively.[19] Lee reports that her Baptist parents "were concerned about these young kids going off on tour…but they didn't have to worry. I was a good daughter."[20]

Nevertheless, the parents of the Shirelles insisted on chaperones on the group's first tour, roles that were ultimately filled by raunchy blues shouters Etta James and Ruth Brown. It is perhaps a mark of the parents' sheltered middle-class lifestyle that they were naïve enough to accept these women as sufficiently matronly to protect their daughters' virtue. Lee fondly recalls the rock'n'roll education she received from James and Brown:

> They taught us a lot, broke us in. When we got on the bus, we were all dressed up in high heels and crinoline skirts. Can you imagine seven hours in a bus in a crinoline skirt? I was seventeen; I though we looked so grown-up and sophisticated. They were so nice to us, though; they just told us, you can't travel like this. You've got to wear jeans, be comfortable, otherwise you'll get tired. They were great friends and great ladies.[21]

Note that Lee bestows the accolade of "ladies" in her praise of these women, although the lessons she learned from them were actually about the importance of abandoning ladylike demeanor in order to survive the discomfort of the road—hardly a proper lifestyle for ladies in the first place, as we have seen. The importance of ladylike respectability is so ingrained in female culture that this kind of compliment seems obligatory, even when demonstrably inapt.

For the audiences who saw girl groups on tour, these performers were living proof of the existence of girls who could survive, and even succeed, in a world that was generally hostile to young females, particularly non-white ones. Even when girl group acts performed conventional, ladylike roles of pining girlfriends and dutiful daughters, their very presence on stage in front of an attentive crowd served to challenge accepted ideas about respectable femininity preferring to avoid the spotlight. Women like writer Kay Sloan recall the exhilaration of outrunning security guards in order to seek out their idols the Beatles as young teens and learning from this experience that they had the power to defy authorities they perceived to be unjust.[22] Just so, fans of girl groups who witnessed their triumphs could be inspired to raise their own voices and resist the status quo. It should perhaps not surprise us, then, to note that girl groups and their repertoire were admired and emulated by several important bands of the New York punk scene in the mid—70s. Musicians associated with this oppositional, often deliberately provocative music style found much to inspire them in decade-old recordings by groups like the Shangri-Las.

Girl Groups and Punk Aesthetics

The New York Dolls were not, of course, the first male group to perform girl group songs—I noted in Chapter 9 that the Beach Boys, the Beatles, and many other male groups of the early 60s scored hits with cover versions of material from this repertoire. Nevertheless, the Dolls' quotation, in the mid-70s, of the spoken dialogue from an old chestnut like the Shangri-Las' "Give Him a Great Big Kiss" in their song "Looking for a Kiss," together with their flamboyant, gender-bending stage attire of teased-up hair, tight pants, and high-heeled boots, suggests that their choice of girl group material aspired toward different goals in terms of listenership and aesthetic.

Donna Gaines asks rhetorically: "Actually, with the grease and glamour hair-dos, all douched up in frilly blouses, what were the New York Dolls anyway but a hard-rock girl-group tribute band?"[23] Similarly, other participants in the New York punk movement have argued that their goal was to restore adolescent enthusiasm and fun to a rock culture that had grown pompous and pretentious. For example, John Doe of the Los Angeles band X recalls the high-spirited camaraderie of the legendary scene at New York's CBGB's in 1977, where he saw bands such as the Ramones: "It was about reclaiming rock'n'roll. It was reclaiming rock'n'roll to a simple message, and wasn't a big, bloated, corporate, limousine, cocaine-ridden bunch of shit. To me, [the Ramones] were pop music, they were what was played on the radio in the sixties. That's what I heard. I thought they were the most commercial band in the world."[24]

The connections between 70s punk and early 60s rock'n'roll are often obscured when we consider punk solely as an angry, confrontational genre, too challenging for the tastes of mainstream radio DJs or sheltered teenage listeners. While political incisiveness and deliberate outrageousness would indeed become crucial components of punk, particularly in the wake of the British band the Sex Pistols, much of the music emerging from the early scene in New York stays faithful to the energy and style of bands like the Beach Boys, the early Beatles, and many girl groups, with upbeat rhythms; simple, catchy melodies; minimal rock'n'roll instrumentation; and two-and-a-half minute songs about girls, going to the beach, attending high school, and other typically adolescent themes. It is no coincidence that the Ramones' 1980 album *End of the Century* was produced by Phil Spector; even the band's name, and the fact that all members adopted the surname Ramone, can be interpreted as a nod to girl groups and other 60s' ensembles made up of family members. What is more, the album actually includes a recording of the Ronettes' "Baby I Love You," an affectionate tribute both to the record producer and to the girl group.

Furthermore, the New York punk band Blondie featured magazine-beautiful Deborah Harry as lead singer, fronting a group of males who dressed carefully like an early 60s beat band. Harry's rendition of the pinup girl was conspicuously flawed, as Charlotte Grieg notes: "[T]here was a tackiness about her bleached blonde hair with its black roots, her cheap mini dresses, and her big sunglasses that was an ironic comment on the sex goddesses of the sixties."[25] Before forming Blondie, Harry had been part of a female harmony group called the Stilettos, singing original songs in the style of 60s girl groups, and the demo record that Blondie sent out to record companies in hopes of a contract included a version of the Shangri-Las' "Out in the Streets"; the band ultimately made their first commercial recording with Richard Gottehrer, who had produced the Angels' "My Boyfriend's Back" in 1963.[26] The band's debt to the music of their teenage years (Harry was born in 1945, the same year as Ronnie Bennett/Spector) is further evident in that their first successful release was a gender-bending version of doo wop quintet Randy and the Rainbows' 1963 "Denise."

What is more, many of the band's original songs are stylistically and thematically reminiscent of girl group material: their 1976 debut album included original songs such as "X Offender," "In the Flesh," and "Rip Her to Shreds," presenting ironic, camp versions of the 60s girl group sound. Ensuing albums featured songs like "(I'm Always Touched by Your) Presence, Dear," "Sunday Girl," "Hanging on the Telephone," and "Dreaming," all of which served to foreground the influence of girl groups and girl culture on the band's work.[27] These songs evoke teenage girl culture with themes of girlish gossip and pining at home, dreaming that a boy will notice; what is more, the musical language often involves distinctive girl group sounds such as the heartbeat snare drum pattern, dialogic vocals (all created by Harry), and a breathy, sweet vocal timbre that Harry uses selectively. In both "Denise" and "Sunday Girl," furthermore, Harry includes a verse in French; I interpret this as a nod to the œuvre of British pop princesses of the 1960s such as Petula Clark or Dusty Springfield, who often made use of their English-accented schoolgirl French to add charm to their songs.

The members of Blondie and other participants in the punk scene had the opportunity to commune with one of the groups they remembered so fondly when the Shangri-Las reunited for a live performance at CBGB's in the summer of 1977, the very year in which punk bands such as Blondie, the Ramones, Talking Heads, and the New York Dolls were beginning to form a community based around that bar. The group (now irrevocably a trio, due to Mary Ganser's 1971 death from encephalitis) had been working together for a few months with the vague idea of releasing an album of new material when they impulsively decided to perform live. The projected album was to have been produced by Andy Paley for Sire Records, the label responsible for punk acts the Ramones, Talking Heads, the Replacements, and eventually Madonna (until she founded her own label, Maverick Records); Sire's founder Seymour Stein had worked briefly at Red Bird Records and was eager to rekindle the career of a group he had known then. Producer Paley reports that the live performance came about on the spur of the moment:

> I called [CBGB's owner] Hilly Kristal and told him what was up, and he said, "Whatever you want. There's nothing happening here tonight." I called Jay Dee Daugherty and Lenny Kaye [drummer and guitarist, respectively, for the Patti Smith Group] to play, and called [rock critic] Lester Bangs and [photographer] Roberta Bayley....[I]t was really, really fun. Everyone had a great time. I remember Lester Bangs jumping up and down screaming, telling me how great it was. Debbie Harry, you know, everybody was really impressed. We had a really good crowd.[28]

Punk's camp revival of the girl group style is evidently steeped in nostalgia, as John Doe's remarks and Blondie's and the New York Dolls' performance choices make clear. Born between the mid-1940s and mid-1950s, punk artists like these—as well as legendary rock critic Lester Bangs and noted sociologist Donna Gaines—were just old enough to look back fondly on the heyday of the girl groups and 60s' rock'n'roll in general. Their efforts to recapture the effervescence of that sound indicate a longing for a hazily remembered time when life, like rock'n'roll, seemed to be simpler (although in many cases, surely, rose-tinted representations of childhood are also an effort to revise childhoods that were not particularly happy). In much the same way, teenagers at the turn of the twenty-first century often display a sentimental enthusiasm for the 1980s' popular culture of their childhoods, often to the bewilderment of members of the generation that actually came of age during that decade.

Gayle Wald argues compellingly that nostalgia played an important role in a later punk movement centered around girls and girl culture, in her discussion of the early 90s' riot grrrl scene. The riot grrrl movement famously emerged from the college student community of Olympia, Washington, and it involved deliberately amateurish musical aesthetics (much like 1970s' punk); outspoken activism on girls' issues such as incestuous abuse, eating disorders, and rape; and an insistence on creating space for girls and women within punk culture (the band Bikini Kill, for example, decreed that male audience members at their shows remain at the back and sides of the performance space, reserving the choicest spots in front of the stage for girls and women). Calling for "Revolution Girl Style Now!" participants in the riot grrrl scene drew on their university education in feminist theory to create a network of resistance to the oppression of girls.[29] Riot grrrl juxtaposed these bold strategies with clichéd images of cloyingly sweet preadolescent girlhood, such as baby-doll dresses, stuffed animals, childhood photographs of musicians on album covers (Hole's explosive 1994 *Live through This*), and song lyrics recalling childish toys such as tricycles (Bikini Kill's 1993 "Rebel Girl"). Wald observes that

> Such a recuperative iconography of girlhood contrasts—markedly, in some cases—with the music itself, which regularly explores themes of incest, the violence of heteronormative beauty culture, and the patriarchal infantalization and sexualization of girls: in short, themes that conjure not a *lost* innocence, a fall from childhood grace, but an innocence that was not owned or enjoyed, a grace that was denied. The performance of nostalgia complicates and extends the Riot Grrrl performance of outrage at patriarchal abuse; in other words, invoking a yearned-for innocence and lightheartedness that retroactively rewrite the script of childhood.[30]

It is surely significant that both the 70s punk scene and the early 90s riot grrrl movement invoked the figures of adolescent and preadolescent girls even as the main participants in the scenes were themselves past adolescence, old enough and sufficiently educated to look back at their teenage years with critical eyes. Indeed, between the mid-1960s and late 1990s, teenage girls themselves seemed almost to vanish entirely from the North American popular music landscape. With the important exceptions of artists such as Debbie Gibson and Tiffany in the late 1980s, musical representations of female adolescence during this period tended to be ironic and performed by young adult women.[31]

The voices of actual teenage girls returned to dominate the airwaves in the mid-1990s, beginning with the 1994 success of a fifteen-year-old African American singer named Brandy. In the following year, a mixed-race vocal ensemble called the Spice Girls—harbingers of what we might call a girl renaissance—emerged with "Wannabe," the first debut single by a female group ever to enter the British charts at number one, and one which sparked a hugely successful international career for the quintet. Although the group members were themselves well into their twenties at the time of their debut, their performance of teenage girlhood made them popular with an audience comprised overwhelmingly of adolescent and preadolescent female fans. In their wake sprang up numerous girl singers actually in their teen years, including Britney Spears, Christina Aguilera, Beyoncé Knowles and Destiny's Child, Jessica Simpson, Hilary Duff, and Avril Lavigne (albeit with markedly different musical aesthetics) all addressing a newly enormous teenage market alongside adolescent boy bands such as Hanson, NSync, and the Backstreet Boys.

"Be a Spice Girl, Not a Nice Girl"[32]

The return of teen pop to center stage of popular culture at the turn of the twenty-first century is one of many cultural phenomena oddly reminiscent of the 1950s and 60s. Once again, mainstream Top Forty radio was dominated by the unsteady voices of singers in the midst of the physical transition from childhood to adulthood, and their rejection of many of the values of middle-class respectability and appropriately demure girlish behavior sparked heated public debate. A widespread fascination with teenage girls in particular extended also to American television, with immensely popular programs such as *Sabrina the Teenage Witch* (1996–2003), *Clueless* (1996–99), *Buffy the Vampire Slayer* (1997–2003), *Lizzie McGuire* (2001–4), and *Joan of Arcadia* (2003–5), among others, focusing on the trials and travails of pretty white girls negotiating their high school years; teen pop sensation Brandy also had a highly successful television career with her comedy series *Moesha* (1996–2001), which featured the singer in the title role as an attractive, upper-middle-class, black teenager. In a further, striking parallel to the teen idols of the late 1950s and early 1960s, many of the television and music stars of this period began their careers as child performers on Disney programs such as *The New Mickey Mouse Club* (Britney Spears, Christina Aguilera, and Justin Timberlake were all performers on this program, with Jessica Simpson narrowly missing a position; Hilary Duff's television series was created for the Disney Channel, and Brandy starred in a Disney film version of the Rodgers and Hammerstein musical *Cinderella* in 1997), much as Annette Funicello, Johnny Crawford, and others had done some forty years earlier.

Yet the girls represented in these fictional texts are understood to participate in 1990s culture, a time period understood variously as the post-feminist era and also as the age of third-wave feminism, and they generated public interest because of their courage and commitment to resisting injustice (often aided, it is true, by supernatural strength, so that the viewer's sense of appropriate body types for pert, pretty girls was not disrupted by unsightly muscles). Even within the mundane world, former Spice Girl Geri Halliwell was appointed a Goodwill Ambassador to the United Nations Population Fund in 1998, with a mission to advocate for "reproductive health care, gender issues, and the empowerment of women throughout the world."[33] This assignment underscores the importance and authority of a figure like Halliwell to girls and women worldwide, even though she and the other Spice Girls were often excoriated as vapid bimbos and poor singers who performed mediocre songs and reinscribed the worst (i.e., most girly) stereotypes about girls.

Earlier in 1998, the Spice Girls released a feature film called *Spice World*, a project that evidently owed a great deal to the Beatles' classic 1964 *Hard Day's Night*, and that similarly appealed to very young girls in its depiction of a zany pop group at the height of stardom. At the seven o'clock opening night show I attended in Westwood, California, many prepubescent girls in the audience were dressed in pajamas, obviously destined for bed as soon as their parents took them home. These girls behaved for the most part like any other audience at a film, until the final credits began to roll and their excitement got the better of them. While the Surround Sound piped in the strains of "The Lady Is a Vamp," a dozen girls sprang squealing from their various seats around the auditorium and rushed to the front of the theater, where they pranced in front of the film screen, singing and enacting all the suggestive bump and grind moves that the music required before being led away by scolding parents. The sight of very small girls in flannel nighties performing the roles of pouty seductresses was certainly disconcerting, but it struck me forcefully that this tiny insurrection could well prove to be a pivotal moment in their coming of age. Shrieking "girl power!" with like-minded strangers may very well have begun to foster in them a thrilling sense of female collectivity and strength. Just so, the girl groups of the 1960s promoted the values of girl solidarity, mutual support, and strength in numbers, and they should be considered anew for their role in the development of youth culture and their importance as models for girls and women.

Notes

Preface and Acknowledgments

1. Lisa Lewis, ed., *The Adoring Audience: Fan Culture and Popular Media* (New York: Routledge, 1992).
2. Gage Averill, *Four Parts, No Waiting: A Social History of American Barbershop Harmony* (Oxford: Oxford University Press, 2003). See also Laurie Stras's "The Voice of the Beehive: Vocal Technique at the Turn of the 60s," in Laurie Stras, ed., *She's So Fine: Whiteness, Femininity, Adolescence and Class in 1960s Music* (Durham, N.C.: Duke University Press, forthcoming).

Introduction

1. The Girl Guides were created as a sister organization to the Boy Scouts in 1910. The American version sought to emphasize itself as distinct from the larger organization and renamed itself the Girl Scouts in 1913. For an examination of this process and its meaning for American girl culture, see Lauren Tedesco, "Making a Girl into a Scout: Americanizing Scouting for Girls," in Sherrie A. Inness, ed., *Delinquents and Debutantes: Twentieth-Century American Girls' Cultures* (New York: New York University Press, 1999), 19–39.
2. Inness, *Delinquents and Debutantes*, "Introduction."
3. Nick Foley, "Barbie All the Rage for Irate Girls," *The Age*, 20 December 2005. http://www.theage.com.au/news/national/barbie-all-the-rage-for-irate-girls/2005/12/19/1134840798477.html, accessed January 10, 2006.
4. Some important texts of girl studies include: Angela McRobbie, ed., *Gender and Generation* (London: MacMillan Publishers Ltd., 1984); *Feminism and Youth Culture: From 'Jackie' to 'Just Seventeen'* (London: MacMillan Publishers Ltd., 1997); Michelle Fine, *Disruptive Voices: The Possibilities of Feminist Research* (Albany: State University of New York Press, 1988); Valerie Walkerdine, *Schoolgirl Fictions* (London: Verso, 1990); *Daddy's Girl: Young Girls and Popular Culture* (Cambridge, Mass.: Harvard University Press, 1997); Wini Breines, *Young, White and Miserable: Growing up Female in the Fifties* (Boston: Beacon Press, 1992); Carol Gilligan and Lyn Mikel Brown, *Meeting at the Crossroads: Women's Psychology and Girls' Development* (Cambridge, Mass.: Harvard Univer-

sity Press, 1992); Lyn Mikel Brown, *Raising Their Voices: The Politics of Girls' Anger* (Cambridge, Mass.: Harvard University Press, 1998); Sherrie Inness, ed., *Delinquents and Debutantes: Twentieth Century American Girls' Cultures* (New York: New York University Press, 1998); Peggy Orenstein, *Schoolgirls: Young Women, Self-Esteem and the Confidence Gap* (New York: Doubleday, 1994); Joan Jacobs Brumberg, *The Body Project: An Intimate History of American Girls* (New York: Random House, 1997); Mary Pipher, *Reviving Ophelia: Saving the Selves of Adolescent Girls* (New York: Ballantine, 1995); and Rachel Simmons, *Odd Girl Out: The Hidden Culture of Aggression in Girls* (New York: Harcourt, 2002).

5. Durwood Ball, "Popular Music," in David Farber and Beth Bailey, eds., *The Columbia Guide to America in the 1960s* (New York: Columbia University Press, 2001), 288–96. There is no essay in the collection addressing other genres of music.
6. Todd Gitlin, *The Sixties: Years of Hope, Days of Rage* (New York: Bantam, 1987), 287–88.
7. Susan Douglas, *Where the Girls Are: Growing up Female with the Mass Media* (New York: Random House, 1994), 5.
8. For further analysis of girls as fans in the 1960s, see Norma Coates, "Teenyboppers, Groupies, and Other Grotesques: Girls and Women and Rock Culture in the 1960s and Early 1970s," *Journal of Popular Music Studies* 15, no. 1 (2003): 65–94; and Barbara Ehrenreich, Elizabeth Hess, and Gloria Jacobs, "Beatlemania: Girls Just Want to Have Fun," in Lisa Lewis, ed., *The Adoring Audience: Fan Culture and Popular Media* (New York: Routledge, 1992), 84–106. Lisa Rhodes, *Electric Ladyland: Women and Rock Culture* (Philadelphia: University of Pennsylvania Press, 2005).
9. Mary Weiss, personal communication, June 19, 2006.
10. Susan McClary, *Feminine Endings: Music, Gender and Sexuality* (Minneapolis: University of Minnesota Press, 1991).
11. Dave Hickey, *Air Guitar: Essays on Art and Democracy* (Los Angeles: Art Issues Press, 1997), 15.
12. Susan McClary, "Terminal Prestige: The Case of Avant-Garde Music Composition," *Cultural Critique* 12 (1989): 57–81.
13. Andreas Huyssen, "Mass Culture as Woman: Modernism's Other," *After the Great Divide: Modernism, Mass Culture, Postmodernism* (Bloomington: Indiana University Press, 1986), 44–62.
14. *One Kiss Can Lead to Another: Girl Group Sounds, Lost and Found*, 2005, Rhino Records R2 74645, and www.spectropop.com. The Rhino CD box set has been reviewed in, among other places, the Dutch newspaper *Het Financieele Dagblad*. Hans Hoes, "Sirenen van de sixties," *Het Financieele Dagblad*, 3 December, 2005, pp. 24–25.
15. The phenomenon of young females singing together for the delectation of spectators has also occurred prior to the 1960s, of course; the famed Three Ladies of Ferrara are an example from late sixteenth-century Italy, and the Three Ladies in Mozart's *Die Zauberflöte* operate in a similar way, trading on Homeric depictions of Sirens twining their melodies

around one another in order to seduce listeners. In twentieth-century North American culture, before the rise of those notions of female adolescence that interest me, female groups such as the Andrews Sisters and the McGuire Sisters developed the demure smiles, matching dresses, and unpretentious singing styles that later became features of girl groups. However, I do not consider these kinds of ensemble girl groups themselves, both because their musical language is so different from early 60s rock'n'roll and because they were not understood as teenagers addressing a teenaged audience.

16. Mary Russo, "Female Grotesques: Carnival and Theory," reprinted in Katie Conboy, Nadia Medina, and Sarah Stanbury, eds., *Writing on the Body: Female Embodiment and Feminist Theory* (New York: Columbia University Press, 1997), 318–36.
17. Earlier writings on girl groups have been invaluable sources for me in my research. Most of the large-scale published work that exists has come from the fields of journalism or cultural studies, so that my interests as a musicologist allow me to elucidate different aspects of the girl-group phenomenon. For other studies of girl groups, see: Alan Betrock, *Girl Groups: The Story of a Sound* (New York: Delilah Books, 1982); Charlotte Grieg, *Will You Still Love Me Tomorrow?: Girl Groups from the 50s On* (London: Virago, 1989); Susan Douglas, "Why the Shirelles Mattered," in *Where the Girls Are: Growing Up Female with the Mass Media* (New York: Random House, 1994), 83–99; and Patricia Juliana Smith, "'Ask Any Girl': Compulsory Heterosexuality and Girl Group Culture," in Kevin J.H. Dettmar and William Richey, eds., *Reading Rock and Roll: Authenticity, Appropriation, Aesthetics* (New York: Columbia University Press, 1999), 93–125. See also articles by musicologists: Barbara Bradby, "Do Talk and Don't Talk: The Division of the Subject in Girl-Group Music," in Simon Frith and Andrew Goodwin, eds., *On Record: Rock, Pop and the Written Word* (New York: Pantheon Books, 1990), 341–69; and Cynthia Cyrus, "Selling an Image: Girl Groups of the 1960s," *Popular Music* 22, no. 2 (2003): 173–93.

Part I

1. Mary Wilson, *Dreamgirl and Supreme Faith: My Life as a Supreme* (New York: Cooper Square Press, 1999).
2. Ibid.

Chapter 1

1. Jay Warner, *American Singing Groups: A History, 1940–1990* (New York: Da Capo, 1992), 104.

2. Charlotte Grieg, *Will You Still Love Me Tomorrow? Girl Groups from the Fifties On* (London: Virago, 1989), 11; and Alan Betrock, *Girl Groups: The Story of a Sound* (New York: Delilah Books, 1982), 9.
3. Michael Redmond and Steven West, liner notes to *The Best of the Chantels*, Rhino Records, R2 70954, 1990, 2; and Warner, *American Singing Groups*, 104.
4. Warner, *American Singing Groups*, 105.
5. Personal interview with Fanita James, December 18, 2004. The jubilee singing style practiced by James's father involved vocal groups modeled after the famous Fisk Jubilee Quartet. By at least the 1920s, these groups combined a restrained concert demeanor and trained vocal sound with the responsorial style of Baptist congregations and the grit of Pentecostal/Holiness singers. Horace Clarence Boyer, *The Golden Age of Gospel* (Urbana: University of Illinois Press, 2000), 29–35.
6. The group's name came from a rival Catholic school, St. Francis de Chantelle. Probably dismissing "the Paduas" as an undesirable name, the singers liked "Chantels" because of its resemblance to the French "chanter," meaning "to sing."
7. Betrock, *Girl Groups*, 10.
8. I thank my colleague Jennifer Bain for drawing on her expertise in chant to comment on this song.
9. Cited in Grieg, *Will You Still Love Me Tomorrow?*, 12. After her recording career as a Chantel, Smith attended the Juilliard School of Music, a fact that further confounds assumptions about untutored pop singers and "legitimate" music study.
10. Mary Wilson, *Dreamgirl & Supreme Faith: My Life as a Supreme* (New York: Cooper Square Press, 1999), 211.
11. See Lynn Abbott and Doug Seroff, *Out of Sight: The Rise of African American Popular Music, 1889–1895* (Jackson: University of Mississippi Press, 2002), 357–60.
12. Gage Averill, *Four Parts, No Waiting: A Social History of American Barbershop Singing* (Oxford: Oxford University Press, 2003), 11.
13. Jeffrey Melnick, "'Story Untold': The Black Men and White Sounds of Doo Wop," in *Whiteness: A Critical Reader*, ed. Mike Hill (New York: New York University Press, 1997), 134–50.
14. Ronnie Spector, with Vince Waldron. *Be My Baby: How I Survived Mascara, Miniskirts and Madness, or My Life as a Fabulous Ronette* (New York: Harmony Books, 1990), 13.
15. Cited in Grieg, *Will You Still Love Me Tomorrow?*, 15.
16. Averill, *Four Parts, No Waiting*, 98.
17. Laurie Stras, "The Voice of the Beehive" (paper presented at the Bucknell University Symposium on 60s Girl Singers, Lewisburg, Pennsylvania, September 2003), 1–16. I thank Laurie for making this version of her paper available to me.

18. Voices come free of charge to amateur musicians and were thus crucial to the rise of new genres in poor inner-city neighborhoods, but professional singers are another matter altogether. At Stax Records in Memphis, Jim Stewart found he could not afford to hire first-rate session singers during the 1960s and reluctantly used a horn section to substitute. Happily, the contributions of the Memphis Horns became an integral element of the Stax sound. Rob Bowman, *Soulsville USA: The Story of Stax Records* (New York: Schirmer Books, 1997), 98.
19. Cited in Gerri Hirshey, *Nowhere to Run: The Story of Soul Music* (New York: Da Capo Press, 1984), 35.
20. See Jeffrey Melnick's "'Story Untold'" for an examination of race and masculinity in doo-wop.
21. Simon Reynolds and Joy Press, *The Sex Revolts: Gender, Rebellion and Rock'n'Roll* (Cambridge, Mass.: Harvard University Press, 1995), 43–65.
22. See, among others: Susan Douglas, *Where the Girls Are: Growing up Female with the Mass Media* (New York: Times Books, 1994); Gayle Wald, "One of the Boys? Whiteness, Gender and Popular Music Studies," in *Whiteness: A Critical Reader*, ed. Mike Hill (New York: New York University Press, 1997), 151–67; and Sheila Whiteley, *Women and Popular Music: Sexuality, Identity and Subjectivity* (New York: Routledge, 2000).
23. Gayle Rubin, "The Traffic in Women: Notes on the 'Political Economy' of Sex," in *Toward an Anthropology of Women*, ed. Rayna Reiter (New York: Monthly Review Press, 1976), 157–210.
24. Elaine Tyler May, *Homeward Bound: American Families in the Cold War Era* (New York: Basic Books, 1988), 11.
25. Wini Breines, *Young, White and Miserable: Growing up Female in the Fifties* (Boston: Beacon Books, 1992), 137.
26. Ibid., xiv.
27. See Germaine Greer and Phil Sommerich, "Why Don't Women Buy CDs?" *BBC Music Magazine* (September 1994), 35–38; and Will Straw, "Sizing up Record Collections: Gender and Connoisseurship in Rock Music Culture," in *Sexing the Groove: Popular Music and Gender*, ed. Sheila Whitely (New York: Routledge, 1997), 3–17. The importance of having the right "look" for girls is examined more thoroughly in Part 2.
28. Angela McRobbie, "Dance and Social Fantasy," in *Gender and Generation*, eds. Angela McRobbie and Mica Nava (London: MacMillan, 1984), 130–61.
29. John Potter, *Vocal Authority: Singing Style and Ideology* (Cambridge: Cambridge University Press, 1998), 162. Potter's provocative observations usefully underscore the notion that successful musical performances in vernacular genres are indeed performances, artistic and carefully designed, and not merely the result of instinctual, innate ability that springs from the unschooled primitive.
30. Cited in Gerri Hirshey, *We Gotta Get Out of This Place: The True, Tough Story of Women in Rock* (New York: Atlantic Monthly Press, 2001), 55.

31. Grieg, *Will You Still Love Me Tomorrow?*, 16. Although Smith was inspired by the falsetto sound of Frankie Lymon, her own female soprano range extended at least an octave higher.
32. My thinking here is greatly influenced by the work of Laurie Stras on pop vocal technique in the 1960s, and I thank her for sharing unpublished versions of her work with me.
33. When Janis Joplin recorded her revisionist version of "Maybe" for her 1969 solo debut album *I Got Dem Ol' Kozmic Blues Again, Mama!*, she performed it in A-flat major.
34. Richie Unterberger, "Biography for Rosie and the Originals," *The All Music Guide*, allmusic.com, accessed June 21, 2005. Lennon actually recorded "Angel Baby" with producer Phil Spector in preparation for his 1975 *Rock and Roll*. The track was not included in the original version of *Rock and Roll* but was issued after Lennon's death.
35. Cited in Gillian Gaar, *She's a Rebel: The History of Women in Rock & Roll* (Seattle: Seal Press, 1992), 29.
36. I examine the strategies with which singers express anger in girl-group songs in "'He Hit Me, and I Was Glad': Violence, Masochism and Anger in Girl Group Music," in *She's So Fine: Whiteness, Femininity and Adolescence in 60s Pop*, Laurie Stras, ed. (Durham, N.C.: Duke University Press, forthcoming).
37. Gaar, *She's a Rebel*, 29. The Bobbettes eventually left Atlantic and recorded with six different labels during the 1960s, but with only moderate success. Warner, *American Singing Groups*, 81. "Mr. Lee" was included in the soundtrack to the 1986 Rob Reiner film *Stand by Me*, and other film fans may know the Bobbettes' "Love That Bomb" from the classic 1964 Peter Sellers' film *Dr. Strangelove*.
38. In fact, the Bobbettes recorded a version of this sequel while still under contract to Atlantic, but the record company shelved the song. This was perhaps the final straw in their strained relationship with the company, and they signed with a new label, where their first release was a new recording of "I Shot Mr. Lee." When this began to sell well, Atlantic was forced to release their first recording, so that two competing versions became available. Warner, *American Singing Groups*, 81.
39. Boyer, *The Golden Age of Gospel*, 11. See note 5 for Chapter 1.
40. Ibid., 30–47.
41. No author listed, http://www.iath.virginia.edu/utc/onstage/duncanhp.html, accessed June 9, 2005.
42. For a sophisticated reading of Topsy, see W. T. Lhamon Jr., *Raising Cain: Blackface Performance from Jim Crow to Hip Hop* (Cambridge, Mass.: Harvard University Press, 1998), 140–5.
43. Valerie Walkerdine, *Daddy's Girl: Young Girls and Popular Culture* (Cambridge, Mass.: Harvard University Press, 1997), 84.
44. Ibid., 93.
45. For a voice in the style of the Shirley Temple model, we might turn to recordings by the Supremes that feature Diana Ross's baby-soft cooing.

46. Walkerdine, *Daddy's Girl*, 162.

Chapter 2

1. Scepter's talent roster would include acts as disparate as Dionne Warwick, the Kingsmen, B. J. Thomas, and Chuck Jackson as well as the Shirelles.
2. Kyra D. Gaunt, "Translating Double-Dutch to Hip-Hop: The Musical Vernacular of Black Girls' Play," in *Language, Rhythm and Sound: Black Popular Cultures into the Twenty-First Century*, eds. Joseph K. Adjaye and Adrianne R. Andrews (Pittsburgh: University of Pittsburgh Press, 1997), 146–65.
3. Eve Harwood, "Go on Girl! Improvisation in African-American Girls' Singing Games," in *In the Course of Performance: Studies in the World of Musical Improvisation*, ed. Bruno Nettl (Chicago: University of Chicago Press, 1998), 113–125.
4. Gaunt, "Translating Double-Dutch to Hip-Hop," 150.
5. The use of nonsense syllables in vocal music is not, of course, an innovation of the girl groups or of doowop. We might also consider the "fa la las" and "hey nonny nonnies" of the English madrigal tradition and other European instances of syllables intending to mimic birds, animals, instruments, and street cries, as well as conspicuously *not* stating something ribald implied by other lyrics.
6. My analysis is influenced by Susan Youens' work on the shape of language in Debussy's *Trois Chansons de Bilitis*. Susan Youens, "Music, Verse, and 'Prose Poetry': Debussy's *Trois Chansons de Bilitis*," *Journal of Musicological Research* VII, no. 1 (1986: 69–94).
7. Charlotte Grieg, *Will You Still Love Me Tomorrow?: Girl Groups from the 50s On* (London: Virago, 1989), 62; and Alan Betrock, *Girl Groups: The Story of a Sound* (New York: Delilah Books, 1982), 92.
8. Grieg, *Will You Still Love Me Tomorrow?*, 62.
9. The Dixie Cups released only one album, but it was issued with three different covers and titles as their different singles waxed and waned in the Billboard charts. It was variously called *Chapel of Love*, *People Say*, and finally *Iko Iko*.
10. Hélène Cixous, "Le Rire de la Meduse," *LIArc* 61 (1975): 48.
11. Theodor Adorno, "The Curves of the Needle," *October* 55 (winter 1990): 48–55. For a feminist reading of this piece, see Barbara Engh, "Adorno and the Sirens: Tele-phono-graphic Bodies," in *Embodied Voices: Representing Female Vocality in Western Culture*, eds. Leslie Dunn and Nancy Jones (Cambridge: Cambridge University Press, 1994), 120–38.

12. Cited in Mary Bufwack and Robert Oermann, *Finding Her Voice: The Saga of Women in Country Music* (New York: Crown Publishing, 1993), 43. This accounts, according to the authors, for the fact that discs by folk singers at the turn of the century were predominantly male, even though folk song traditions were primarily the domain of women.
13. The ribbon microphone of the 1930s became popular with singers such as Bing Crosby because of its great sensitivity and ability to eliminate unwanted sounds from the sides, and this directionality in microphones became increasingly sophisticated during the 1940s and 50s, to the point that legendary singer Frank Sinatra became closely associated with the Telefunken brand polydirectional microphone and reportedly would not sing without his "Telly." Steven E. Schoenherr, "Microphones, Part 3: The Modern Era" http://history.acusd.edu/gen/recording/microphones3.html, accessed June 16, 2005.
14. Craig Monson, "Disembodied Voices: Music in the Nunneries of Bologna in the Midst of the Counter-Reformation," in *The Crannied Wall: Women, Religion, and the Arts in Early Modern Europe*, ed. Craig Monson (Ann Arbor: University of Michigan Press, 1992), 191–210.
15. Ellen Koskoff, *Music in Lubavitcher Life* (Chicago: University of Illinois Press, 2001), 136–37.
16. Roland Barthes, "The Grain of the Voice," in *On Record: Pop, Rock and the Written Word*, eds. Simon Frith and Andrew Goodwin (New York: Routledge, 1990), 293–300.
17. M. G. Lord, *Forever Barbie: The Unauthorized Biography of a Real Doll* (New York: Avon Books, 1994), 136–7.
18. Grieg, *Will You Still Love Me Tomorrow?*, 51. I am less sure, though, that the objectification of boys—along the lines by which girls and women can be reduced to the status of "things" by a male gaze—is actually to be celebrated as a feminist victory.
19. The quasi-religious fervor surrounding boys in this genre is the joke underlying the 1992 Disney film *Sister Act* (starring baby boomers Whoopi Goldberg, Maggie Smith, and Harvey Keitel), in which a choir of nuns transforms girl-group classics into devotional anthems with very little alteration of lyrics, musical language, or general affect. Mary Wells's "My Guy" becomes "My God" and Little Peggy March's "I Will Follow Him" does not require even this degree of change.
20. Patricia Juliana Smith, "Ask Any Girl: Compulsory Heterosexuality and Girl Group Culture," in *Reading Rock and Roll: Authenticity, Appropriation, Aesthetics*, eds. Kevin J.H. Dettmar and William Richey (New York: Columbia University Press, 1999), 93–125.
21. Barbara Bradby, "Do-Talk and Don't Talk: The Division of the Subject in Girl-Group Music," in *On Record: Rock, Pop and the Written Word*, eds. Simon Frith and Andrew Goodwin (New York: Routledge, 1990), 341–68.
22. Marc Taylor, *The Original Marvelettes: Motown's Mystery Girl Group* (Jamaica, N.Y.: Aloiv Publishing, 2004), 19–20.

23. See Fred Bronson, liner notes to *Deliver: the Marvelettes' Singles 1961–1971*, Motown 37463-6259, 1993-2; Susan Whitall, *Women of Motown: An Oral History* (New York: Avon Books, 1998); Gerry Hirshey, *Nowhere to Run: The Story of Soul Music* (New York: Da Capo Press, 1984); and Grieg, *Will You Still Love Me Tomorrow?*
24. Cited in Taylor, *The Original Marvelettes*, 129.
25. Cited in Bronson, liner notes to *Deliver.*
26. Ballard also had her devotees, and Randy Taraborelli relates that Jules Podell, owner of the Copa Cabana in New York, cancelled a performance by the Supremes after learning of Gordy's plan to replace Ballard in the act. J. Randy Taraborelli, *Call Her Miss Ross: The Unauthorized Biography of Diana Ross* (New York: Birch Lane Press, 1989), 143.
27. Susan Douglas, *Where the Girls Are: Growing up Female with the Mass Media* (New York: Times Books, 1994), 304.

Part II

1. *Rock and Roll*, "Respect." (PBS & BBC co-production, produced by Elizabeth Deane, Robert Palmer, and Hugh Thomson, 1995). In his autobiography, Berry Gordy indicates that the idea of having an Artist Development Department came first from his three sisters, all closely involved with Motown and Gordy's other business ventures. Berry Gordy, *To Be Loved: The Music, the Magic, the Memories of Motown* (New York: Warner Books, 1994), 176.

Chapter 3

1. Cholly Atkins and Jacqui Malone, *Class Act: the Jazz Life of Cholly Atkins* (New York: Columbia University Press, 2001), xviii. Italics in original.
2. Seen in *Shindig! Presents Groovy Gals*, Rhino Home Video RNVD 1457, 1991.
3. Marc Taylor, *The Marvelettes: Motown's Mystery Girl Group* (Jamaica, N.Y.: Aloiv Publishing, 2004), 121.
4. Seen in *Girl Groups.* Delilah Films Production M600194.
5. Ibid.
6. The Marvelettes would, of course, return to the Top Forty with "Too Many Fish in the Sea" in December of 1964, but in 1963 they were in the middle of a dry spell, with no chart entries since "Beechwood 4-5789" in the fall of 1962.
7. J. Randy Taraborrelli, *Call Her Miss Ross* (New York: Birch Lane Press, 1989), 110; and Mary Wilson, *Dreamgirl & Supreme Faith: My Life as a Supreme* (New York: Cooper Square Press, 1999), 163.

8. Atkins and Malone, *Class Act*, 131. My italics.
9. John Berger, *Ways of Seeing* (London: Penguin Books, 1972), 46.
10. Susan Bordo, *Unbearable Weight: Feminism, Western Culture, and the Body* (Berkeley: University of California Press, 2003), 166.
11. Ibid., 169–70.
12. See Mark Johnson, *The Body in the Mind: The Bodily Basis of Meaning, Imagination, and Reason* (Chicago: University of Chicago Press, 1987); and Paul Connerton, *How Societies Remember* (Cambridge: Cambridge University Press, 1989).
13. Susan Douglas, *Where the Girls Are: Growing up Female with the Mass Media* (New York: Times Books, 1994), 93.
14. Judith Lynne Hanna, *Dance, Sex and Gender: Signs of Identity, Dominance, Defiance, and Desire* (Chicago: University of Chicago Press, 1988), 75.
15. Ibid., 78–9.
16. Michel Foucault, *Discipline and Punish* (New York: Vintage, 1979).
17. Sandra Lee Bartky, "Foucault, Femininity and Patriarchal Power," in *Writing on the Body: Female Embodiment and Feminist Theory* (New York: Columbia University Press, 1997), 129–55.
18. Ibid., 136.
19. Wilson, *Dreamgirl and Supreme Faith*, 151.
20. David Schepp, "Bitchy Bosses Go to Boot Camp," http://news.bbc.co.uk/1/hi/business/1476762.stm, accessed July 27, 2005. Jean Hollands, the founder of Bully Broads, published a book called *Same Game, Different Rules: How to Get Ahead without Being a Bully Broad, Ice Queen, or "Ms. Understood"* in 2002.
21. RDF Media promotes *Ladette to Lady* thus: "The New Oxford English Dictionary officially lists 'ladette' as a word for the first time, defining it as 'young women who behave in a boisterously assertive or crude manner and engage in heavy drinking sessions.' We have just 5 weeks to reform 10 loudmouthed ladettes in a finishing school of etiquette, manners and social graces. The ladettes move into Eggleston Hall, a traditional finishing school, brought back to life for the purpose. The girls' clothing will be binned and replaced by traditional daywear as their institutionalisation begins. There will also be numerous challenges which will have to be completed successfully in order for them to avoid elimination, and be in with a chance to win the final prize. The tasks will include attending a dinner dance and a country house weekend, cooking a cordon bleu diner party, wine tasting and dressmaking. Will the girls be able to walk in their new shoes, choose Champagne over Babysham and cope with the eccentricities of high society life to pull it off and reveal a true female sensibility? Catfights, burnt souffles and drunken debauchery aside, one thing is certain, the girl who walks away with the prize will be a lady." No author listed, http://www.rdfmedia.com/reality/LadetteToLady.asp, accessed January 19, 2006.
22. Marjorie Garber, *Vested Interests: Cross-Dressing and Cultural Anxiety* (New York: Routledge, 1992), 357–74.

Chapter 4

1. Cited in Charlotte Grieg, *Will You Still Love Me Tomorrow?: Girl Groups from the 50s On* (London: Virago, 1989), 48.
2. Jay Warner, *American Singing Groups: A History 1940–1990* (New York: Da Capo, 1992), 353. Of course, the Wall of Sound was a production style that involved more than a generous use of echo, as we shall see in the next section.
3. Gillian Gaar, *She's a Rebel: The History of Women in Rock & Roll* (Seattle: Seal Press, 1992), 44; and Alan Betrock, *Girl Groups: The Story of a Sound* (New York: Delilah Books, 1982), 35.
4. Cited in Gaar, *She's a Rebel*, 44.
5. Cited in Betrock, *Girl Groups*, 35.
6. Cited in Gaar, *She's a Rebel*, 45.
7. Three different voices provided leads on records by the Crystals: Barbara Alston was the soloist on their first recordings, "There's No Other Like My Baby," "Uptown," and "He Hit Me"; Darlene Love (who was never actually a member of the group) sang lead on "He's a Rebel" and "He's Sure the Boy I Love"; and Dolores "Lala" Brooks was the lead singer on the group's remaining releases.
8. Cited in Warner, *American Singing Groups*, 352.
9. McCrea's version of the song was intended to be a demo, but it was, like "The Locomotion," considered a good enough version of the song to be released in its own right. Songwriters King and Goffin subsequently sold the song to Herman's Hermits, who chose it before McCrea's recording had been released. Betrock, *Girl Groups*, 49.
10. One source suggests that Eve Boyd (Little Eva) often sang with the Cookies and can be heard on "Chains." John Frank, "The Cookies," http://spectropop.com/gg/cookies.html, accessed July 11, 2005. In my repeated listening to the song, I can discern only three voices; it is possible that Boyd filled in for another singer on this session.
11. Betrock, *Girl Groups,* 49.
12. Naomi Wolf, *The Beauty Myth* (Toronto: Random House of Canada, 1990), 157.
13. This valuable and influential essay has enabled much work by feminist theorists, including the ensuing quoted excerpts from McRobbie and Lamb. Laura Mulvey, "Visual Pleasure and Narrative in Cinema," in *Visual and Other Pleasures* (Bloomington: Indiana University Press, 1989), 14–26.
14. Angela McRobbie, "Dance and Social Fantasy," in *Gender and Generation*, eds. Angela McRobbie and Mica Nava (London: MacMillan, 1984), 130–61.
15. Sharon Lamb, *The Secret Lives of Girls: What Good Girls Really Do—Sex Play, Aggression, and Their Guilt* (New York: The Free Press, 2001), 41, 44.
16. Valerie Walkerdine, *Daddy's Girl: Young Girls and Popular Culture* (New York: Routledge, 1998).

Chapter 5

1. Alison Lurie, *The Language of Clothes* (New York: Henry Holt and Company, 1981), 18. Lurie goes on to discuss the ways in which a uniform can also be strangely liberating because the wearer can feel unaccountable for her actions, and I will return to this idea shortly.
2. Mary Wilson, *Dreamgirl & Supreme Faith: My Life as a Supreme* (New York: Cooper Square Press, 1999), 200–211. Wilson identifies Ballard as a high soprano; as I noted in the previous section, the terms used to describe voice types in this genre do not correspond with the usage of the same terminology in opera or other kinds of classical singing.
3. bell hooks, "Selling Hot Pussy," in *Writing on the Body: Female Embodiment and Feminist Theory*, eds. Katie Conboy, Nadia Medina, and Sarah Stanbury (New York: Columbia University Press, 1997), 113–29.
4. Fanita James, personal interview, and Jay Warner, *American Singing Groups* (New York: Da Capo Press, 1992), 450.
5. Mark Ribowsky, *He's a Rebel: The Truth about Phil Spector—Rock and Roll's Legendary Madman* (New York: EP Dutton, 1989), 155.
6. Cynthia Cyrus, "Selling an Image: Girl Groups of the 1960s," *Popular Music* 22, no. 2 (2003): 173–93.
7. Georganne Scheiner, *Signifying Female Adolescence: Film Representations and Fans, 1920–1950* (Westport, Conn.: Praeger Publishers, 2000), 91–115.
8. Carolyn Kay Steedman, *Landscape for a Good Woman: A Story of Two Lives* (London: Virago, 1987), 15.
9. See W. T. Lhamon Jr., *Raising Cain: Blackface Performance from Jim Crow to Hip Hop* (Cambridge, Mass.: Harvard University Press, 1998); and Marjorie Garber, "Black and White TV: Cross-Dressing the Color Line," in *Vested Interests: Cross-Dressing and Cultural Anxiety* (New York: Routledge, 1992), 267–303.
10. Billie Holiday, "On the Road with Count Basie," in *Keeping Time: Readings in Jazz History*, ed. Robert Walser (New York: Oxford University Press, 1999), 96–100; and Garber, *Vested Interests*, 279–81. Tina Turner has also challenged notions of black femininity by playing with the minstrel mask, appearing eating watermelon while wearing white face paint on the cover of a 1969 record, *Outta Season*. See Susan Fast, "Bold Soul Sister: Why Can Tina Play with the (White) Guys?" in *She's So Fine: Whiteness, Femininity and Adolescence in 60s Music*, ed. Laurie Stras (Durham, N.C.: Duke University Press, forthcoming).
11. Tina Turner, in Obie Benz, Ted Haimes, and Andrew Solt, directors, *The History of Rock'n'Roll*, Time Life Video 34991-90-IN, 2004.

12. See Dale Cockrell, *Demons of Disorder: Early Blackface Minstrels and Their World* (Cambridge: Cambridge University Press, 1997); Eric Lott, *Love and Theft: Blackface Minstrelsy and the American Working Class* (Oxford: Oxford University Press, 1993); William J. Mahar, *Behind the Burnt Cork Mask: Early Blackface Minstrelsy and Antebellum American Popular Culture* (New York: Scholarly Book Services, 2002).
13. Lhamon Jr., *Raising Cain*, 97.
14. Berry Gordy, To Be Loved: The Music, the Magic, the Memories of Motown (New York: Warner Books, 1994), 206.
15. Rachel Rubin, "Sing me Back Home: Nostalgia, Bakersfield, and Modern Country Music," in *American Popular Music*, eds. Rachel Rubin and Jeffrey Melnick (Amherst: University of Massachussetts Press, 2001), 93–110.
16. Garber, *Vested Interests*, 313.
17. Esther Newton, "Role Models," in *Camp Grounds: Style and Homosexuality*, ed. David Bergman (Amherst: University of Massachusetts Press, 1993), 39–54. Italics in original.
18. Mark Booth, *Camp* (London: Quartet Books, 1983), 18. Italics in original.
19. Pamela Robertson, *Guilty Pleasures: Feminist Camp from Mae West to Madonna* (Durham, N.C.: Duke University Press, 1996), 17.
20. See also Susan Sontag's famous "Notes on Camp," in *Against Interpretation and Other Essays* (New York: Dell, 1966) 275–92.
21. Patricia Juliana Smith, "'You Don't Have to Say You Love Me': The Camp Masquerades of Dusty Springfield," in *Camp Grounds: Style and Homosexuality*, ed. David Bergman (Amherst: University of Massachusetts Press, 1993), 185–206.
22. Smith, "'You Don't Have to Say You Love Me,'" 188; and Lucy O'Brien, *SheBop: The Definitive History of Women in Rock, Pop and Soul* (London: Penguin Books, 1995), 61–4.
23. Homosexual relations between adults over the age of twenty-one were decriminalized in Britain in 1967, and the last anti-homosexual laws in the United States were overturned in 2003.
24. Joan Rivière, "Womanliness as a Masquerade," in *Formations of Fantasy*, eds. Victor Burgin, James Donald, and Cora Kaplan (London: Methuen, 1986), 35–44.
25. Ibid., 38.
26. Sharon Lamb, *The Secret Lives of Girls: What Good Girls Really Do—Sex Play, Aggression, and Their Guilt* (New York: The Free Press, 2001), 46.
27. hooks, "Selling Hot Pussy," 116.
28. Susan Douglas, *Where the Girls Are: Growing up Female with the Mass Media* (New York: Random House, 1994), 96. Of course, bell hooks critiques this kind of envy in her analysis of Madonna's declaration of having wanted to be black as a young girl. See bell hooks, "Madonna: Plantation Mistress or Soul Sister?" in *Black Looks: Race and Representation* (Toronto: Between the Lines, 1992), 157–64.

29. Mary Russo, "Female Grotesques," in *Writing on the Body*, 318–37. Italics in original.
30. Lyn Mikel Brown, *Raising Their Voices: The Politics of Girls' Anger* (Cambridge, Mass.: Harvard University Press, 1998), 16.

Part III

1. Some of the ideas discussed in this section appear also in my essay "'He's Got the Power': The Politics of Production in Girl Group Music," in *Music, Space and Place: Popular Music and Cultural Identity*, eds. Sheila Whiteley, Andy Bennett, and Stan Hawkins (Aldershot, UK: Ashgate Press, 2004), 191–200.
2. Kristine McKenna, liner notes to *RESPECT: A Century of Women in Music*, Rhino Records R2 75815, 31, 1999, 34.
3. The obstacles facing a female musician in the realm of Western European art music are examined in Marcia Citron's *Gender and the Musical Canon*, while the struggles of female jazzers and rockers are explored in Linda Dahl's *Stormy Weather* and Reynolds and Press's *The Sex Revolts*. Marcia Citron, *Gender and the Musical Canon* (Cambridge: Cambridge University Press, 1993); Linda Dahl, *Stormy Weather: The Music and Lives of a Century of Jazz Women* (London: Quartet Books, 1984); Simon Reynolds and Joy Press, *The Sex Revolts: Gender, Rebellion and Rock'n'Roll* (Cambridge, Mass.: Harvard University Press, 1995).

Chapter 6

1. Jerry Wexler, cited in Albin J. Zak III, *The Poetics of Rock: Cutting Tracks, Making Records* (Berkeley: University of California Press, 2001), 164.
2. Kari McDonald and Sarah Hudson Kaufman, "Tomorrow Never Knows: The Contribution of George Martin and His Production Team to the Beatles' New Sound," in *'Every Sound There Is': The Beatles'* Revolver *and the Transformation of Rock and Roll*, ed. Russell Reising (Aldershot, UK: Ashgate Publishing, 2002), 139–57.
3. Berry Gordy, *To Be Loved: The Music, the Magic, the Memories of Motown* (New York: Time Warner, 1994), 131.
4. Zak III, *The Poetics of Rock*, 178.
5. Gerald Early, *One Nation under a Groove: Motown and American Culture* (Hopewell, N.J.: Ecco Press, 1995), 117–8.

6. The inability of musicians to hear what they sound like was revolutionized with the development of recording, as Mark Katz shows: "In 1905 soprano Adelina Patti was finally persuaded to commit her famous voice to wax…she heard her recorded voice for the first time. 'My God!' she reportedly exclaimed, 'Now I understand why I am Patti! What a voice! What an artist!'" Mark Katz, *Capturing Sound: How Technology Has Changed Music* (Berkeley: University of California Press, 2004), 28.
7. Nancy Hartsock, "The Feminist Standpoint: Developing the Ground for a Specifically Feminist Historical Materialism," reprinted in *Feminism and Methodology*, ed. Sandra Harding (Oxford: Oxford University Press, 1997), 157–80. Originally in Nancy Hartsock, *Money, Sex and Power: Toward a Feminist Historical Materialism* (Boston: New England University Press, 1984).
8. Peter Mercer-Taylor, "Songs from the Bell Jar: Autonomy and Resistance in the Music of the Bangles," *Popular Music* 17, no. 2 (1998): 187–204.
9. Will Straw, "Authorship," in *Key Terms in Popular Music and Culture*, eds. Bruce Horner and Thomas Swiss (Oxford: Blackwell, 1999), 199–208.
10. In the early twentieth century, this way of thinking seems largely intact; witness the critical acclaim for albums by groups such as Coldplay, Radiohead, Greenday, and the White Stripes as compared to the condescension greeting best-selling singles by Jennifer Lopez, Britney Spears, and Hilary Duff. Note also that this binary is invariably gendered.
11. Alan Betrock, *Girl Groups: The Story of a Sound* (New York: Delilah Books, 1982), 42.
12. Tom Wolfe, "The First Tycoon of Teen," in *The Kandy-Kolored Tangerine-Flake Streamline Baby* (New York: Bantam, 1999).
13. In particular, see Betrock, *Girl Groups*, and Gerri Hirshey, *Nowhere to Run: The Story of Soul Music* (New York: Da Capo Press, 1984).
14. Mike Stoller, in *Girl Groups: The Story of a Sound*, Delilah Films M600194, 1994.
15. Ellie Greenwich, "How to Write a Hit Song," http://www.spectropop.com/EllieGreenwich/index.htm, accessed August 3, 2005 (first published in *Disco Scene* magazine in 1968).
16. Fourth Bluebelle Cindy Birdsong left the group in 1967 to become a Supreme, replacing Florence Ballard. Labelle continued as a trio.
17. Cited in Lucy O'Brien, *SheBop: The Definitive History of Women in Rock, Pop, and Soul* (New York: Penguin, 1995), 273.
18. Cited in Diana Reid Haig, "Interview with Florence Greenberg," in liner notes to *The Scepter Records Story*, Capricorn Records 9 42003–2, 2001.
19. Diana Reid Haig, "The Scepter Records Story," liner notes to *The Scepter Records Story*. Capricorn Records 9 42003, 2001, 12–27.
20. Haig, "Interview with Florence Greenberg."
21. Bill Ragogna, linter notes to *The Shirelles: 25 All-Time Greatest Hits*, Varèse Sarabande VSD-6029, 1999.

22. Carol Kaye, "Carol Kaye on Bass, Brian and the Beach Boys," http://abbeyrd.best.vwh.net/carolkay.htm, accessed August 3, 2005.
23. Ibid.
24. Ibid.
25. Cited in Mark Cunningham, *Good Vibrations: A History of Record Production* (Chessington, Surrey: Castle Communications, 1996), 58–59.
26. Karl Marx, "Estranged Labour," reprinted in *Social Theory: The Multicultural and Classic Readings*, ed. Charles Lemert (Boulder, Colo.: Westview Press, 1999), 30–36. Emphasis in original.
27. Cited in Charlotte Grieg, *Will You Still Love Me Tomorrow?: Girl Groups from the 50s On* (London: Virago, 1989), 54.
28. See Louise Kapp Howe, *Pink Collar Workers* (New York: Putnam, 1977). Dolly Parton's self-written 1981 hit "9 to 5" (from the film of the same name) critiques this system.
29. Zak III, *The Poetics of Rock*, 179.
30. Mark Ribowsky, *He's a Rebel: The Truth about Phil Spector: Rock and Roll's Legendary Madman* (New York: EP Dutton, 1989), 118–25. Indeed, when Spector and then-partner Lester Sill were working on the master recording, they overheard musicians playing "He's a Rebel" in an adjoining studio, creating a record for white pop singer Vikki Carr—Carr's record did well in Australia, but could not outdo the Crystals' version in North America.
31. Ibid., 145.
32. Ibid., 147–8.
33. Cited in Grieg, *Will You Still Love Me Tomorrow?*, 52.
34. Fanita James, personal interview, December 2004.
35. Ibid.
36. Ibid.
37. Ibid.
38. Kaye, "Carol Kaye on Bass, Brian and the Beach Boys," http://abbeyrd.best.vwh.net/carolkay.htm, accessed August 3, 2005.
39. Cited in Viv Groskop, "We Weren't Lovers—Dusty Wasn't My Type," *Daily Express Micro Edition*, 13 August 2000. Available at http://www.lineone.net/express/00/08/13/features/f0200-d.html
40. Cited in Haig, "Interview with Florence Greenberg."

Chapter 7

1. Allison Anders's 1996 film *Grace of My Heart* is a thoughtful account of a young woman songwriter's career from the Brill Building days to the era of psychedelic concept albums. Though largely based on the life of Carole King, the central character Denise Waverley bears resemblances also to Cynthia Weil and Ellie Greenwich, and other characters in the film are clearly modeled on such figures as Phil Spector, Brian Wilson, and

former girl pop star Lesley Gore. Many of the film's songs were written or cowritten by King's former husband and writing partner Gerry Goffin, and one, "My Secret Love," is a collaboration between Goffin and Lesley Gore.

2. Alan Betrock, *Girl Groups: The Story of a Sound* (New York: Delilah Books, 1982), 43–4.
3. James Perone, *Carole King: A Bio-Bibliography* (Westport, Conn.: Greenwood Press, 1999), 132–38.
4. Ibid., 14; and Ken Emerson, *Always Magic in the Air: The Bomp and Brilliance of the Brill Building Era* (New York: Viking, 2005), 90. The mind fairly boggles at the idea of Mathis, a barely closeted crooner with a largely young, female fan base, maintaining his dreamboat status with a song about the possibly dire consequences of submitting to a lover's entreaties. The conspiracy of blindness that enveloped men like Mathis, Little Richard, and Liberace would surely have stirred in the face of such unabashed vulnerability and sexual insecurity. It is tempting to speculate about the extent to which the Women's Liberation movement and the Gay Civil Rights movement might have unfolded differently had Mathis's A&R man not turned the song down before Mathis heard it.
5. Perone, *Carole King*, 14.
6. In the final mix of "Will You Love Me Tomorrow?" the kettle drums are deeply submerged and audible only in the song's bridge, so that the listener has to work hard to discern them. In King's 1971 recording of the song, the kettle drums are more prominent, though still gentle in this softer, more intimate arrangement of acoustic instruments.
7. Susan Douglas, *Where the Girls Are: Growing up Female with the Mass Media* (New York: Times Books, 1994), 85.
8. Cited in Diana Reid Haig, "Interview with Florence Greenberg," in liner notes to *The Scepter Records Story*, Capricorn Records 9 42003-2, 2001.
9. Betrock, *Girl Groups*, 84. Ellie Greenwich's 1958 single featured two of her own songs but did not do well enough to keep RCA interested in her as a recording artist.
10. For my analysis of "Johnny Get Angry," see my article "'He Hit Me and I Was Glad': Violence, Masochism and Anger in Girl Group Music," in *She's So Fine: Whiteness, Femininity and Adolescence in 60s Music*, ed. Laurie Stras (Duke University Press, forthcoming). For an analysis of kd lang's interpretation of the song, see Lori Burns, "'Joanie' Get Angry: kd lang's Feminist Revision," in *Understanding Rock: Essays in Music Analysis*, eds. John Covach and Graeme Boone (New York: Oxford University Press, 1997), 93–112.
11. Betrock, *Girl Groups*, 102. In spite of—or perhaps partly because of—the ban, it reached #11 on the British charts.
12. Charlotte Grieg, *Will You Still Love Me Tomorrow?: Girl Groups from the 50s On* (London: Virago, 1989), 80.
13. Betrock, *Girl Groups*, 89.

14. Don Charles, "Shout my Name! The Jeff Barry Story," http://spectropop.com/brill/jeff_barry.html, accessed August 9, 2005.

Chapter 8

1. Evan Eisenberg, *The Recording Angel: Explorations in Phonography* (New York: McGraw-Hill, 1987), 126.
2. Mark Ribowsky, *He's a Rebel: The Truth about Phil Spector: Rock and Roll's Legendary Madman* (New York: EP Dutton, 1989), 122.
3. Ibid., 205.
4. Ibid., 88.
5. Both cited in Gillian G. Gaar, *She's a Rebel: The History of Women in Rock & Roll* (Seattle: Seal Press, 1992), 49.
6. Ronnie Spector, with Vince Waldron, *Be My Baby: How I Survived Mascara, Miniskirts and Madness, or My Life as a Fabulous Ronette* (New York: Harmony Books, 1990), 107.
7. Ibid., 52.
8. I thank David Ake and Matthew Bannister for sharing their thoughts on the origins of the baion beat with me.
9. The producer's efforts to isolate Ronnie Spector from her sister and cousin so that he could pursue a romance with her later led him to send the group on tour with Dick Clark in 1963 with another cousin filling in as lead singer. The fact that fans did not complain about this substitution (and in many cases might not have noticed) reinforces the fact that the Ronettes were above all a studio group, and that listeners interacted with them primarily through records and not live concerts. Spector, *Be My Baby*, 51, 63, 66.
10. Alan Betrock, *Girl Groups: The Story of a Sound* (New York: Delilah Books, 1982), 136.
11. Eddie Holland, cited in Charlotte Grieg, *Will You Still Love Me Tomorrow?: Girl Groups from the 50s On* (London: Virago, 1989), 134.
12. Sharon Krum, "Ready, Girls?" *Manchester Guardian*, 13 July 1998, 6. Ronnie and Phil Spector had divorced in 1972; she asserts that her mother had to help her escape from their Beverly Hills mansion barefoot, because Phil kept her shoes in order to control her movements. Spector, *Be My Baby*, 200.
13. Cited in "Ronettes Entitled to Back Pay from Phil Spector, Judge Rules," *Los Angeles Times*, 17 June 2000, A14. Although Phil Spector was required to pay far less than he was sued for, he appealed the ruling, but was ordered in 2001 to pay. "Appeals Court Upholds $3M Award to Ronettes," *Billboard Online*, 14 November 2001. Available at http://www.billboard.com/billboard/daily/article_display.jsp?vnu_content/id=110545

14. Cited in Lucy O'Brien, *SheBop: The Definitive History of Women in Rock, Pop and Soul* (London: Penguin, 1995), 71.
15. Maria Mies, *Patriarchy and Accumulation on a World Scale* (London: Zed Books, 1986).
16. Nancy Hartsock, "The Feminist Standpoint: Developing the Ground for a Specifically Feminist Historical Materialism," in *Feminism and Methodology*, ed. Sandra Harding (Bloomington: Indiana University Press, 1987), 171.
17. J. Randy Taraborelli, *Call Her Miss Ross* (New York, Birch Lane Press, 1989), 282. This quip is found in an account of a recording session for her 1973 hit "Touch Me in the Morning," which she had learned in Ab. At the session, the engineer and musicians switched to Bb without telling her; tempers flared when she began to sing, still in Ab, and arranger Ron Miller convinced her that the mistake was hers. What is remarkable to me about this anecdote is not so much that Ross—a singer not known for being acquiescent—gave in, but that far from not knowing her keys, her sense of Ab was so strong that she could sing it over an accompaniment *a major second higher*. Even more astounding, the story is presented as one in which Ross demonstrated musical ignorance and behaved badly, although the account shows that her singer's sense of how pitches feel in the throat was entirely accurate.
18. Dorothy Smith, "Women's Perspective as a Radical Critique of Sociology," in *Feminism and Methodology*, ed. Sandra Harding (Bloomington: Indiana University Press, 1987); and Hartsock, "The Feminist Standpoint."
19. Cited in *Girl Groups: The Story of a Sound*, Delilah Films M600194., 1994
20. Kylie Minogue's 1988 version of the song is a self-conscious attempt to recapture the effect of the original, while Grand Funk Railroad's 1974 recording is best understood as an ironic and light-hearted response to Little Eva, and a pun on the band's name. In 2000, a "Locomotion" by Atomic Kitten, like Minogue's effort, aimed for the style of the original but fell short largely because the bland, polished voices lack the affable character of Boyd's.
21. Ronnie Spector relates how the Shirelles, queens of girl groups, praised the Ronettes' first hit in 1963: "Shirley [Owens] surprised me by saying right out how much she liked the record. 'Especially the part where you go "*Be my little bay-bee*," she told me.'" Ronnie Spector, *Be My Baby*, 56.
22. Valerie Walkerdine, *Daddy's Girl: Young Girls and Popular Culture* (Cambridge, Mass.: Harvard University Press, 1997), 166. Of course, Walkerdine's project is to complicate Mulvey's theory.
23. In her study of middle school girls in Northern California in the early 1990s, investigative journalist Peggy Orenstein interviews a social studies teacher who regularly asks her students to make oral presentations in which they speak as a significant historical figure. Upon noticing that, while her female students were quite comfortable taking on a male character, her male students would never choose to speak as a woman, the teacher took the unusual step of requiring that all students make one

presentation as a male and one as a female. She explains that "as long as it's required, [the boys] accept it, but it wouldn't occur to them to choose it." Cited in Peggy Orenstein, *SchoolGirls: Young Women, Self-Esteem, and the Confidence Gap* (New York: Doubleday, 1994), 249.

24. John Berger, *Ways of Seeing* (London: Penguin Books, 1972), 46.
25. W.E.B. Du Bois, *Souls of Black Folk* (Greenwich, Conn.: Fawcett Publications, 1961), 16–17.

Part IV

1. Toni Morrison, *The Bluest Eye* (New York: Alfred A. Knopf, 1970), 83.
2. Ibid., 87.
3. Cecil Brown, *Stagolee Shot Billy* (Cambridge, Mass.: Harvard University Press, 2003).
4. Nadine George-Graves, *The Royalty of Negro Vaudeville: The Whitman Sisters and the Negotiation of Race, Gender and Class in African American Theatre, 1900–1940* (New York: St. Martin's Press, 2000).
5. Lyn Mikel Brown, *Raising Their Voices: The Politics of Girls' Anger* (Cambridge, Mass.: Harvard University Press, 1998), 148.

Chapter 9

1. Beverley Skeggs, *Formations of Class and Gender: Becoming Respectable* (London: Sage Publications, 1997), 3, 5.
2. David Considine, *The Cinema of Adolescence* (Jefferson, N.C.: McFarland, 1985), 213.
3. Barbara Christian, "The Race for Theory," reprinted in Sandra Kemp and Judith Squires, *Feminisms* (Oxford: Oxford University Press, 1997), 69–78. Originally in Linda Kauffman (ed.), *Gender and Theory* (Oxford: Blackwell, 1989), 225-36.
4. Patricia Hill Collins, "Mammies, Matriarchs and Other Controlling Images," in *Black Feminist Thought: Knowledge, Consciousness, and the Politics of Empowerment* (New York: Routledge, 1990), 76–91.
5. Sheila Whiteley, "Little Red Rooster v. the Honky Tonk Woman: Mick Jagger, Sexuality, Style and Image," in *Sexing the Groove: Popular Music and Gender*, ed. Sheila Whiteley (New York: Routledge, 1997), 67–99.
6. Terri Sutton, "Janis Joplin," in *The Rolling Stone Book of Women in Rock*, ed. Barbara O'Dair (New York: Random House, 1997), 157–66; and Randy Bachman, *Randy's Vinyl Tap*, CBC Radio One, August 13, 2005.
7. Susan McClary, "Thinking Blues," in *Conventional Wisdom: The Content of Musical Form* (Berkeley: University of California Press, 2000), 32–62, 59.

8. Timothy White, *The Nearest Faraway Place: Brian Wilson, the Beach Boys and the Southern California Experience* (New York: Henry Holt, 1994), 356.
9. Sarah Banet-Weiser, *The Most Beautiful Girl in the World: Beauty Pageants and National Identity* (Berkeley: University of California Press, 1999), 38.
10. Patricia Juliana Smith, "'Ask Any Girl': Compulsory Heterosexuality and Girl Group Culture," in *Reading Rock'n'Roll: Authenticity, Appropriation, Aesthetics*, ed. Kevin Dettmar and William Richey (New York: Columbia University Press, 1999), 93–125.
11. J. Randy Taraborrelli, *Call Her Miss Ross* (New York: Birch Lane Press, 1989), 109.
12. For more on the Supremes' meeting with the Beatles, see Gerri Hirshey, *Nowhere to Run: The Story of Soul Music* (New York: Da Capo Press, 1984), 181; and Mary Wilson, *Dreamgirl & Supreme Faith: My Life as a Supreme* (New York: Cooper Square Press, 1999), 177–8.
13. Cited in Reebee Garofalo, *Rockin' Out: Popular Music in the USA* (Boston: Allyn & Bacon, 1997), 190.
14. Emily White, *Fast Girls: Teenage Tribes and the Myth of the Slut* (New York: Scribner, 2002).
15. Charlotte Grieg, *Will You Still Love Me Tomorrow?: Girl Groups from the 50s On* (London: Virago, 1989), 57.
16. Suzanne Smith, *Dancing in the Street: Motown and the Cultural Politics of Detroit* (Cambridge, Mass.: Harvard University Press, 1999), 15.

Chapter 10

1. Gerald Early, *One Nation under a Groove: Motown and American Culture* (Hopewell, N.J.: Ecco Press, 1995), 54.
2. Cited in Gerri Hirshey, *Nowhere to Run: The Story of Soul Music* (New York: Da Capo Press, 1984), 189.
3. Early, *One Nation under a Groove*, 48–9.
4. Berry Gordy, *To Be Loved: The Music, the Magic, the Memories of Motown* (New York: Warner Books, 1994), 59–61.
5. Because of a general concern with thriftiness at Motown, very few takes were ever recorded of any song, and artists who could deliver the goods accurately the first time were prized. Diana Ross's ability to perform a tune exactly the same way more than once—and with little need for lengthy and costly rehearsal—made her the ideal singer for Gordy's money.
6. Rob Bowman, *Soulsville USA: The Story of Stax Records* (New York: Schirmer Books, 1997), 98.
7. Iain Chambers, *Urban Rhythms: Pop Music and Pop Culture* (New York: St. Martin's Press, 1985), 44.

8. Patricia Juliana Smith, "Ask Any Girl: Compulsory Heterosexuality and Girl Group Culture." In *Reading Rock and Roll: Authenticity, Appropriation, Aesthetics*, eds. Kevin J. H. Dettmar and William Richey (New York: Columbia University Press, 1999), 93-125, 94.
9. Quincy Jones, *Q: The Autobiography of Quincy Jones* (New York: Doubleday, 2001), 173.
10. Ibid., 174.
11. Shauna Swartz, "Interview with Lesley Gore," http://www.afterellen.com/People/2005/6/lesleygore.html, accessed August 15, 2005.
12. Lucy O'Brien, *She Bop II: The Definitive History of Women in Rock, Pop and Soul* (London: Continuum, 2002), 77.
13. Randall Wilson, *Forever Faithful: Florence Ballard and the Supremes* (San Francisco: Renaissance Sound and Publications, 1999), 40; and Gordy, *To Be Loved*, 254–6. See also Mary Wilson, *Dreamgirl & Supreme Faith: My Life as a Supreme* (New York: Cooper Square Press, 1999); and Randy Taraborrelli, *Call Her Miss Ross: the Unauthorized Biography of Diana Ross* (New York: Birch Lane Press, 1989).
14. Taraborrelli, *Call Her Miss Ross*, 16.
15. Ibid., 45, and Wilson, *Dreamgirl & Supreme Faith*, 63–7.
16. Wilson, *Dreamgirl and Supreme Faith*, 187–89.
17. Gerri Hirshey, *Nowhere to Run*, 171.
18. Taraborrelli, *Call Her Miss Ross*, 73.
19. Of course, the voices of Baker, Brown, James, and Thornton were largely considered unsuitable for white middle-class ears, and their songs were generally re-recorded by "nice" white girls such as Patti Page, Doris Day, and Georgia Gibbs, who tended to enjoy far greater commercial success with them. Ruth Brown was eventually compelled to seek work as a maid in white middle-class suburbia and listened to her own songs performed by Page on the radio; perhaps, after all, Florence Ballard would not have found greater happiness in the 50s.
20. Aida Pavletich, *Sirens of Song: The Popular Female Vocalist in America* (New York: Da Capo Press, 1980), 107.
21. Early, *One Nation under a Groove*, 58–9.
22. Fred Ross (Diana's father), cited in Taraborrelli, *Call Her Miss Ross*, 37.
23. Ibid., 448.
24. Cited in Susan Whitall, *Women of Motown: An Oral History* (New York: Avon Books, 1998), 68.
25. Cited in *Rock and Roll*, "Respect" (PBS).
26. Ibid.
27. Susan Douglas, *Where the Girls Are: Growing up Female with the Mass Media* (New York: Random House, 1994), 96.
28. "Diana Ross and Brandy," Episode 91, Season 13, *The Oprah Winfrey Show*, May 10, 1999.

29. The British Invasion is generally held to have taken place between 1964 and 1966, although many British acts had trans-Atlantic successes before and after these dates. Indeed, I consider that identifying 1966 as the end of the Invasion is inaccurate and falsely bolsters the importance of male beat bands, if only because it excludes one of its most effective texts; namely, the Sidney Poitier vehicle *To Sir With Love*, a film about gritty working-class London that was explicitly aimed at North American viewers. The title track to the film, performed by Glaswegian moppet Lulu, became the top U.S. single of the year, far outstripping any of the Beatles' singles or tracks from their *Sgt. Pepper's Lonely Heart's Club Band*.

Chapter 11

1. Barbara Christian, "The Race for Theory," in *Feminisms*, eds. Sandra Kemp and Judith Squires (Oxford: Oxford University Press, 1997), 71; and Tania Modleski, *Old Wives' Tales and Other Women's Stories* (New York: New York University Press, 1998), 27.
2. Cited in Susan Whitall, *Women of Motown: An Oral History* (New York: Avon Books, 1998), 126.
3. Jennifer Barnes, "Where Are the Mothers in Opera?" in *Girls! Girls! Girls! Essays on Women and Music*, ed. Sarah Cooper (New York: New York University Press, 1996), 86–97.
4. Marianne Hirsch, *The Mother/Daughter Plot: Narrative, Psychoanalysis, Feminism* (Bloomington: Indiana University Press, 1989), 10–11. See also Naomi Scheman, "Missing Mothers/Desiring Daughters: Framing the Sight of Women," in *Engenderings: Constructions of Knowledge, Authority, and Privilege* (New York: Routledge, 1993), 126–54.
5. Joan Jacobs Brumberg, *The Body Project: An Intimate History of American Girls* (New York: Vintage Books, 1997), 41.
6. Wini Breines, *Young, White, and Miserable: Growing up Female in the Fifties* (Boston: Beacon Books, 1992), 79.
7. An example of girl-group singers playing different characters in a song can be found in the Shirelles' 1963 "Foolish Little Girl." In this song, Shirley Owens addresses a foolish girl who has failed to keep a desirable boyfriend. Playing the role of the foolish girl, Beverley Lee sighs "But I love him" in slow, plaintive half notes, to which the backing Shirelles reply in brisk eighths "No you don't, it's just your pride that's hurt!"
8. The quintet did have a #15 hit with their recording of "I Sold My Heart to the Junkman" in 1962, but they recorded this with the Newton label while still under contract to PAM Records. The producer of the record released the Starlets' recording under the name of the Bluebelles, launching the decades-long career of Patti LaBelle and her group members. The Starlets were eventually compensated for their role in the recording, but their own

career proved impossible to resume. Jay Warner, *American Singing Groups* (New York: Da Capo Press, 1992), 456. The recording is correctly credited to the Starlets in the 2005 box set *One Kiss Can Lead to Another: Girl Group Sounds Lost and Found*, Rhino Records 8122 74645 2.

9. In Chapter 1, I pointed out that the Marvelettes were unusual among girl groups in that lead vocals were shared more or less equally by two vocalists; Horton, whose full, brassy timbre is heard on records such as "Please Mr. Postman" and "Beechwood 4-5789"; and Wanda Young, whose softer, huskier voice characterizes "Destination: Anywhere" and "Don't Mess with Bill."
10. Cited in Charlotte Grieg, *Will You Still Love Me Tomorrow?: Girl Groups from the 50s On* (London: Virago, 1989), 104.
11. Ibid., 105–6.

Part V

1. Cited in Diana Reid Haig, liner notes to *The Scepter Records Story*, Capricorn Records 9 52003-2, 1992.
2. See, for example, Lori Burns and Mélisse Lafrance, *Disruptive Divas: Feminism, Identity and Popular Music* (New York: Routledge, 2002).
3. Lyn Mikel Brown and Carol Gilligan, *Meeting at the Crossroads: The Landmark Book about the Turning Point in Girls' and Women's Lives* (Cambridge, Mass.: Harvard University Press, 1992), 195.
4. Mary Pipher, *Reviving Ophelia: Saving the Selves of Adolescent Girls* (New York: Ballantine Books, 1994), and Rachel Simmons, *Odd Girl Out: The Hidden Culture of Aggression in Girls* (New York: Harcourt, 2004). I myself have explored the problems girls face in speaking out for themselves in "'He Hit Me, and I Was Glad': Anger, Violence and Masochism in Girl Group Music," in Laurie Stras, ed., *She's So Fine: Whiteness, Femininity and Adolescence in 60s Pop* (Durham, N.C.: Duke University Press, forthcoming).
5. Meda Chesney-Lind and Katherine Irwin, "From Badness to Meanness: Popular Contructions of Contemporary Girlhood," in Anita Harris, ed., *All about the Girl: Culture, Power, and Identity* (New York: Routledge, 2004), 45–56, 51.
6. Bonnie J. Ross Leadbeater and Niobe Way, eds., *Urban Girls: Resisting Stereotypes, Creating Identities* (New York: New York University Press, 1996), 6; and Peggy Orenstein, *SchoolGirls: Young Women, Self-Esteem, and the Confidence Gap* (New York: Doubleday, 1994).

Chapter 12

1. Angela McRobbie, *Feminism and Youth Culture: From 'Jackie' to 'Just Seventeen'* (Cambridge, Mass.: Unwin Hyman, 1991), 205.
2. Mary Jane Rotheram-Borus et al., "Personal and Ethnic Identity, Values, and Self-Esteem among Black and Latino Adolescent Girls," in *Urban Girls: Resisting Stereotypes, Creating Identities*, eds. Bonnie J. Ross Leadbeater and Niobe Way (New York: New York University Press, 1996), 35–52, 50.
3. Susan Douglas, *Where the Girls Are: Growing up Female with the Mass Media* (New York: Random House, 1994), 140–1.
4. Ronnie Spector, with Vince Waldron, *Be My Baby: How I Survived Mascara, Miniskirts and Madness, or My Life as a Fabulous Ronette* (New York: Harmony Books, 1990), 3.
5. The Ronettes had a complicated ethnic background, as their mothers (who were sisters) had an African American father and a Native American mother, and the father of Ronnie and Estelle Bennett was of Irish descent, while Nedra Talley's father was Hispanic.
6. Spector, *Be My Baby*, 26–28.
7. Ibid., 27.

Chapter 13

1. John J. Grecco, "Out in the Streets: The Story of the ShangriLas," http://www.redbirdent.com/slas1.htm, accessed October 1, 2005.
2. Miriam Linna, "Good Bad, but not Evil," http://www.nortonrecords.com/index2.html, accessed June 23, 2006.
3. *The ShangriLas: Myrmidons of Melodrama*, "Good Taste Tip from Mary Weiss," (FKR Productions). RPM Records RPM 136, 1994.
4. Although Betty Weiss did not even participate in this recording, the Gansers address the protagonist (Mary Weiss) as "Betty" in this song.
5. See Bonnie J. Dow, *Prime-Time Feminism: Television, Media Culture, and the Women's Movement Since 1970* (Philadelphia: University of Pennsylvania Press, 1996); and Dorothy E. Smith, "Women's Perspective as a Radical Critique of Sociology," reprinted in *Feminism and Methodology*, ed. Sandra Harding (Oxford: Oxford University Press, 1997), 84–96. Originally a conference paper for the American Academy for the Advancement of Science (Pacific Division), Eugene, Oregon, 1972.
6. Patricia Juliana Smith, "Ask Any Girl: Compulsory Heterosexuality and Girl Group Culture," in *Reading Rock and Roll: Authenticity, Appropriation, Aesthetics*, eds. Kevin J. H. Dettmar and William Richey (New York: Columbia University Press, 1999), 107.

7. The track is also included, happily, in the Rhino Records 2005 box set *One Kiss Can Lead to Another: Girl Group Sounds Lost & Found*. Rhino Records R2 74645.
8. Ken Emerson, "It Was Just Jewish Latin," in *Always Magic in the Air: The Bomp and the Brilliance of the Brill Building Era* (New York: Viking, 2005), 121–40.
9. Donna Gaines, "Girl Groups: A Ballad of Codependency," in *Trouble Girls: The Rolling Stone Book of Women in Rock*, ed. Barbara O'Dair (New York: Random House, 1997), 103–16.
10. Rachel Devlin, "Female Juvenile Delinquency and the Problem of Sexual Authority in America, 1945–1965," in *Delinquents and Debutantes: Twentieth-Century American Girls' Cultures*, ed. Sherrie A. Inness (New York: New York University Press, 1998), 83–108.
11. Simon Reynolds and Joy Press, *The Sex Revolts: Gender, Rebellion and Rock'n'Roll* (Cambridge, Mass.: Harvard University Press, 1995), 45.
12. When the Chiffons' record label sued Harrison for closely imitating the melody, harmonic framework, and texture of "He's So Fine," the former Beatle was found guilty of "subconscious plagiarism." Considering Harrison's close relationship to girl groups in the early days of his career—the Beatles had performed many girl group songs, and Harrison had dated one of the Ronettes—as well as the fact that "My Sweet Lord" was produced by Phil Spector, it is surprising that no one involved in making his record noticed the striking similarity to the Chiffons. The girl group underscored their moral victory by releasing a cover version of "My Sweet Lord" in 1975. Jay Warner, *The Da Capo Book of American Singing Groups*, (New York: Da Capo Press, 1992), 344.
13. Warner, *The Da Capo Book of American Singing Groups*, 325.
14. Sheila Burgel, liner notes to *One Kiss Can Lead to Another: Girl Group Sounds, Lost and Found*, Rhino Records R2 74645, 54, 2005. The Rolling Stones did record the song in 1965, and it is included on the 1975 album *Metamorphosis*, a compilation of outtakes and other unreleased material.

Chapter 14

1. *The Academy of Achievement*, "Rosa Parks Biography: Pioneer of Civil Rights," http://www.achievement.org/autodoc/page/par0bio-1, accessed August 16, 2005. Similarly, Parks was generally understood to be a work-worn elderly woman; in fact, she was forty-two at the time of her activism.
2. My thinking here is much influenced by Mark Anthony Neal, *What the Music Said: Black Popular Music and Black Public Culture* (New York: Routledge, 1999).

3. Billie Holiday, with William Dufty, *Lady Sings the Blues* (New York: Penguin, 1984), 74. Holiday recounts that her difficulties using public toilets were so demoralizing and exhausting that she eventually contracted a bladder infection because of her efforts to avoid confrontation. Insult was later added to injury when she consulted a doctor, who misdiagnosed her problem as a venereal infection. Holiday, *Lady Sings the Blues*, 77.
4. Greta Schiller and Andrea Weiss, directors, *International Sweethearts of Rhythm*, Jezebel Productions documentary 1563584883, 1986.
5. Berry Gordy, *To Be Loved: The Music, the Magic, the Memories of Motown* (New York: Time Warner, 1994), 165; and Martha Reeves in *Rock and Roll*, "Respect," (PBS).
6. Gladys Knight, cited in "Episode 5:The Sounds of Soul," *The History of Rock'n'Roll*, Time-Life Television series, 34991-90-IN 1995.
7. Cited in Marc Taylor, *The Original Marvelettes: Motown's Mystery Girl Group* (Jamaica, N.Y.: Aloiv Publishing Group, 2004), 66.
8. Ibid., 21.
9. Cited in Gerri Hershey, *We Gotta Get out of This Place: The True, Tough Story of Women in Rock* (New York: Atlantic Monthly Press, 2001), 51.
10. Ibid., 12.
11. Cited in Taylor, *The Original Marvelettes*, 69.
12. Ibid.
13. Suzanne Smith, *Dancing in the Street: Motown and the Cultural Politics of Detroit* (Cambridge, Mass.: Harvard University Press, 1999), 1–2.
14. Cited in Vicky Lebeau, "The Unwelcome Child: Elizabeth Eckford and Hannah Arendt," *Journal of Visual Culture* 3, no. 1, April 2004: 51–62.
15. Cited in Peggy Orenstein, *SchoolGirls: Young Women, Self-Esteem, and the Confidence Gap* (New York: Doubleday Books, 1994), 60–61.
16. Cited in Charlotte Grieg, *Will You Still Love Me Tomorrow?: Girl Groups from the 50s On* (London: Virago, 1989), 17.
17. Ronnie Spector, with Vince Waldron, *Be My Baby: How I Survived Mascara, Miniskirts and Madness, or My Life as a Fabulous Ronette* (New York: Harmony Books, 1990), 73–4.
18. Linna, "Good Bad, but not Evil," http://www.nortonrecords.com/maryweiss, accessed June 10, 2006.
19. The term "chitlin' circuit" has been used to designate the group of large theater venues catering primarily to African American audiences in the first half of the twentieth century. The name "chitlin'" derives from "chitterling," fried pig intestines that are a familiar dish in soul food.
20. Cited in Grieg, *Will You Still Love Me Tomorrow?*, 34.
21. Ibid.
22. Kay Sloan, "You Say You Want a Revolution," in *In My Life: Encounters with the Beatles*, eds. Robert Carding, Shelli Jankowski-Smith, and E.J. Miller Laino (New York: Fromm International, 1998), 26–32.

23. Donna Gaines, "Girl Groups: A Ballad of Codependency," in *The Rolling Stone Book of Women in Rock*, ed. Barbara O'Dair (New York: Rolling Stone Press, 1997), 103.
24. Cited in "Episode 9: Punk," *The History of Rock'n'Roll*, Time-Life Television series, 34991, 1995.
25. Grieg, *Will You Still Love Me Tomorrow?*, 184.
26. Ibid., 183.
27. For an analysis of camp aesthetics in Blondie's "Rip Her to Shreds," see Judith Peraino, "*Rip Her to Shreds*: Women's Music According to a Butch-Femme Aesthetic," *Repercussions* 1, no. 1 (1992): 19–47.
28. Cited in Phil Milstein, "ShangriLas 77!," http://www.spectropop.com/Shangri-Las/index.htm, accessed February 10, 2006. Lenny Kaye's devotion to girl-group music was manifested again in 2005, when he served as Master of Ceremonies at a New York party for the release of Rhino Records' *One Kiss Can Lead to Another: Girl Group Sounds, Lost and Found*, R2 74645. David A. Young, "Please Don't Wake Me: Rhino's *Girl Group Sounds*," http://www.spectropop.com/recommends/index2006.htm#Rhino, accessed February 20, 2006.
29. Marion Leonard, "Rebel Girl, You Are the Queen of My World" in *Sexing the Groove: Popular Music and Gender*, ed. Sheila Whitely (New York: Routledge, 1997), 230–56. See also some primary sources of riot grrrl reprinted in David Brackett, ed., *The Pop, Rock, and Soul Reader: Histories and Debates* (Oxford: Oxford University Press, 2005).
30. Gayle Wald, "Just a Girl? Rock Music, Feminism, and the Cultural Construction of Female Youth," in *Rock over the Edge: Transformations in Popular Music Culture*, eds. Roger Beebe, Denise Fulbrook, and Ben Saunders (Durham, N.C.: Duke University Press, 2002), 191–215. Italics in original.
31. A partial list of adult female bands and artists who have played with the iconography of teenage girls might include the Runaways, Toni Basil, the GoGos, Cyndi Lauper, the Bangles, Bananarama, and Gwen Stefani (of the band No Doubt). Note that all of these examples are of white women whose most obvious musical influences are hard rock and punk music.
32. Spice Girls' slogan, cited in Sheila Whitely, *Women and Popular Music: Sexuality, Identity and Subjectivity* (New York: Routledge, 2000), 226.
33. Press release, no author cited, "United Nations Population Fund Names Geri Halliwell Goodwill Ambassador," http://www.unfpa.org/news/news.cfm?ID=324%20, accessed February 20, 2006.

Bibliography

Aapola, Sinikka, Marnina Golnick, and Anita Harris. *Young Femininity: Girlhood, Power and Social Change*. New York: Palgrave MacMillan, 2005.

Abbott, Lynn, and Doug Seroff. *Out of Sight: The Rise of African American Popular Music, 1889–1895*. Jackson: University of Mississippi Press, 2002.

Adjaye, Joseph K., and Adrianne R. Andrews, eds. *Language, Rhythm, and Sound: Black Popular Cultures into the Twenty-First Century*. Pittsburgh: University of Pittsburgh, 1997.

Adorno, Theodor. "The Curves of the Needle." *October* 55 (winter 1990): 48–55.

Albright, Ann Cooper. *Choreographing Difference: the Body and Identity in Contemporary Dance*. Hanover, N.H.: Wesleyan University Press, 1997.

Averill, Gage. *Four Parts, No Waiting: A Social History of American Barbershop Harmony*. New York: Oxford University Press, 2003.

Ball, Durwood. "Popular Music." In *The Columbia Guide to America in the 1960s*, edited by David Farber and Beth Bailey, 288–96. New York: Columbia University Press, 2001.

Banes, Sally. *Dancing Women: Female Bodies on Stage*. London: Routledge, 1998.

Banet-Weiser, Sarah. *The Most Beautiful Girl in the World: Beauty Pageants and National Identity*. Berkeley: University of California Press, 1999.

Barnes, Jennifer. "Where Are the Mothers in Opera?" In *Girls! Girls! Girls! Essays on Women and Music*, edited by Sarah Cooper, 86–97. New York: Vintage Books, 1996.

Barthes, Roland. "The Grain of the Voice." In *On Record: Rock, Pop and the Written Word*, edited by Simon Frith and Andrew Goodwin, 293–300. New York: Routledge, 1990.

Bartky, Sandra Lee. "Foucault, Femininity and Patriarchal Power." In *Writing on the Body: Female Embodiment and Feminist Theory*, edited by Katie Conboy, Nadia Medina, and Sarah Stanbury, 129–55. New York: Columbia University Press, 1997.

Baty, S. Page. *American Monroe: The Making of a Body Politic*. Berkeley: University of California Press, 1995.

Beebe, Roger, Denise Fulbrook, and Ben Saunders. *Rock over the Edge: Transformations in Popular Music Culture*. Durham, N.C.: Duke University Press, 2002.

Bell, John. "Puppets and Performing Objects in the Twentieth Century." *Performing Arts Journal* 19, no. 2 (1997): 29–46.

Berger, John. *Ways of Seeing*. London: Penguin, 1972.

Bergman, David, ed. *Camp Grounds: Style and Homosexuality*. Amherst: University of Massachusetts Press, 1993.

Betrock, Alan. *Girl Groups: The Story of a Sound*. New York: Delilah Books, 1982.

Blackmer, Corinne, and Patricia Juliana Smith, eds. *En Travesti: Women, Gender Subversion, Opera*. New York: Columbia University Press, 1995.

Booth, Mark. *Camp*. London: Quartet Books, 1983.

Bordo, Susan. *Unbearable Weight: Feminism, Western Culture and the Body*. Berkeley: University of California Press, 1992.

Bordo, Susan. "The Body and the Reproduction of Femininity." In *Writing on the Body: Female Embodiment and Feminist Theory*, edited by Katie Conboy, Nadia Medina, and Sarah Stanbury, 90–110. New York: Columbia University Press, 1997.

Bowman, Rob. *Soulsville USA: The Story of Soul Music*. New York: Schirmer Books, 1997.

Boyer, Horace Clarence. *The Golden Age of Gospel*. Urbana: University of Illinois Press, 2000.

Brackett, David. *Interpreting Popular Music*. Berkeley: University of California Press, 2000.

Brackett, David, ed. *The Pop, Rock, and Soul Reader: Histories and Debates*. New York: Oxford University Press, 2005.

Bradby, Barbara. "Do-Talk and Don't-Talk: The Division of the Subject in Girl-Group Music." In *On Record: Rock, Pop and the Written Word*, edited by Simon Frith and Andrew Goodwin, 341–69. New York: Routledge, 1990.

Bradby, Barbara, and Brian Torode. "Pity Peggy Sue." In *Reading Pop: Approaches to Textual Analysis in Popular Music*, edited by Richard Middleton, 203–28. Oxford: Oxford University Press, 2000.

Breines, Wini. *Young, White, and Miserable: Growing up Female in the Fifties*. Boston: Beacon Books, 1992.

Brett, Philip, Elizabeth Wood, and Gary C. Thomas, eds. *Queering the Pitch: The New Gay and Lesbian Musicology*. New York: Routledge, 1994.

Brown, Cecil. *Stagolee Shot Billy*. Cambridge, Mass.: Harvard University Press, 2003.

Brown, Lyn Mikel. *Raising Their Voices: The Politics of Girls' Anger*. Cambridge, Mass.: Harvard University Press, 1998.

Brown, Lyn Mikel, and Carol Gilligan. *Meeting at the Crossroads: The Landmark Book about the Turning Point in Girls' and Women's Lives*. Cambridge, Mass.: Harvard University Press, 1992.

Brumberg, Joan Jacobs. *The Body Project: An Intimate History of American Girls*. New York: Random House, 1997.

Bufwack, Mary, and Robert Oermann. *Finding Her Voice: The Saga of Women in Country Music*. New York: Crown, 1993.

Burgel, Sheila. Liner notes to *One Kiss Can Lead to Another: Girl Group Sounds, Lost and Found*, Rhino Records R2 74645.

Burns, Lori. "'Joanie' Get Angry: kd lang's Feminist Revision." In *Understanding Rock: Essays in Music Analysis*, edited by John Covach and Graeme Boone, 93–112. Oxford: Oxford University Press, 1997.

Burns, Lori, and Mélisse Lafrance. *Disruptive Divas: Feminism, Identity & Popular Music*. New York: Routledge, 2002.

Burt, Ramsay. *Alien Bodies: Representations of Modernity, "Race" and Nation in Early Modern Dance*. New York: Routledge, 1998.

Butler, Judith. *Gender Trouble: Feminism and the Subversion of Identity*. New York: Routledge, 1990.

Butler, Judith. *Bodies That Matter: On the Discursive Limitations of "Sex."* New York: Routledge, 1993.

Butler, Judith. "Performative Acts and Gender Constitution: An Essay in Phenomenology and Feminist Theory." In *Writing on the Body: Female Embodiment and Feminist Theory*, edited by Katie Conboy, Nadia Medina, and Sarah Stanbury, 400–417. New York: Columbia University Press, 1997.

Carby, Hazel. "'It Jus' Be's Dat Way Sometime': The Sexual Politics of Women's Blues." In *Keeping Time: Readings in Jazz History*, edited by Robert Walser, 351–64. Oxford: Oxford University Press, 1999.

Chambers, Iain. *Urban Rhythms: Pop Music and Pop Culture*. New York: St. Martin's Press, 1985.

Chesney-Lind, Meda, and Katherine Irwin. "From Badness to Meanness: Popular Contructions of Contemporary Girlhood," in *All about the Girl: Culture, Power, and Identity*, edited by Anita Harris, 45–56. New York: Routledge, 2004.

Christian, Barbara. "The Race for Theory." In *Feminisms*, edited by Sandra Kemp and Judith Squires, 69–78. Oxford: Oxford University Press, 1997.

Citron, Marcia. *Gender and the Musical Canon*. Cambridge: Cambridge University Press, 1993.

Cixous, Hélène. "Le Rire de la Meduse." *LIArc* 61 (1975): 39–54.

Clément, Catherine. *Opera, or the Undoing of Women*. Minneapolis: University of Minnesota Press, 1988.

Coates, Norma. "Teenyboppers, Groupies, and Other Grotesques: Girls and Women and Rock Culture in the 1960s and early 1970s," *Journal of Popular Music Studies* 15, no. 1 (2003): 65–94.

Cockrell, Dale. *Demons of Disorder: Early Blackface Minstrels and Their World*. Cambridge: Cambridge University Press, 1997.

Collins, Patricia Hill. *Black Feminist Thought: Knowledge, Consciousness, and the Politics of Empowerment*. New York: Routledge, 1990.

Conboy, Karen, Nadia Medina, and Sarah Stanbury, eds. *Writing on the Body: Female Embodiment and Feminist Theory*. New York: Columbia University Press, 1997.

Connerton, Paul. *How Societies Remember*. Cambridge: Cambridge University Press, 1989.

Considine, David. *The Cinema of Adolescence*. Jefferson, N.C.: McFarland, 1985.

Cook, Susan, and Judy Tsou, eds. *Cecilia Reclaimed: Feminist Perspectives on Gender and Music*. Chicago: University of Illinois Press, 1994.

Coontz, Stephanie. *The Way We Never Were: American Families and the Nostalgia Trap*. New York: Basic Books, 1992.

Cooper, Kim, and David Smay, eds. *Bubblegum Music Is the Naked Truth: The Dark History of Prepubescent Pop, from the Banana Splits to Britney Spears*. Los Angeles: Feral House, 2001.

Cooper, Sarah, ed. *Girls! Girls! Girls! Essays on Women and Music*. New York: New York University Press, 1996.

Cording, Robert, Shelli Jankowski-Smith, and E.J. Miller Laino, eds. *In My Life: Encounters with the Beatles*. New York: Fromm International, 1998.

Covach, John, and Graeme Boone, eds. *Understanding Rock: Essays in Music Analysis*. Oxford: Oxford University Press, 1997.

Cunningham, Mark. *Good Vibrations: A History of Record Production*. Chessington: Castle Communications, 1996.

Cyrus, Cynthia J. "Selling an Image: Girl Groups of the 1960s." *Popular Music* 22, no. 2 (2003): 173–93.

Dahl, Linda. *Stormy Weather: The Music and Lives of a Century of Jazz Women*. London: Quartet Books, 1984.

Davis, Angela. *Women, Race and Class*. New York: Vintage, 1983.

de Beauvior, Simone. *The Second Sex,* 267. London: Vintage, 1989 (reissue).

Dettmar, Kevin J. H., and William Richey, ed. *Reading Rock and Roll: Authenticity, Appropriation, Aesthetics*. New York: Columbia University Press, 1999.

Devlin, Rachel. "Female Juvenile Delinquency and the Problem of Sexual Authority in America, 1945–1965." In *Delinquents and Debutantes: Twentieth-Century American Girls' Cultures*, edited by Sherrie A. Inness, 83–108. New York: New York University Press, 1998.

Dijkstra, Bram. *Evil Sisters: The Threat of Female Sexuality and the Cult of Manhood*. New York: Alfred A. Knopf, 1996.

di Leonardo, Micaela, ed. *Gender at the Crossroads of Knowledge: Feminist Anthropology in the Postmodern Era*. Berkeley: University of California Press, 1991.

Dolenz, Micky, with Mark Bego. *I'm a Believer: My Life of Monkees, Music, and Madness*. New York: Cooper Square Press, 1993.

Dougher, Sarah. "Authenticity, Gender and Personal Voice: She Sounds So Sad, Do You Think She Really Is?" In *This Is Pop: In Search of the Elusive at Experience Music Project*, edited by Eric Weisbard, 145–54. Cambridge, Mass.: Harvard University Press, 2004.

Douglas, Susan. *Where the Girls Are: Growing up Female with the Mass Media*. New York: Random House, 1994.

Dow, Bonnie J. *Prime-Time Feminism: Television, Media Culture, and the Women's Movement Since 1970*. Philadelphia: University of Pennsylvania Press, 1996.

Du Bois, W.E.B. *Souls of Black Folk*. Greenwich, Conn.: Fawcett Publications, 1961.

Dunn, Leslie, and Nancy Jones, eds. *Embodied Voices: Representing Female Vocality in Western Culture*. Cambridge: Cambridge University Press, 1994.

Early, Gerald. *One Nation under a Groove: Motown and American Culture*. Hopewell, N.J.: Ecco Press, 1995.

Echols, Alice. *Shaky Ground: The Sixties and Its Aftershocks*. New York: Columbia University Press, 2002.

Eisenberg, Evan. *The Recording Angel: Explorations in Phonography*. New York: McGraw-Hill, 1987.

Emerson, Ken. *Always Magic in the Air: The Bomp and Brilliance of the Brill Building Era*. New York: Viking, 2005.

Engh, Barbara. "Adorno and the Sirens: Tele-phono-graphic Bodies." In *Embodied Voices: Representing Female Vocality in Western Culture*, edited by Leslie Dunn and Nancy Jones, 120–38. Cambridge: Cambridge University Press, 1994.

Evans, Liz. *Women, Sex and Rock'n'Roll*. London: Pandora, 1994.

Faludi, Susan. *Backlash: The Undeclared War against American Women*. New York: Anchor Books, 1991.

Farber, David, and Beth Bailey, eds. *The Columbia Guide to America in the 1960s*. New York: Columbia University Press, 2001.

Fast, Susan. *In the Houses of the Holy: Led Zeppelin and the Power of Rock Music*. New York: Oxford University Press, 2001.

Fast, Susan. "Why Can Tina Play with the (White) Guys?" In *She's So Fine: Whiteness, Femininity, Adolescence and Class in 1960s Music*, edited by Laurie Stras. Durham, N.C.: Duke University Press, forthcoming.

Feld, Steven. *Sound and Sentiment*. Chicago: University of Chicago Press, 1988.

Fine, Michelle. *Disruptive Voices: The Possibilities of Feminist Research*. Albany: State University of New York Press, 1988.

Floyd, Samuel A. *The Power of Black Music: Interpreting Its History from Africa to the United States*. New York: Oxford University Press, 1995.

Foucault, Michel. *Discipline and Punish*. New York: Vintage, 1979.

Foucault, Michel. *The History of Sexuality: Volume I, an Introduction*. New York: Vintage, 1980.

Frank, Thomas. *The Conquest of Cool: Business Culture, Counterculture, and the Rise of Hip Consumerism*. Chicago: University of Chicago Press, 1997.

Frith, Simon. "Towards an Aesthetic of Popular Music." In *Music and Society: The Politics of Composition, Performance and Reception*, edited by Richard Leppert and Susan McClary, 133–49. Cambridge: Cambridge University Press, 1987.

Frith, Simon, and Andrew Goodwin, eds. *On Record: Rock, Pop and the Written Word*. New York: Pantheon Books, 1990.

Gaar, Gillian. *She's a Rebel: The History of Women in Rock & Roll*. Seattle: Seal Press, 1992.

Gaines, Donna. *Teenage Wasteland: Suburbia's Deadend Kids*. New York: Pantheon, 1991.

Gaines, Donna. "Girl Groups: A Ballad of Codependency." In *The Rolling Stone Book of Women in Rock*, edited by Barbara O'Dair, 103–16. New York: Rolling Stone Press, 1997.

Gallop, Jane. *Thinking through the Body*. New York: Columbia University Press, 1988.

Garber, Marjorie. *Vested Interests: Cross-Dressing and Cultural Anxiety*. New York: Harper, 1992.

Garofalo, Reebee. *Rockin' Out: Popular Music in the USA*. Boston: Allyn & Bacon, 1997.

Gaunt, Kyra D. "Translating Double-Dutch to Hip-Hop: The Musical Vernacular of Black Girls' Play." In *Language, Rhythm, and Sound: Black Popular Cultures into the Twenty-First Century*, edited by Joseph K. Adjaye and Adrianne R. Andrews, 146–73. Pittsburgh: University of Pittsburgh, 1997.

George-Graves, Nadine. *The Royalty of Negro Vaudeville: The Whitman Sisters and the Negotiation of Race, Gender and Class in African American Theatre, 1900–1940*. New York: St. Martin's Press, 2000.

Gilligan, Carol. *In a Different Voice: Psychological Theory and Women's Development*. Cambridge, Mass.: Harvard University Press, 1982.

Gitlin, Todd. *The Sixties: Years of Hope, Days of Rage*. New York: Bantam Books, 1987.

Gordy, Berry. *To Be Loved: The Music, the Magic, the Memories of Motown*. New York: Time Warner, 1994.

Gracyk, Theodore. *I Wanna Be Me: Rock Music and the Politics of Identity*. Philadelphia: Temple University Press, 2001.

Grecco, John J. "Out in the Streets: The Story of the ShangriLas." Available at http://www.redbirdent.com/slas1.htm, accessed October 1, 2005.

Greenblatt, Stephen. *Renaissance Self-Fashioning from More to Shakespeare*. Chicago: University of Chicago Press, 1980.

Greer, Germaine, and Phil Sommerich. "Why Don't Women Buy CDs?" *BBC Music Magazine* (September 1994): 35–8.

Grieg, Charlotte. *Will You Still Love Me Tomorrow?: Girl Groups from the 50s On*. London: Virago, 1989.

Hamm, Charles. *Yesterdays: Popular Song in America*. New York: Norton, 1979.

Hanna, Judith Lynne. *Dance, Sex and Gender: Signs of Identity, Dominance, Defiance, and Desire*. Chicago: University of Chicago Press, 1988.

Harding, Sandra, ed. *Feminism and Methodology*. Bloomington: Indiana University Press, 1987.

Harris, Anita, ed. *All about the Girl: Culture, Power and Identity*. New York: Routledge, 2004.

Hartsock, Nancy. "The Feminist Standpoint: Developing the Ground for a Specifically Feminist Historical Materialism." In *Feminism and Methodology*, edited by Sandra Harding, 157–81. Bloomington: Indiana University Press, 1987.

Harwood, Eve. "Go on Girl! Improvisation in African-American Girls' Singing Games." In *In the Course of Performance: Studies in the World of Musical Improvisation*, edited by Bruno Nettl and Melinda Russell, 113–125. Chicago: University of Chicago Press, 1998.

Hebdige, Dick. *Subculture: the Meaning of Style*. London: Methuen, 1979.

Hewett, Heather. "In Search of an 'I': Embodied Voice and the Personal Essay." *Women's Studies* 33 (2004): 719–41.

Hickey, Dave. *Air Guitar: Essays on Art and Democracy*. Los Angeles: Art Issues Press, 1997.

Hill, Mike, ed. *Whiteness: A Critical Reader*. New York: New York University Press, 1997.

Hirsch, Marianne. *The Mother/Daughter Plot: Narrative, Psychoanalysis, Feminism*. Bloomington: Indiana University Press, 1989.

Hirshey, Gerri. *Nowhere to Run: The Story of Soul Music*. New York: Da Capo Press, 1984.

Hirshey, Gerri. *We Gotta Get out of This Place: The True, Tough Story of Women in Rock*. New York: Atlantic Monthly Press, 2001.

Holiday, Billie, with William Dufty. *Lady Sings the Blues*. New York: Penguin, 1984.

hooks, bell. *Black Looks: Race and Representation*. Toronto: Between the Lines Press, 1992.

hooks, bell. "Madonna: Plantation Mistress or Soul Sister?" In *Black Looks: Race and Representation*, 157–64. Toronto: Between the Lines Press, 1992.

hooks, bell. "Selling Hot Pussy." In *Writing on the Body: Female Embodiment and Feminist Theory*, edited by Katie Conboy, Nadia Medina, and Sarah Stanbury, 113–29. New York: Columbia University Press, 1997.

Horner, Bruce, and Thomas Swiss, ed. *Key Terms in Popular Music and Culture*. Oxford: Blackwell, 1999.

Huyssen, Andreas. "Mass Culture as Woman: Modernism's Other." In *After the Great Divide: Modernism, Mass Culture, Postmodernism*, 44–62. Bloomington: Indiana University Press, 1986.

Inness, Sherrie A. *Tough Girls: Women Warriors and Wonder Women in Popular Culture*. Philadelphia: University of Pennsylvania Press, 1999.

Inness, Sherrie A., ed. *Delinquents and Debutantes: Twentieth-Century American Girls' Cultures*. New York: New York University Press, 1998.

Jackson, John A. *American Bandstand: Dick Clark and the Making of a Rock'n'Roll Empire*. New York: Oxford University Press, 1997.

Johnson, Mark. *The Body in the Mind: The Bodily Basis of Meaning, Imagination, and Reason*. Chicago: University of Chicago Press, 1987.

Jones, Quincy. *Q: The Autobiography of Quincy Jones*. New York: Doubleday, 2002.

Justice-Malloy, Rhona. "Little Girls Bound: Costume and Coming of Age in the Sears Catalog 1906–1927." In *Delinquents and Debutantes: Twentieth-Century American Girls' Cultures*, edited by Sherrie A. Inness, 109–33. New York: New York University Press, 1998.

Kaplan, E. Ann. *Rocking around the Clock: Music Television, Postmodernism, and Consumer Culture*. New York: Methuen, 1987.

Kapp Howe, Louise. *Pink Collar Workers*. New York: Putnam, 1977.

Katz, Mark. *Capturing Sound: How Technology Has Changed Music*. Berkeley: University of California Press, 2004.

Kay, Carol. "On Bass, Brian and the Beach Boys." Available at http://abbeyrd.best.vwh.net/carolkay.htm, accessed March 10, 2006.

Keil, Charles. "Participatory Discrepancies and the Power of Music." In *Music Grooves*, edited by Charles Keil and Steven Feld, 96–108. Chicago: University of Chicago Press, 1994.

Kemp, Sandra, and Judith Squires, eds. *Feminisms*. Oxford: Oxford University Press, 1997.

Kenny, Dianna T., and Gavin Faunce. "The Impact of Group Singing on Mood, Coping and Perceived Pain in Chronic Pain Patients Attending a Multidisciplinary Pain Clinic." *Journal of Music Therapy* XLI, no. 3 (2004): 241–58.

Kingston, Anne. *The Meaning of Wife*. Toronto: HarperCollins, 2004.

Knight, Gladys. *Between Each Line of Pain and Glory: My Life Story*. New York: Hyperion, 1997.

Koskoff, Ellen. *Music in Lubavitcher Life*. Chicago: University of Illinois Press, 2001.

Koskoff, Ellen, ed. *Women and Music in Cross-Cultural Perspective*. New York: Greenwood Press, 1987.

Kureishi, Hanif, and Jon Savage, eds. *The Faber Book of Pop*. London: Faber & Faber, 1995.

Lamb, Sharon. *The Secret Lives of Girls: What Good Girls Really Do—Sex Play, Aggression, and Their Guilt*. New York: The Free Press, 2001.

Lebeau, Vicky. "The Unwelcome Child: Elizabeth Eckford and Hannah Arendt," *Journal of Visual Culture* 3 (April 2004), no. 1: 51–62.

Leonard, Marion. "Rebel Girl, You Are the Queen of My World." In *Sexing the Groove: Popular Music and Gender*, edited by Sheila Whitely, 230–56. New York: Routledge, 1997.

Lewin, David. "Women's Voices and the Fundamental Bass." *Journal of Musicology* XIV, no. 1 (1992): 1–34.

Lewis, Lisa. *Gender Politics and MTV: Voicing the Difference*. Philadelphia: Temple University Press, 1990.

Lewis, Lisa, ed. *The Adoring Audience: Fan Culture and Popular Media*. New York: Routledge, 1992.

Lhamon, W. T., Jr. *Raising Cain: Blackface Performance from Jim Crow to Hip Hop*. Cambridge, Mass.: Harvard University Press, 1998.

Linna, Miriam. "Good-Bad, but not Evil." Available at http://www.nortonrecords.com/maryweiss, accessed June 10, 2006.

Lipsitz, George. *A Rainbow at Midnight: Class and Culture in Cold War America*. South Hadley, Mass.: Bergin and Harvey, 1982.

Lipsitz, George. *Dangerous Crossroads: Popular Music, Postmodernism, and the Poetics of Place*. London: Verso, 1994.

Lord, M. G. *Forever Barbie: The Unauthorized Biography of a Real Doll*. New York: Avon Books, 1994.

Lott, Eric. *Love and Theft: Blackface Minstrelsy and the American Working Class*. Oxford: Oxford University Press, 1993.

Love, Preston. *A Thousand Honey Creeks Later: My Life in Music from Basie to Motown*. Hanover, N.H.: Wesleyan University Press, 1997.

Lurie, Alison. *The Language of Clothes*. New York: Henry Holt and Co., 1981.

Mahar, William J. *Behind the Burnt Cork Mask: Early Blackface Minstrelsy and Antebellum American Popular Culture.* New York: Scholarly Book Services, 2002.

Marx, Karl. "Estranged Labour." In *Social Theory: The Multicultural and Classic Readings*, edited by Charles Lemert, 30–36. Boulder, Colo.: Westview Press, 1999.

May, Elaine Tyler. *Homeward Bound: American Families in the Cold War Era.* New York: Basic Books, 1988.

McClary, Susan. "Terminal Prestige: The Case of Avant-Garde Music Composition." *Cultural Critique* 12 (1989): 57–81.

McClary, Susan. *Feminine Endings: Music, Gender and Sexuality.* Minneapolis: University of Minnesota Press, 1991.

McClary, Susan. "Music, the Pythagoreans, and the Body." In *Choreographing History*, edited by Susan Foster. Bloomington: Indiana University Press, 1995: 82-104.

McClary, Susan. *Conventional Wisdom: The Content of Musical Form.* Berkeley: University of California Press, 2000.

McClary, Susan, and Richard Leppert, eds. *Music and Society: The Politics of Composition, Performance, and Reception.* Cambridge: Cambridge University Press, 1987.

McCracken, Allison. "'God's Gift to Us Girls': Crooning, Gender and the Re-Creation of American Popular Song, 1928–1933." *American Music* 17, no. 4 (Winter, 1999): 365–95.

McCracken, Grant. *Big Hair: A Journey into the Transformation of Self.* Woodstock, N.Y.: The Overlook Press, 1996.

McDonald, Janet. *Project Girl.* Berkeley: University of California Press, 1999.

McDonald, Kari, and Sarah Hudson Kaufman. "Tomorrow Never Knows: The Contribution of George Martin and His Production Team to the Beatles' New Sound." In *'Every Sound There Is': The Beatles'* Revolver *and the Transformation of Rock and Roll*, edited by Russell Reising, 139–57. Aldershot, UK: Ashgate Publishing, 2002.

McLuhan, Marshall. *Understanding Media: The Extensions of Man.* Cambridge, Mass.: MIT Press, 1994.

McNeill, William H. *Keeping Together in Time: Dance and Drill in Human History.* Cambridge, Mass.: Harvard University Press, 1995.

McRobbie, Angela. "Dance and Social Fantasy." In *Gender and Generation*, edited by Angela McRobbie and Mica Nava, 130–61. London: MacMillan, 1984.

McRobbie, Angela. *Feminism and Youth Culture: From 'Jackie' to 'Just Seventeen.'* London: MacMillan, 1997.

Mead, Margaret. *Male and Female.* New York: Quill, 1967.

Melnick, Jeffrey. "'Story Untold': The Black Men and White Sounds of Doo Wop." In *Whiteness: A Critical Reader*, edited by Mike Hill, 134–50. New York: New York University Press, 1997.

Mercer-Taylor, Peter. "Songs from the Bell Jar: Autonomy and Resistance in the Music of the Bangles." *Popular Music* 17, no. 2 (1998): 187–204.

Middleton, Richard. *Studying Popular Music*. Milton Keynes: Open University Press, 1990.

Middleton, Richard, ed. *Reading Pop: Approaches to Textual Analysis in Popular Music*. Oxford: Oxford University Press, 2000.

Mies, Maria. *Patriarchy and Accumulation on a World Scale*. London: Zed Books, 1986.

Milstein, Phil. "ShangriLas 77!" Available at http://www.spectropop.com/Shangri-Las/index.htm. Accessed February 10, 2006.

Modleski, Tania. *Old Wives' Tales and Other Women's Stories*. New York: New York University Press, 1998.

Moisala, Pirkko, Beverly Diamond, and Ellen Koskoff, eds. *Music and Gender*. Chicago: University of Illinois Press, 2000.

Monks, Susan. "Adolescent Singers and Perceptions of Vocal Identity." *British Journal of Music Education* 20, no.3 (2003): 243–56.

Monson, Craig. "Disembodied Voices: Music in the Nunneries of Bologna in the Midst of the Counter-Reformation." In *The Crannied Wall: Women, Religion, and the Arts in Early Modern Europe*, edited by Craig Monson, 191–210. Ann Arbor: University of Michigan Press, 1992.

Morrison, Toni. *The Bluest Eye*. New York: Alfred A. Knopf, 1970.

Neal, Mark Anthony. *What the Music Said: Black Popular Music and Black Public Culture*. New York: Routledge, 1999.

Negus, Keith. *Popular Music in Theory*. Hanover, N.H.: Wesleyan University Press, 1996.

Newton, Esther. "Role Models." In *Camp Grounds: Style and Homosexuality*, edited by David Bergman, 39–54. Amherst, Mass.: University of Massachusetts Press, 1993.

O'Brien, Lucy. *SheBop: The Definitive History of Women in Rock, Pop and Soul*. London: Penguin, 1995.

O'Dair, Barbara, ed. *Trouble Girls: The Rolling Stone Book of Women in Rock*. New York: Rolling Stone Press, 1997.

Okely, Judith. "Privileged, Schooled and Finished: Boarding Education for Girls." In *Defining Females: The Nature of Women in Society*, edited by Shirley Ardener, 109–39. London: Croom Helm in association with Oxford University Women's Studies Committee, 1978.

Orenstein, Peggy. *SchoolGirls: Young Women, Self-Esteem, and the Confidence Gap*. New York: Doubleday, 1994.

Orgill, Roxane. *Shout, Sister, Shout! Ten Girl Singers Who Shaped a Century*. New York: McElderry, 2001.

Pavletich, Aida. *Sirens of Song: The Popular Female Vocalist in America*. New York: Da Capo Press, 1980.

Pegley, Karen, and Virginia Caputo. "Growing up Female(s): Retrospective Thoughts on Musical Preferences and Meanings." *Repercussions* 1, no. 1 (1992): 65–80.

Peraino, Judith. "'Rip Her to Shreds': Women's Music According to a Butch/Femme Aesthetic." *Repercussions* 1, no. 1 (1992), 19–47.

Perone, James E. *Carole King: A Bio-Bibliography*. Westport, Conn.: Greenwood Press, 1999.

Pipher, Mary. *Reviving Ophelia: Saving the Selves of Adolescent Girls*. New York: Ballantine Books.

Potter, John. *Vocal Authority: Singing Style and Ideology*. Cambridge: Cambridge University Press, 1998.

Rabinow, Paul, ed. *The Foucault Reader*. New York: Pantheon Books, 1984.

Radway, Janice. *Reading the Romance: Women, Patriarchy, and Popular Literature*. Chapel Hill: University of North Carolina Press, 1991.

Reising, Russell, ed. *'Every Sound There Is': The Beatles'* Revolver *and the Transformation of Rock and Roll*. Aldershot, UK: Ashgate Publishing, 2002.

Reynolds, Simon, and Joy Press. *The Sex Revolts: Gender, Rebellion, and Rock'n'Roll*. Cambridge, Mass.: Harvard University Press, 1995.

Rhodes, Lisa. *Electric Ladyland: Women and Rock Culture*. Philadelphia: University of Pennsylvania Press, 2005.

Ribowsky, Mark. *He's a Rebel: The Truth about Phil Spector: Rock and Roll's Legendary Madman*. New York: EP Dutton, 1989.

Rivière, Joan. "Womanliness as a Masquerade." In *Formations of Fantasy*, edited by Victor Burgin, James Donald, and Cora Kaplan, 35–44. London: Methuen, 1986.

Robertson, Pamela. *Guilty Pleasures: Feminist Camp from Mae West to Madonna*. Durham, N.C.: Duke University Press, 1996.

Roberts, Robin. *Ladies First: Women in Music Videos*. Jackson, Mississippi: University of Mississippi Press, 1996.

Roman, Leslie. "Intimacy, Labor, and Class: Ideologies of Feminine Sexuality in the Punk Slam Dance." In *Becoming Feminine: The Politics of Popular Culture,* edited by Leslie Roman and Linda K. Christian-Smith, 25–37. London: Falmer Press, 1988.

Rose, Tricia. *Black Noise: Black Cultural Resistance in Contemporary American Popular Culture*. Ann Arbor: University of Michigan Press, 1994.

Ross, Andrew, and Tricia Rose, eds. *Microphone Fiends: Youth Music and Youth Culture*. New York: Routledge, 1994.

Ross Leadbeater, Bonnie J., and Niobe Way, eds. *Urban Girls: Resisting Stereotypes, Creating Identities*. New York: New York University Press, 1996.

Rotheram-Borus, Mary Jane, Steve Dopkins, Nuria Sabate, and Marguerita Lightfoot. "Personal and Ethnic Identity, Values, and Self-Esteem among Black and Latino Adolescent Girls." In *Urban Girls: Resisting Stereotypes, Creating Identities*, edited by Bonnie J. Ross Leadbeater and Niobe Way, 35–52. New York: New York University Press, 1996.

Rubin, Gayle. "The Traffic in Women: Notes on the 'Political Economy' of Sex." In *Toward an Anthropology of Women*, edited by Rayna Reiter. New York: Monthly Review Press, 1976: 157–210.

Rubin, Rachel. "Sing Me Back Home: Nostalgia, Bakersfield, and Modern Country Music." In *American Popular Music: New Approaches to the Twentieth Century*, edited by Rachel Rubin and Jeffrey Melnick, 93–110. Amherst: University of Massachussetts Press, 2001.

Rubin, Rachel, and Jeffrey Melnick, eds. *American Popular Music: New Approaches to the Twentieth Century*. Boston: University of Massachusetts Press, 2001.

Russo, Mary. "Female Grotesques: Carnival and Theory." In *Writing on the Body: Female Embodiment and Feminist Theory*, edited by Katie Conboy, Nadia Medina, and Sarah Stanbury, 318–36. New York: Columbia University Press, 1997.

Scheman, Naomi. "Missing Mothers/Desiring Daughters: Framing the Sight of Women." In *Engenderings: Constructions of Knowledge, Authority, and Privilege*, 126–54. New York: Routledge, 1993.

Scheiner, Georganne. *Signifying Female Adolescence: Film Representations and Fans, 1920–1950*. Westport, Conn.: Praeger, 2000.

Sharpe, Sue. *Just Like a Girl: How Girls Learn to be Women from the Seventies to the Nineties*. London: Penguin, 1994.

Skeggs, Beverley. *Formations of Class and Gender: Becoming Respectable*. London: Sage Publications, 1997.

Simmons, Rachel. *Odd Girl Out: The Hidden Culture of Aggression in Girls*. New York: Harcourt, 2002.

Sloan, Kay. "You Say You Want a Revolution." In *In My Life: Encounters with the Beatles*, edited by Robert Cording, Shelli Jankowski-Smith, and E.J. Miller Laino, 26–32. New York: Fromm International: 1998.

Small, Christopher. *Musicking: The Meanings of Performing and Listening*. Hanover, N.H.: Wesleyan University Press, 1998.

Smith, Dorothy. "Women's Perspective as a Radical Critique of Sociology." In *Feminism and Methodology*, edited by Sandra Harding, 84–97. Bloomington: Indiana University Press, 1987.

Smith, Joan. *Different for Girls: How Culture Creates Women*. London: Chatto & Windus, 1997.

Smith, Patricia Juliana. "'You Don't Have to Say You Love Me': The Camp Masquerades of Dusty Springfield." In *Camp Grounds: Style and Homosexuality*, edited by David Bergman, 185–206. Amherst: University of Massachusetts Press, 1993.

Smith, Patricia Juliana. "Ask Any Girl: Compulsory Heterosexuality and Girl Group Culture." In *Reading Rock and Roll: Authenticity, Appropriation, Aesthetics*, edited by Kevin J. H. Dettmar and William Richey, 93–125. New York: Columbia University Press, 1999.

Smith, Suzanne E. *Dancing in the Street: Motown and the Cultural Politics of Detroit*. Cambridge, Mass.: Harvard University Press, 1999.

Snyder, Rachel Louise. "Will You Still Love Me Tomorrow?" Available at http://www.salon.com/people/feature/1999/06/19/king, accessed October 10, 2000.

Solie, Ruth, ed. *Musicology and Difference: Gender and Sexuality in Music Scholarship*. Berkeley: University of California Press, 1993.

Sontag, Susan. "Notes on Camp." In *Against Interpretation and Other Essays*, 275-92. New York: Dell, 1966.

Spector, Ronnie, with Vince Waldron. *Be My Baby: How I Survived Mascara, Miniskirts and Madness, or My Life as a Fabulous Ronette*. New York: Harmony Books, 1990.

Steedman, Carolyn Kay. *Landscape for a Good Woman: A Story of Two Lives*. London: Virago, 1987.

Sterne, Jonathan. *The Audible Past: Cultural Origins of Sound Reproduction*. Durham, N.C.: Duke University Press, 2004.

Stras, Laurie. "Voice of the Beehive: Vocal Technique at the Turn of the 60s." In *She's So Fine: Whiteness, Femininity, Adolescence and Class in 1960s Music*, edited by Laurie Stras. Durham, N.C.: Duke University Press, forthcoming.

Stras, Laurie, ed. *She's So Fine: Whiteness, Femininity, Adolescence and Class in 1960s Music*. Durham, N.C.: Duke University Press, forthcoming.

Straw, Will. "Sizing up Record Collections: Gender and Connoisseurship in Rock Music Culture." In *Sexing the Groove: Popular Music and Gender*, edited by Sheila Whitely, 3–17. New York: Routledge, 1997.

Straw, Will. "Authorship." In *Key Terms in Popular Music and Culture*, edited by Bruce Horner and Thomas Swiss, 199–208. Oxford: Blackwell, 1999.

Sugarman, Jane. *Engendering Song: Singing and Subjectivity at Prespa Albanian Weddings*. Chicago: University of Chicago Press, 1997.

Sutton, Terri. "Janis Joplin." In *The Rolling Stone Book of Women in Rock*, edited by Barbara O'Dair, 157–66. New York: Random House, 1997.

Tagg, Philip. "Analyzing Popular Music: Theory, Method, and Practice." In *Popular Music* 2 (1982): 37–67.

Taraborrelli, J. Randy. *Call Her Miss Ross*. New York: Birch Lane Press, 1989.

Taylor, Marc. *The Original Marvelettes: Motown's Mystery Girl Group*. Jamaica, N.Y.: Aloiv Publishing, 2005.

Tedesco, Lauren. "Making a Girl into a Scout: Americanizing Scouting for Girls." In *Delinquents and Debutantes: Twentieth-Century American Girls' Cultures*, edited by Sherrie A. Inness, 19–39. New York: New York University Press, 1998.

Thomas, Helen. *Dance, Modernity and Culture: Explorations in the Sociology of Dance*. New York: Routledge, 1995.

Thomas, Helen, ed. *Dance, Gender and Culture*. New York: St. Martin's Press, 1993.

Tick, Judith, and Jane Bowers, eds. *Women Making Music: The Western Art Tradition 1150–1950*. Chicago: University of Illinois Press, 1987.

Tyler May, Elaine. *Homeward Bound: American Families in the Cold War Era*. New York: Basic Books, 1988.

Vale, V., ed. *Angry Women*. San Francisco: RE/Search, 1991.

Wald, Gayle. "One of the Boys? Whiteness, Gender and Popular Music Studies." In *Whiteness: A Critical Reader*, edited by Mike Hill, 151–67. New York: New York University Press, 1997.

Wald, Gayle. "Just a Girl? Rock Music, Feminism, and the Cultural Construction of Female Youth." In *Rock over the Edge: Transformations in Popular Music Culture*, edited by Roger Beebe, Denise Fulbrook, and Ben Saunders, 191–215. Durham, N.C.: Duke University Press, 2002.

Walkerdine, Valerie. *Schoolgirl Fictions*. London: Verso, 1990.

Walkerdine, Valerie. *Daddy's Girl: Young Girls and Popular Culture*. New York: Routledge, 1998.

Walser, Robert. "The Body in the Music: Epistemology and Musical Semiotics." *College Music Symposium* 31 (1991): 117–26.

Walser, Robert. *Running with the Devil: Power, Gender and Madness in Heavy Metal Music*. Hanover, N.H.: Wesleyan University Press, 1993.

Walser, Robert, ed. *Keeping Time: Readings in Jazz History*. Oxford: Oxford University Press, 1999.

Warner, Jay. *American Singing Groups*. New York: Da Capo Press, 1992.

Warwick, Jacqueline. "'He's Got the Power': The Politics of Production in Girl Group Music." In *Music, Space and Place: Popular Music and Cultural Identity*, edited by Sheila Whitely, Andy Bennett, and Stan Hawkins, 191–200. Aldershot, UK: Ashgate, 2004.

Warwick, Jacqueline. "'He Hit Me, and I Was Glad': Violence, Masochism, and Anger in Girl Group Music." In *She's So Fine: Whiteness, Femininity, Adolescence and Class in 1960s Music*, edited by Laurie Stras. Durham, N.C.: Duke University Press, forthcoming.

Washburne, Christopher J., and Maiken Derno, eds. *Bad Music: The Music We Love to Hate*. New York: Routledge, 2004.

Weisbard, Eric, ed. *This Is Pop: In Search of the Elusive at Experience Music Project*. Cambridge, Mass.: Harvard University Press, 2004.

Whitall, Susan. *Women of Motown: An Oral History*. New York: Avon Books, 1998.

White, Emily. *Fast Girls: Teenage Tribes and the Myth of the Slut*. New York: Scribner, 2002.

Whitely, Sheila, ed. *Sexing the Groove: Popular Music and Gender*. New York: Routledge, 1997.

Whitely, Sheila. "Little Red Rooster v. the Honky Tonk Woman: Mick Jagger, Sexuality, Style and Image." In *Sexing the Groove: Popular Music and Gender*, edited by Sheila Whiteley. New York: Routledge, 1997: 67–99.

Whitely, Sheila. *Women and Popular Music: Sexuality, Identity and Subjectivity*. New York: Routledge, 2000.

Whitely, Sheila, Andy Bennett, and Stan Hawkins, eds. *Music, Space and Place: Popular Music and Cultural Identity*. Aldershot, UK: Ashgate, 2004.

Wilcox, Rhonda V., and David Lavery. *Fighting the Forces: What's at Stake in* Buffy the Vampire Slayer. Lanham, MD.: Rowman & Littlefield, 2002.

Williams, Juan. *Eyes on the Prize: America's Civil Rights Years, 1954–65*. New York: Penguin, 1987.

Willis, Paul. *Learning to Labour: How Working Class Kids Get Working Class Jobs*. New York: Columbia University Press, 1977.

Wilson, Mary. *Dreamgirl & Supreme Faith: My Life as a Supreme*. New York: Cooper Square Press, 1999.

Wilson, Randall. *Forever Faithful! Florence Ballard and the Supremes*. San Francisco: Renaissance Sound and Publications, 1999.

Wiseman, Rosalind. *Queen Bees and Wannabes: Helping Your Daughter Survive Cliques, Gossip, Boyfriends and Other Realities of Adolescence*. New York: Crown Publishers, 2002.

Wolf, Naomi. *The Beauty Myth*. Toronto: Random House, 1990.

Wolfe, Tom. "The First Tycoon of Teen." In *The Kandy-Kolored Tangerine-Flake Streamline Baby,* 32-37. New York: Bantam, 1999.

Yalom, Marilyn. *A History of the Breast*. New York: Ballantine Books, 1997.

Youens, Susan. "Music, Verse, and 'Prose Poetry': Debussy's Trois Chansons de Bilitis." *Journal of Musicological Research* VII, no. 1 (1986): 69–95.

Young, David A. "Please Don't Wake Me: Rhino's Girl Group Sounds." Available at http://www.spectropop.com/recommends/index2006.htm#Rhino, accessed January 14, 2006.

Young, Iris. *Throwing Like a Girl and Other Essays in Feminist Philosophy and Social Theory*. Bloomington: Indiana University Press, 1990.

Zak, Albin J., *The Poetics of Rock: Cutting Tracks, Making Records*. Berkeley: University of California Press, 2001.

Index

H

I

J